Use this worksheet to keep track of all the fees involved in financing and closing on your new home. Carry it with you as a handy reminder. Refer to Chapter 20 for more information on closing costs.

Buying a House: Planning Worksheet

Offer Price   _____

Down Payment   _____

Loan Amount   _____

Interest Rate   _____

Closing Costs:

Points   _____

Origination Fee   _____

Appraisal Fee   _____

Credit Report   _____

Insurance   _____

Inspection   _____

Title Search/Insurance   _____

Mortgage Insurance Premium   _____

Insurance Reserve   _____

Tax Reserve   _____

Attorney's Fees   _____

Document Preparation Fees   _____

Recording Fees   _____

Survey   _____

Other   _____

TOTAL   [_____]

alpha books

cut here

Part V walks you step-by-step through the process of selling your home. Chapter 24 explains what is involved in setting the price for your house. Use this worksheet to figure the costs and profits based on three different selling prices. This will help you decide what the lowest possible price is that you can accept for your home.

Selling A House: Planning Worksheet

	Price 1	Price 2	Price 3
Sales Price			
1st Mortgage Payoff			
2nd Mortgage Payoff			
Brokerage Fee			
Title Insurance			
Mortgage Discount Points			
Origination Fee			
Deed and Affidavit			
Document Preparation			
Taxes			
Buyer's Closing Costs			
Closing Fee			
Assessments			
Inspections			
Underwriting Fee			
Tax Service Fee			
Repairs			
Other			
TOTAL			
NET AT CLOSING			

The

COMPLETE
IDIOT'S
GUIDE TO
Buying and Selling
a Home

by Shelley O'Hara
with Maris Bluestein

alpha
books

A Division of Macmillan Computer Publishing
with a Prentice Hall Macmillan Company
201 W. 103rd Street, Indianapolis, IN 46290

International Standard Book Number: 1-56761-510-4

Library of Congress Catalog Card Number: 94-71781

96 95 94   8 7 6 5 4 3 2 1

Interpretation of the printing code: the rightmost number of the first series of numbers is the year of the book's printing; the rightmost number of the second series of numbers is the number of the book's printing. For example, a printing code of 94-1 shows that the first printing of the book occurred in 1994.

Printed in the United States of America

Publisher
Marie Butler-Knight

Product Manager
Thomas F. Godfrey III

Managing Editor
Elizabeth Keaffaber

Acquisitions Manager
Barry Pruett

Production Editor
Michelle Shaw

Development/Copy Editor
Howard Peirce

Cover Designer
Scott Cook

Designer
Barb Webster

Indexer
Charlotte Clapp

Production Team
*Gary Adair, Dan Caparo, Brad Chinn, Kim Cofer,
Lisa Daugherty, David Dean, Jennifer Eberhardt,
Erika Millen, Beth Rago, Bobbi Satterfield,
Carol Stamile, Karen Walsh, Robert Wolf*

*Special thanks to Judd Winick for drawing the clever
illustrations used throughout this book.*

A good laugh is sunshine in a house.

—William Makepeace Thackeray

ABOUT THE AUTHORS

Shelley O'Hara

Shelley O'Hara is a best-selling author from Indianapolis, Indiana. She has written over 30 books, dealing with difficult or technical topics. Shelley has a BA in English from the University of South Carolina and an MA in English from the University of Maryland.

Maris Bluestein

Maris Bluestein graduated from the City College of New York with a teaching degree in Spanish. Her many moves as a corporate wife led her into real estate in 1977. She has been a successful and active broker in the Indianapolis area for over 17 years. She is also an appraiser and does private consulting. This is her first book.

Our Team of Experts Also Includes

Sarah M. Diana
Realtor Associate
RE/MAX Elite

Tom Mattingly
Real Estate Broker
RE/MAX Real Estate Group

Katherine Rock Ray
Mortgage Banker/Broker
Mortgage Corporation of America

Steve Surette
Home Inspector
Surette & Associates

Todd Tarbutton
Custom Home Builder

Contents at a Glance

Contents

Part II: Make an Offer — 91

8 Making an Offer — 93

9 Negotiating — 107

10 Buying a New Home — 117

13 Getting a Fixed-Rate Mortgage **153**

14 Getting an Adjustable-Rate Mortgage **161**

15 Understanding Other Financing **173**

Introduction

When it comes to some topics (computers, buying and selling a home, Wall Street), you may feel like an idiot. The terms used in each field are confusing, and the experts lord their knowledge over you. For example, if you are buying a house, your lender may say "You'll want to consider a conventional ARM with a 90LTV for that house. The qualifying ratios used are 28/36." Excuse me?

You're an expert in your own field. You have your own lingo and expert knowledge that you use day-to-day. No, you aren't an idiot. But when it comes to real estate, you need explanations in terms anyone can understand. You don't need a degree in real estate law; you just need someone to tell you what you need to know and what's important. That's what this book does.

So You Want to Buy a House

Owning a home is probably the quintessential American dream. From the first days of settling this country, our forebears (either in spirit or in blood) fought hard to earn the right to own a spot of land. That right and dream has been passed down ever since, not only to their descendents, but to every newcomer who sets foot on this soil.

At times, you may feel as if buying a house is as hard as riding across the plains in a wagon train for months, bouncing over mile after mile of flat land, covered in dust, wearing the same outfit for an entire year, until you reach that little piece of land somewhere in the West. Or as hard as riding in the immigrant hull of a ship, your children crowded around your feet, with little to eat, awaiting the start of a new life in a strange land. Once you start the house-buying process, you may actually imagine that those obstacles would be *easier* to surmount than the ones you face. With this book, though, you'll find your struggle manageable, sometimes even fun.

The Complete Idiot's Guide to Buying and Selling A Home strives to make understanding the home-buying process easy. The book is divided into five parts, each part focusing on a particular step in the home buying process:

Part I, "Find Your Dream Home," covers getting ready to buy a house. You have to prepare mentally and financially, and this part tells you want to expect. Part I also covers finding a house—knowing what you want and finding it.

Part II, "Make an Offer," covers the offer process. Once you find the house you want, you have to convince the sellers to sell it to you at the price you want to pay. This part covers how to make an offer, review a counteroffer, and get an offer accepted.

Part III, "Get Financing," focuses on the next step in the home-buying process—getting financing so that you can pay for the home. This part covers, in simple terms, the financial options available for purchasing your home.

Part IV, "Close on the House," brings you to the final step: closing on the house. Before you can move in, you have to have a few things done, such as having the house inspected and getting insurance. Then you have the final showdown when you sign a couple hundred documents, turn over your money, and finally get the keys to your new house.

Part V, "Sell Your House," covers selling your home—making the decision to sell, getting the house ready, deciding whether to use an agent or go it alone, pricing and marketing the house, negotiating offers, and closing on the house.

If you are buying your first home, Parts I–IV will lead you through the intricacies of the home-buying market, teaching you essential strategies for dealing with Realtors,® lenders, inspectors, building contractors, and other scary people. If you have already bought a house and are now buying a new one, this book can help you, too. During the first purchase, you may have felt like a horse being led around by its nose. "Sign here. You need this. Pay for this." And so on. This book can give you a better understanding of what you are signing, what you need, and what you pay.

So You Want to Sell Your House

If you are selling a house, you must have bought it sometime in the past, so you are at least a little familiar with the process. You can use this book to help you through the sometimes difficult process of preparing your home, having it appraised, deciding on an asking price, signing on with an agent or deciding to go it alone, and finally, closing on the deal.

If you get through that, you can go back to square one and bone up on the buying process because in most cases you will turn around and buy another house after you sell yours.

Extras

In addition to clear explanations and advice, this book offers vital information that can help you accomplish a difficult task more easily, or caution you about a common pitfall. These tips are splashed generously throughout the book and are easily recognizable with the following icons:

Tips mention a better way to accomplish a task, a way to save money, a way to get a better deal, or some shortcut. Read these to get short bits of advice on buying and selling a home.

To avoid common mistakes, look for this pitiful house. Here you'll find warnings and cautions against potential problems or misunderstandings.

A Bit of Background

These handy sidebars contain useful background information, such as the history of interest rates from 1972–1993. They also introduce you to the mysterious lingo used in real estate. After reading these, you can throw around terms such as *LTV* and *settlement sheet* like the pros.

Acknowledgments

Special thanks to Michelle Shaw, Production Editor, for handling a difficult project so skillfully, and for her meaningful changes, corrections, and suggestions. Also, special thanks to the technical reviewers, Sarah Diana, Tom Mattingly, Katherine Rock Ray, Steve Surette, and Todd Tarbutton for their suggestions and comments. Finally, thanks to Marie Butler-Knight, Publisher; Barry Pruett, Acquisitions Manager; Tom Godfrey, Product Manager; and Howard Peirce, Editor.

Part I
Find Your Dream Home

Owning a home can provide you with many benefits. Once you make the decision to purchase a home, you need to become financially prepared to make that commitment. You want to find out how big a down payment you can afford and how much you can spend for a house.

Once you define a price range, you can start looking at houses until you find one that you like. You may fall in love with the first one, or you may look at house after house after house. Somewhere out there, though, you'll find the house for you.

Chapter 1

The Dream of Owning a Home

In This Chapter
➤ Understanding the advantages and disadvantages of owning a home
➤ When you shouldn't buy a home
➤ Some home-buying information you may not know

Almost everyone dreams of owning his or her own home. After all, that's part of the American dream. Think of all the movies you've seen dramatizing the struggle to own a piece of America. Picture Tom Cruise racing wildly on a horse in the Oklahoma land rush. Picture him dramatically plunging his stake into the plot of land by the river, triumphant at last.

For generations, most Americans have been driven to own a piece of America. As America gets parceled into smaller and smaller pieces, and those pieces get more and more expensive, that drive isn't growing any less intense. Owning a home is still as enticing as it ever was, but is owning a home right for everyone? Is it right for you? If so, when is the best time to buy a house? When is the worst time? This chapter explores these questions and more.

The Advantages of Owning a Home

When the roof is leaking, your mortgage payment is late, and your new neighbors move in with a 90-pound German shepherd that likes to howl at the moon every night, you may seriously wonder whether buying a home has any advantages. Of course, it does. Here are a few of the important ones:

Uncle Sam likes to encourage home ownership, so you get a **big tax break** when you own your own home. You get to deduct some, if not all, of the interest you pay on the loan as well as some of the costs involved in financing the home (points paid, for instance). Your property taxes are also deductible. On a modest home, you may be able to deduct, for example, $8,000 to $10,000 a year. That's quite a tax break.

Home ownership brings with it the advantage of **enforced savings**. Unlike a rent payment, which goes bye-bye once you pay it, some of the money you pay on your home goes toward building up your equity. You can take out a loan against your equity, and you can get back the equity when you sell your house.

If you rent an apartment or home, you don't have too much control over the rent. Your landlord can raise the rent, sometimes as much as he wants. As a homeowner, on the other hand, you have the advantage of **fixed housing costs**. If you pay $800 the first month of a 30-year fixed mortgage, you'll pay $800 the last month, for principal and interest. If you get an adjustable-rate mortgage, however, the payments may vary some. The different types of financing are covered in Chapter 12. Taxes and insurance costs may vary.

WHOA!

How Much Is Your Bucket Worth?

Equity is the percentage of the house you own. When you first purchase a house, the bank owns most of it. When you start making payments, most of the payment goes toward paying the interest on the loan, but a drop or two goes toward the equity bucket. As you pay off more of the loan, more drops go into the equity bucket. When you sell your home, that bucket is yours. To figure out how much equity you have, take the selling price of the home and subtract the amount you still owe. For example, if you sold your house for $100,000 and owed $80,000, you'd have $20,000 in equity.

Most homes **appreciate**, or increase in value, over time. Your house is likely to be worth more when you sell it than when you purchased it. You can use the money you make on the sale of your home to finance a bigger and better home or to finance your retirement. (Keep in mind that not all homes will appreciate in value.)

Making timely mortgage payments builds a great **credit history**. If you want to purchase a car or get a credit card, most lenders look favorably on homeowners.

The financial and rational advantages are great, but probably the best advantages of owning a home are the control and autonomy that ownership affords you, and the sense of pride in that ownership. You can paint all the rooms chartreuse and knock out walls to remodel if you want. You can add an enclosed porch or put in solar panels. It's your house, and you can do what you want. There's just something special about owning your own place.

The Disadvantages of Owning a Home

Moving to the flip side of the coin, the disadvantages of buying a home are mostly financial. You must make the monthly mortgage payments; if you don't, the lender can *foreclose* on the house, meaning they can take it away from you. In addition to the actual loan, you will have property taxes and homeowner's insurance. Other expenses that you probably don't have as a renter are: **all** the utility bills (landlords usually cover some if not most utilities for apartment dwellers), and maintenance and upkeep on the house and property, such as fixing the leaking roof, mowing the grass, painting the garage, and so on and so on.

Finally, you can't pull up stakes and leave as easily if you own a home. If you're a renter, you can give your notice and take off. You don't have any financial responsibilities to the landlord. When you have a house, on the other hand, you have commitments that you will have to settle before you move on.

When Not to Buy a Home

In some cases, buying a house isn't the best idea. When are you better off not buying? Consider these examples:

If you're buying a home solely as an investment, you should be aware that, though most homes do appreciate in value, appreciation is not guaranteed. Many things that you have no control over affect the value of your home—local economy, national economy, abandoned buildings or new businesses in the neighborhood, a land fill, tacky neighbors who paint their houses chartreuse. Real estate investments can pay off, but you may also want to consider other investment opportunities.

If you know you're going to keep the house for only a short time, for instance, if you may be transferred to a new job or get married and move, you may want to consider renting rather than buying. When you haven't owned a house for very long, it's difficult to break even, let alone make a profit, when you sell it. You don't have much equity built up, plus you have all the costs of selling the home to consider.

If you aren't sure that you're going to like the area where you're considering a purchase, do your homework first. Don't just jump in and buy a house because it's, say, close to where you work. Try visiting a block-club meeting, grocery shopping in the local supermarket, taking your kids to the neighborhood park—anything that will allow you to get to know some of the neighbors and get a "feel" for the area.

If you cannot count on a steady income to make your payments, the lender may not approve you for a loan. If you're approved and you cannot make the payments, the lender may foreclose. You will lose all the money you have invested, and your credit rating will be ruined. If you have an unsteady income, you may want to wait until you're sure you can make the long-term financial commitment of buying a home.

Little-Known Facts about Buying a Home

Knowledge is the key to making your home-buying or -selling experience successful. The more you know, the more prepared you will be. That doesn't mean you need to understand every intricacy of the real estate market. It does mean that you should be aware of the process. The rest of this book will prepare you for the process of both buying and selling a home; here I want to just touch on some of the little-know facts about buying a home.

Everything is negotiable   From the price you pay for the house to when you move in, negotiate, negotiate, negotiate. When you make an offer, you can and should ask for the moon, if that's what you want.

Everything varies   You'll find that there aren't many tried, true, and trusted facts about the home-buying and home-selling process. Every home buyer and home seller's experience is going to vary wildly. One person may sell his house in the first month it is on the market; it may take another person six months. One person may feel an adjustable mortgage is the only way to finance. Another person may say it's insane to gamble like that and insist on a fixed-rate mortgage. Everything will vary according to your situation and what you want.

Everything changes   Laws about what tax benefits you get, laws about what the seller must tell you, and real-estate practices can change at any time.

There is no perfect time to buy   Some buyers get caught in the "I'll wait until I can afford my dream home" trap. These buyers wait and wait until they think the market will be perfect or until they find the house they've always wanted or until they can afford the house they've always wanted. Unless you have a compelling reason to wait, you shouldn't. The perfect market, perfect house, perfect price may not come along. Buy what you can afford and then trade up.

Don't fall for the no-money-down deal   You may see advertisements saying you can buy a house with no money down. Most too-good-to-be-true deals are just that. You can certainly get a good deal, but you should be skeptical of any plan that is big on promise and vague on delivery.

Win-win negotiating   A lot of people think that a successful deal happens only when they impose their will on another and get their way entirely (a win-lose situation). The best deals, though, are when both negotiating parties are happy (a win-win situation). If you buy a house at the price you want and the terms you want, and the sellers also get the price they want at acceptable terms, you both benefit.

> You can learn a lot from this book about buying and selling a home, but remember to ask friends and colleagues about their experiences, and when dealing with agents and homeowners, don't be afraid to interrogate them about everything.

The little-known physics Law of Expanding Possessions   If you're moving from a small house to a larger house, be prepared for the Law of Expanding Possessions. Physicists have yet to understand what causes this phenomenon, which simply stated says, "If you have a two-bedroom house full of junk and move to a four-bedroom house, you will have a four-bedroom house full of junk."

The redecorating cycle   Be prepared for the redecorating cycle. When you move in, you'll probably find that the couch isn't going to go with the carpet in the living room. Then when you recarpet, the recliner is going to look shabby, so you're going to need a new recliner. And while you're getting the recliner, you might as well pick out a new coffee table, which will bring you full circle back to the couch, which now doesn't seem to fit in with the new carpet, recliner, and coffee table. And after you paint the room to go with the new couch, carpet, recliner, and coffee table, the dining room will need work. Rest assured that one day everything will be perfect. That's the day you put the "For Sale" sign up and hope to recoup all your redecorating dollars.

The Least You Need to Know

Getting ready to buy a home is a big decision. This chapter gave you a basis for making that decision by teaching you that:

➤ There are many advantages to buying a home, including tax savings, appreciation in the value of your home, enforced savings, and having a place to call your own.

➤ You should carefully consider the wisdom of purchasing a home if you don't plan to live in the area for long, you're buying the home strictly as an investment, or you do not have a steady income.

➤ When buying a home, everything is negotiable.

Chapter 2

Understanding the Up-Front Costs of Buying a Home

To acquire most anything, you need money. That's what this chapter is all about. When you buy a house, you should expect to pay out two big amounts—one for the down payment and one for the closing costs. How much you pay for each depends on your particular situation. This chapter gives you an overview of what you can expect. For more details on financing and closing costs see Chapter 17 "Applying for the Mortgage."

Down Payments

You may see no-money-down deals advertised, but these types of deals usually carry the validity of those scandal newspapers that proclaim "Elvis Delivers Quintuplets in West Virginia" or "Eat All the Chocolate You Want and Lose 50 Pounds." The headlines are big on promise and hype, but when you read the small print, you discover the only witness to the event was a little space alien who looks like Ross Perot, or there's some odd, little ritual you have to perform to achieve success. In short, you're lured in by the catchy headline, but all you're left with is a fifty-cent tabloid and unfulfilled promises. Unfortunately, if you allow yourself to be lured in by a no-money-down scheme, it'll likely be more than a fifty-cent mistake.

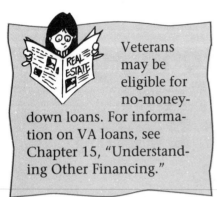

Veterans may be eligible for no-money-down loans. For information on VA loans, see Chapter 15, "Understanding Other Financing."

In nearly all instances, you're going to have to put some money down to purchase a house. Lenders don't like to give out loans that are risky to them. If a borrower doesn't have any money invested in a property, he may be more likely to default on the loan. The more money the borrower puts down, the happier (and more lenient) the lender is.

How Much Down Payment Do You Need?

The amount of down payment you need depends on many things: the type of financing, what payment you qualify for, and the purchase price of the home.

The down payment is usually figured as a percentage of the purchase price. The percentage you must pay depends on the type of financing you receive. (Financing is covered in detail in Part III of this book.) Conventional financing offers programs with as little as 5% down. With this type of down payment, you would also be required to pay private mortgage insurance (PMI). PMI reduces the risk to the mortgage company when there is less than 20% equity invested by the borrowers (see Chapter 18). For a conservative example, let's use a down payment of 20% of the purchase price. If you're buying a home for $100,000, you'd be expected to pay $20,000 down. Other types of loans—for example, government-assisted loans—require a smaller down payment. For this type of loan, you may need to put down only 5% or less.

Loan-To-Value

You may hear lenders use the term **loan-to-value** or LTV. If you put down 10% and finance 90%, that's called a 90% LTV loan.

Where to Get the Down Payment

If you already own a home and are moving to a new home, you can probably use the equity from the sale of your first home as the down payment on your second home. If you're a first-time buyer, you may use your savings for the down payment. If you have stocks, bonds, or other assets, you may want to sell these to raise the money for the down payment.

You may have assets that you aren't even aware of. For instance, perhaps you have a stamp collection that you can sell. Or perhaps you have a life insurance policy with some cash value. Consider all sources of income.

What If You Don't Have Money for the Down Payment?

If you don't have the money for a down payment, you can try one of the following strategies for getting the money:

Start a savings program and wait until you have 3-5% of the purchase price saved. If you don't have any savings, you probably aren't ready to buy a home. You should have at least some savings for the down payment. Also, you should be sure that you can afford the monthly payments. Open a savings account now and start saving.

When you're thinking about buying a home, you may want to create a budget and try to stick to it. Take some time to analyze where your money is going and look for places to save. Make your savings a basic expense; don't just save what is leftover every month from your paycheck.

Consider asking your parents or relative for a gift for the down payment. According to a 1987 study by the National Association of Realtors, 31 percent of all first-time buyers were aided by parents. If your parents are in a position to help, they can be a valuable resource when you're just starting out. Most lenders require a *gift letter*, showing that the money was a gift and does not have to be repaid. If you are getting a conventional loan, at least 5% of the down payment has to come from your money. The gift can be used for the closing costs or reserves (two months of house payments). FHA, on the other hand, allows a gift for the entire down payment and closing costs.

If you're purchasing a new home, **look for a builder who will consider "sweat equity."** In exchange for doing some of the work on the house—painting the interior, for example—the builder may reduce or waive the down payment. Sometimes the builder will issue credits for appliances, carpet, and so on, if the buyers have other sources who can give them a better price.

Consider using a different type of financing—for instance, seller take-backs or using a co-borrower. These alternative strategies are covered in Chapter 15.

When Do You Fork Over the Down Payment?

When you make an offer on the house, you're going to have to show the seller that you're sincere. An earnest smile and firm handshake won't do it. The seller will want a deposit on the house, sometimes called *earnest money*. The amount of money required for the deposit will vary depending on the local practices, the offer you're making on the house, and the market (whether it's a buyer's or a seller's market). The nuances of making an offer are covered in Chapter 8.

The earnest money will go toward your down payment. The down payment is payable at the closing. See Chapter 20 for closing strategies.

Closing Costs

In addition to the down payment, you also have to pay *settlement* or *closing costs* when you close on the loan. When you apply for a loan, the lender will give you an estimate of the closing costs, and you will probably feel like crying when you see the total. Typically, closing costs depend on the local costs and loan arrangement.

Before you give up, keep in mind that the costs you're required to pay and the amount will vary depending on your situation. You may be required to pay some costs; the seller may pick up other costs. Remember to bargain. Depending on how motivated the sellers are, you could get them to pick up quite a bit of the closing costs. Also, with some types of loans, you can finance some of the closing costs (that is, you can add them to your loan amount).

The following chapters will give you an idea of some of the closing costs involved: Chapter 8 considers closing costs as part of negotiating a sale; Chapter 16 shows how to use them for comparing lenders; Chapter 17 shows you how to get an estimate of closing costs, and Chapter 20 walks you through actually paying the fees.

Lender Fees

A lot of money you pay in closing goes into the lenders' pockets. They are the money people. Here are some fees you can expect to pay to the lender:

Points   A prepayment of interest. One point is equal to one percent of the mortgage or loan amount. Depending on the type of loan you get and the current mortgage market, you may have to pay points. For example, you may get an 8% loan with two points. If you're financing $100,000, one point would be equal to $1,000. Two points would total $2,000. Points are tax-deductible in the year they are paid.

You can keep down your points in two ways. First, you can shop for a loan with the lowest number of points and interest rates. Rates and points will vary from lender to lender (see Chapter 16). Second, you can ask the seller to pay points (see Chapter 8).

Loan origination fee   This fee covers the costs of the time for finalizing and reviewing the loan. Though it is basically a prepaid point, or one percent of the loan amount, it is not tax deductible.

Loan application fee   Usually around $200 to $300, this fee is payable when you apply for the loan. The lender uses it immediately to cover the costs of verifying your income, checking your credit, getting an appraisal, and so on. Be sure to inquire about this fee when you apply for the loan (see Chapter 16).

Interest payment   Depending on when you close on your house, you may have to pay interest for that month. (See the "Paying in Arrears" sidebar on the following page.)

Document preparation fee   Some lenders charge you an additional amount for preparing the loan documents. This may be a fluff fee, especially if you paid a loan application fee. When you're shopping around for a lender, ask about these fees.

Credit check fee   As part of the loan application process, you may be charged a fee for running a credit check. It's usually around $50. This fee doesn't actually go into the lender's pocket. He has to pay it out to have the credit check done.

Appraisal fee   Before a lender will approve a loan, the house will need to be appraised. The lender usually arranges the appraisal, but you may have to pay the fee. Expect to pay $250 to $300. Again, the lender has to pay this fee to the appraiser. See Chapter 17 to learn more about appraisals.

Paying in Arrears

Many buyers are confused about how house payments are paid and why interest is due at closing in some cases. When you rent an apartment, you pay in advance. On August 1, you pay the rent for the month of August.

When you purchase a house, you *pay in arrears*, or back pay on the house. For instance, your payment for August 1 pays for the month of July.

When you close on a house, you need to pay for the part of the month that you will be living in the house. If you close on July 29th, you have to pay for July 29th, 30th, and 31st. You're then paid up for that month. Your next payment won't be until September 1st; this payment will cover the month of August.

Advance and Reserve Payments

In addition to lender fees, you have to pay some other fees up front, including your insurance. You also have to set aside some money for your *escrow account*.

All lenders require that the home you purchase be insured. If your spouse sneaks a cigarette in the garage and burns the house down, the lender wants to be sure the damage is covered (more on insurance in Chapter 18). You usually have to pay up front and show a receipt and a one-year policy. You may also be required to pay a few months of insurance to put into an escrow account.

Escrow

What's an **escrow account**? Basically, the lender doesn't trust you to save up the money to pay taxes and insurance when they come due. So the lender requires you to pay 1/12 of your insurance and tax amount each month. This money is kept in an escrow account. When the tax and insurance bills come due, your lender pays them from this account. Escrow accounts are negotiable; see Chapter 18 for details.

You may be required to pay a few months of taxes to put into the escrow account, as well. If you opt not to do that, you may have to pay for a tax service contract. This contract is used to hire a company to watch your taxes and make sure that you pay them. If you don't, the lender is alerted, pays the taxes, adds the amount to your mortgage, and may foreclose.

Taxes are included as part of your monthly mortgage payment. Ask your agent to give you an estimate of taxes in the area you're looking. When you're considering a particular house, the listing should give you an exact amount for current taxes, but if you have any questions, you should check with the local tax assessor office to be sure.

If you put down less than 20% for a down payment, you will probably be required to pay private mortgage insurance (PMI). This insurance protects the lender in case you default on the loan. For some loans, you must pay this insurance fee up front. For other types of loans, you pay a monthly fee (sometimes in addition to the up-front fee) as part of your mortgage payment. PMI adds 0.25% to your interest rate. Chapter 18 discusses this type of insurance. For some loans, you may be able to finance the cost of mortgage insurance.

Other Fees

You may also be charged for other miscellaneous fees. If you have hired an attorney to handle the transaction, you will have an **attorney fee**. You should negotiate this fee with your attorney. Also, sometimes the lender charges you an attorney fee for their attorney, who ensures that local, state, and federal regulations are adhered to.

The **title search** ($25 to $50) checks to be sure there are no outstanding liens, unpaid loans, or other claims against the property. This fee varies according to the price you paid for the house. **Title insurance** is required and guarantees the title search if any claims or discrepancies pop up. The cost of title insurance varies depending on the price of the house, but count on several hundred dollars. Usually the buyer pays a portion of it and the seller pays the balance.

You're charged a fee for **recording** the sale with the proper county courthouse. Usually this fee is split by the buyer and seller, but this varies from state to state. You may also have to pay fees for an **inspection** and **survey**. The inspector will check for pests, roof damage, problems with the plumbing, wiring, heating, water, structure, and more. Inspections are covered in Chapter 19. There may be other **government fees** such as tax stamps, transfer taxes, and other fees due upon the sale. These fees vary by area.

Adding Up All the Costs

Table 2.1 shows an example of what you might pay up front for buying a home. Keep in mind that each of these figures will vary—the sales price, the required down payment, the closing costs, everything. This table should give you a rough idea of what to expect.

The Least You Need to Know

Once you've decided to purchase a home, you have to prepare financially. You need to round up some money for the down payment and the closing costs.

➤ You will be required to make a down payment of between 3% and 20% depending on the type of financing you get.

➤ You will also have to pay closing costs, which run from 3–6% of the sales price.

➤ Keep in mind that closing costs can be negotiable. You can ask the seller to pay some. You can shop around for a lender that doesn't charge a lot of closing costs, and for some loans, you can finance the closing costs.

Table 2.1   Estimate of Up-Front Costs

Purchase Price	$100,000
Interest Rate	8%
Total Amount Financed	$95,000

Type of Fee	Amount	Description
Down Payment	$5,000.00	5% of purchase price
Loan Origination Fee	950.00	1% of loan amount
Points	950.00	1 point or 1% of loan amount
Appraisal Fee	300.00	
Credit Report	60.00	
Insurance	350.00	
Mortgage Insurance Premium		
Insurance Reserve	58.33	2 months (350/12)
Tax Reserve	280.00	2 months at 140
Attorney's Fees	300.00	
Recording Fees	20.00	
Survey	125.00	
Total	8,393.33	

No man acquires property without acquiring with it a little arithmetic also.

—Ralph Waldo Emerson

Chapter 3

Figuring Out How Much You Can Borrow

In This Chapter

➤ Calculating your total income and monthly expenses

➤ Figuring out how much you can borrow

➤ Prequalifying for a loan

➤ Checking your credit history

If you had enough money to pay cash for your home, buying a home would be fairly simple—find the house and write the check. Unfortunately, there are very few people who can pay cash for a home. Around 99% of home buyers borrow money to buy their home. You probably fall into this 99%.

How much you can borrow is the critical question. All lenders are going to take a close look at your financial situation. You can't finance a house on your looks, unless, of course, you happen to look like Cindy Crawford or Richard Gere, in which case maybe you **could** pay cash for your home. This chapter covers the up-front costs of buying a home and then helps you take a close, perhaps painful look at your financial situation.

Before All the Numbers Make You Dizzy

This chapter is heavy on the number crunching—figuring this, subtracting that, multiplying by 28%, and so on. If you like to work with numbers, you will find this chapter useful in figuring out the amount of loan you can afford. Basically, you're prequalifying yourself.

If you don't want to wade through all the worksheets, you can ask your agent to give you an estimate of how much house you can afford and what the up-front costs will be. You can also go to a lender and be prequalified, as described in the section "Prequalifying for a Loan," later in this chapter.

How Much Are You Worth?

Before a lender will give you a loan, he will take a close look at the money you make and the money you spend. So that you're prepared, you should also scrutinize your income and debts.

Totaling Your Income

The first thing you should do in figuring out how much money you can spend on a house is to take a good look at your income. You need to total your annual and monthly gross income (before taxes). To do so, gather all your savings account information and check stubs (I know you keep them all in a shoebox somewhere). If you have other income, gather that information also. If you will be buying the house with a partner—for example, your spouse—gather income information for this person as well.

Keep in mind that lenders will look for an *average income*. They will want to evaluate your income for the past two years to make sure that it has been steady, and to take into consideration any seasonal jumps. Usually two years' continuous employment proves to the lender that you have a steady income. If you're recently out of college, lenders may take into consideration your future earning power.

If you're self-employed, the lender will usually consider as gross income the amount of money on which you paid taxes. For instance, if your business grossed $100,000, but you paid taxes on only $35,000, the lender will consider $35,000 as your gross annual income. You will have to show several years' tax returns to verify your income.

Bonuses don't always count, because this money is not guaranteed. If you want to have your bonus money considered as part of your gross salary, you need to prove that bonuses are a regular part of your pay. You must show a track record of receiving bonuses rather than just relying on the promise of a bonus. Your employer, for instance, may be able to write a letter saying that the bonus is dependable.

If you receive alimony or child support, you can include this money in your total, if you want. You must show that this is a dependable source of income. You may need a settlement statement from your divorce that states the amount. Most lenders will consider only income that can be verified—from your employer or past tax returns.

Use the worksheet in Table 3.1 to record your income. Total the income for yourself and your partner (line 8), then add your income to your partner's income to come up with the grand total (line 9). This figure represents your annual gross income. To calculate your monthly gross income, divide this figure (line 9) by 12.

Table 3.1 Calculate Your Income

	A You	B Co-purchaser
1. Gross Salary	135,000 – 210,000	
2. Bonuses		
3. Interest	3,000	
4. Dividends		
5. Social Security/Pension		
6. Child Support		
7. _____ (OTHER)		
8. **TOTAL** (add lines 1 - 7)		
9. **GRAND TOTAL** (add line 8, columns A and B)	138,000 – 213,000	
10. **Monthly Income** (divide line 9 by 12)	11,500 – 17,750	.28% = 3,220 – 4,970

You now know how much money you and your partner make each year and each month. You will use the figures you came up with here to calculate some qualifying ratios in "How Much Can You Borrow?," later in this chapter.

Totaling Your Monthly Expenses

You know the money that is coming in. Now you need to figure out the total money that is going out. Lenders will also want to know what monthly expenses you have. For conventional loans, lenders don't care that you spend five dollars every day to eat at Pizza Hut; they are concerned with long-term debt—debt that will take you longer than 10 months to pay off. For VA and FHA loans, monthly expenses such as utilities are taken into consideration.

You need to collect all your required monthly payments and total them. This includes car loans, student loans, payments you must make on any and all credit cards, and so on. Use the worksheet in Table 3.2 to record your monthly debts.

Table 3.2 Calculate Monthly Payments

	A You	B Co-purchaser
1. Car Payment		
2. Student Loan		
3. Credit Card #1	1,200	
4. Credit Card #2		
5. Credit Card #3		
6. Other Loan		
7. _____ _(OTHER)		
8. **TOTAL** (add lines 1 - 7)		
9. **GRAND TOTAL** (add line 8, columns A and B)	1200	

Enter all your debts in one column. If you're purchasing the house with a partner, enter that person's monthly payments as well. Then total the two to come up with your monthly debt amount. You will use this figure in the next section to compare some lending ratios.

How Much Can You Borrow?

The first part of the loan equation is complete: you know how much you make and how much you spend. Step two is to figure out how much you can borrow.

> If you have less than 10 months left on an installment loan, don't include it in your total monthly debt payments. If you're close to 10 months, consider paying off the loan enough to bring it under the 10-month mark. Then you don't have to count it.

Getting a Ballpark Figure

270 - 335,000
— 420 - 525,000

If you're getting tired of all the number crunching, you can use a ballpark method for figuring out how much you can borrow. Roughly, you can borrow up to 2–2½ times your annual salary. If you and your partner make $50,000, you can buy a house in the $100,000 to $125,000 price range.

You can also use Table 3.3 to estimate the amount of loan you can finance. This table assumes that you're getting a 30-year fixed-rate mortgage. Follow these steps:

1. Find your gross annual income in the far left column of the table.

2. The second column represents 25% of your gross annual income, divided by 12. The assumption is that 25% of your income will pay for principal and interest and 3% will pay for taxes and insurance.

3. In the top row, find the interest rate that you qualify for and is available.

4. Find the value where the interest rate and gross annual income intersect.

The resulting value shows you the amount of mortgage you can afford.

Table 3.3 Estimate Your Mortgage

Gross Annual Income	Monthly Payment	6.0%	6.5%	7.0%	7.5%	8.0%	8.5%
$20,000	$417	69,497	65,921	62,628	59,591	56,785	54,189
25,000	521	86,871	82,401	78,285	74,488	70,981	67,736
30,000	625	104,245	98,882	93,942	89,386	85,177	81,284
35,000	729	121,619	115,362	109,599	104,284	99,373	94,831
40,000	833	138,993	131,842	125,256	119,181	113,570	108,378
45,000	938	156,367	148,323	140,913	134,079	127,766	121,925
50,000	1,042	173,741	164,803	156,570	148,977	141,962	135,473
55,000	1,146	191,115	181,283	172,227	163,874	156,158	149,020
60,000	1,250	208,490	197,764	187,884	178,772	170,354	162,567
65,000	1,354	225,864	214,244	203,541	193,670	184,551	176,114
70,000	1,458	243,238	230,724	219,199	208,567	198,747	189,662
75,000	1,563	260,612	247,204	234,856	223,465	212,943	203,209
80,000	1,667	277,986	263,685	250,513	238,363	227,139	216,756
85,000	1,771	295,360	280,165	266,170	253,260	241,335	230,303
90,000	1,875	312,734	296,645	281,827	268,158	255,532	243,851
95,000	1,979	330,108	313,126	297,484	283,056	269,728	257,398
100,000	2,083	347,483	329,606	313,141	297,953	283,924	270,945
110,000	2,292	382,231	362,566	344,455	327,749	312,316	298,040
120,000	2,500	416,979	395,527	375,769	357,544	340,709	325,134
130,000	2,708	451,727	428,488	407,083	387,339	369,101	352,229
140,000	2,917	486,476	461,448	438,397	417,135	397,494	379,323
150,000	3,125	521,224	494,409	469,711	446,930	425,886	406,418
160,000	3,333	555,972	527,369	501,025	476,725	454,278	433,512
170,000	3,542	590,720	560,330	532,339	506,521	482,671	460,607
180,000	3,750	625,469	593,291	563,653	536,316	511,063	487,701
190,000	3,958	660,217	626,251	594,967	566,111	539,455	514,796
200,000	4,167	694,965	659,212	626,282	595,907	567,848	541,890

9.0%	9.5%	10.0%	10.5%	11.0%	11.5%	12.0%	12.5%
51,784	49,553	47,480	45,550	43,753	42,075	40,508	39,041
64,730	61,941	59,349	56,938	54,691	52,594	50,635	48,801
77,676	74,329	71,219	68,325	65,629	63,113	60,761	58,561
90,622	86,717	83,089	79,713	76,567	73,632	70,888	68,322
103,568	99,106	94,959	91,101	87,505	84,150	81,015	78,082
116,514	111,494	106,829	102,488	98,443	94,669	91,142	87,842
129,460	123,882	118,699	113,876	109,382	105,188	101,269	97,602
142,406	136,270	130,569	125,263	120,320	115,707	111,396	107,362
155,352	148,658	142,439	136,651	131,258	126,225	121,523	117,123
168,298	161,047	154,308	148,039	142,196	136,744	131,650	126,883
181,244	173,435	166,178	159,426	153,134	147,263	141,777	136,643
194,190	185,823	178,048	170,814	164,072	157,782	151,904	146,403
207,136	198,211	189,918	182,201	175,011	168,301	162,031	156,163
220,082	210,599	201,788	193,589	185,949	178,819	172,157	165,924
233,028	222,988	213,658	204,976	196,887	189,338	182,284	175,684
245,975	235,376	225,528	216,364	207,825	199,857	192,411	185,444
258,921	247,764	237,398	227,752	218,763	210,376	202,538	195,204
284,813	272,540	261,137	250,527	240,640	231,413	222,792	214,725
310,705	297,317	284,877	273,302	262,516	252,451	243,046	234,245
336,597	322,093	308,617	296,077	284,392	273,489	263,300	253,766
362,489	346,869	332,357	318,852	306,269	294,526	283,553	273,286
388,381	371,646	356,096	341,627	328,145	315,564	303,807	292,806
414,273	396,422	379,836	364,403	350,021	336,601	324,061	312,327
440,165	421,199	403,576	387,178	371,897	357,639	344,315	331,847
466,057	445,975	427,316	409,953	393,774	378,676	364,569	351,368
491,949	470,751	451,055	432,728	415,650	399,714	384,823	370,888
517,841	495,528	474,795	455,503	437,526	420,752	405,076	390,409

Keep in mind that ballpark figures aren't always reliable. For one thing, ballpark figures make a lot of assumptions about your situation. You will probably want to take the time to work through the lender's ratios.

Use Your Computer...

If you have a computer and a spreadsheet program, you can build your own worksheets that figure monthly payments and other calculations.

If you really want to explore all the possibilities, you may want to purchase software designed for buying a home. Parsons Technology, for example, sells the "Home Buying Companion," a program that can calculate a loan amount, create an amortization table, figure out a maximum loan amount, and help you with other aspects of buying a home. Information about this product is included in Appendix B.

You can also use a financial calculator to figure payments.

Using a Lender's Ballpark Figure

Lenders and agents are a little leery of the ballpark method. For one thing, this method is too easy, and if they allow things to look too easy, you may figure out you don't need them. More importantly, rough estimates can't take into consideration individual circumstances. For example, if one couple with a $50,000 income has $20,000 in savings, and no a car payment, they may be able to afford an even more expensive house than a ballpark figure would indicate. If another couple with a $50,000 income has two car payments, maxed-out credit cards, and intend to get their down payment by winning the lottery, they might not qualify for a home in any price range.

Lenders compare your income and monthly payments to certain qualifying ratios. You will see these ratios expressed like this: 28/36 (the ratios most often used for conventional loans) or 29/41 (ratios used for FHA loans). If you have a particular lender in mind, call the lender and ask what ratios they use.

The first number, sometimes called the *front* or *housing ratio,* is that percentage of your income you can spend on housing. For example, most lenders say your monthly house payment (including loan payment, property taxes, and insurance) shouldn't total more than 28 percent of your gross monthly income (that is, your gross annual income, divided by 12). The ratio used depends on the amount of money you put down.

The second number, the *back* or *overall debt ratio,* totals your housing expenses plus your long-term monthly debt, then figures this total as a percentage of your monthly gross income. For example, most lenders say that your housing expenses plus your monthly debt should not be more than 36 percent of your monthly income.

The Guessing Game

How did they come up with these ratios? Lenders don't like guesses, but that's basically what the ratios are. The lenders feel if they follow these guidelines, homeowners will be able to payoff the loan. The ratios are arbitrary, though, and are based on studies done in the 1930s and 1940s by the Federal Housing Administration.

Most lenders sell the loans to a secondary market (as described in Chapter 16), and therefore follow the guidelines set by the agencies that purchase the loans.

The ratios will vary depending on the area. For instance, if these ratios were used in California, it is likely that very few people would be able to afford a home.

Also, the bigger your down payment, the less significant the ratios become.

What's Your Ratio?

To figure out your housing ratio, use the worksheet in Table 3.4 and follow these steps:

1. Enter your gross monthly income from line 10 of Table 3.1.

2. Multiply this amount by 28% (.28). The resulting figure is the most you can afford for a monthly mortgage payment.

Table 3.4   Maximum Mortgage Payment Housing Ratio

1. Monthly Gross Income	_____
	×.28
2. Maximum Mortgage Payment	3220 – 4970

To figure out your overall debt ratio, use the worksheet in Table 3.5 and follow these steps:

1. Write down your monthly gross income.

2. Multiply this amount by 36% (.36). This figure is the total amount of money you can spend on all debts—housing and other.

3. Write in your current monthly debts from line 9 of Table 3.2.

4. Subtract your present debt from your maximum allowable debt to find out how much you have left over for your house payment.

Table 3.5   Maximum Mortgage Payment Overall Debt Ratio

1. Monthly Gross Income	11,500 – 17,750
	×.36
2. Maximum Monthly Debt	4,140 – 6,390
3. Present Monthly Debt	_____
4. Maximum Mortgage Payment	_____

The amount left over is the amount you can spend on a mortgage payment. Translating this monthly payment to a loan amount can be tricky. Your housing expenses include what is known as PITI (principal, interest, taxes, and insurance—pronounced pity). The principal and interest will vary depending on the amount of the loan, type of loan, and interest rate. You can use the tables in Appendix A to look up the principal and interest amount for different loans and interest rates.

Just because a lender says you can afford house payments of $1,200 doesn't mean you actually can. On top of the principal and interest, you need to add taxes and insurance. Taxes will vary depending on where you live, and insurance will vary depending on the policy you purchased. You can ask your agent to give you estimates of these payments.

With an experienced agent, you can sometimes do some creative financing to be able to qualify for a loan. Your agent won't recommend anything illegal, but he or she may be able to make suggestions about how to lower your monthly debts or how to finance your loan. Just be careful not to get in over your head.

Looking at an Example

Table 3.6 shows the annual gross income and monthly payments for Jim and Betty Shikenjanski. In this example, the combined income of the couple totals $55,250. Their monthly gross income, then, is $4,604.

Table 3.6 Jim and Betty's Annual Gross Income

	A Jim	B Betty
1. Gross Salary	$30,000	$25,000
2. Bonuses		
3. Interest		250
4. Dividends		
5. Social Security/Pension		
6. Child Support		
7. _____ (OTHER)		
8. **Total** (add lines 1-7)	30,000	25,250
9. **Grand Total** (add line 8, columns A and B)	$55,250	
10. **Monthly Income** (divide line 9 by 12)	$4,604	

Table 3.7, on the following page, gives a breakdown of Jim & Betty's monthly debt.

Table 3.7 Jim and Betty's Monthly Debt

	A Jim	B Betty
1. Car Payment	$240	$325
2. Student Loan	85	
3. Credit Card #1		25
4. Credit Card #2		
5. Credit Card #3		
6. Other Loan		
7. _____ (OTHER)		
8. **Total** (add lines 1-7)	325	350
9. **Grand Total** (add line 8, columns A and B)	$675	

If you apply the first ratio, you can see from Table 3.8 that the Shikenjanskis can afford a maximum house payment of $1,289. If you use the second ratio (overall debt), Table 3.9 shows that the Shikenjanskis can afford a maximum payment of $983. When qualifying the loan, the lender will use the lowest figure ($983).

Table 3.8 Jim and Betty's Monthly Payment Housing Ratio

1. Monthly Gross Income	$4,604
	× .28
2. Maximum Monthly Payment	1,289

Table 3.9 Jim and Betty's Overall Debt Ratio

1. Monthly Gross Income	$4,604
	× .36
2. Maximum Monthly Debt	1,658
3. Present Monthly Debt	– 675
4. Maximum Monthly Payment	983

Prequalifying for a Loan

If you have followed all the worksheets in this chapter, you have prequalified yourself. You should feel pretty confident about what you can afford, and you should know your financial situation.

If you choose not to do the worksheets, you may want to have a lender prequalify you. (You may want to do this in addition to qualifying yourself so you're sure your figures are accurate.)

You can prequalify informally or formally; each has its advantages and drawbacks.

Prequalifying Informally

When you prequalify informally, you don't pay a fee. You usually spend 20 to 30 minutes on the phone with a lender. The lender will ask you questions about your income and monthly debt (similar to topics covered in this chapter). Then the lender will do some quick calculations to let you know how much you can finance. This type of prequalifying is good when you want a rough estimate.

Keep in mind that the lender is not guaranteeing you a loan; you will still have to go through a formal qualification. Also, the lender is basing his estimate on what you tell him. If you exaggerate your income, make up an amount because you don't know, or forget about monthly payments, you won't get an accurate figure.

Formally Prequalifying

If you prefer, you can also make a written application for a loan. In this case, you will need to bring in all your financial information (tax receipts, bank statements, and so on), and the qualification will take longer. You will also be charged for the loan application. After a day or so, the lender will give you an estimate of the loan amount you can qualify for.

Because you have supplied accurate information, you can pretty much count on qualifying for the loan amount. Also, sellers like buyers who have been formally prequalified because they know that the buyer will not (or should not) have problems qualifying for a loan.

On the down side, when you prequalify, you're guaranteed a loan with that particular lender. Another lender may offer better terms, and if you want to use that lender, you will have to qualify with them. As you learn in Chapter 16, you will probably want to shop around and select a lender with the most favorable terms.

Checking Your Credit Record

When you qualify for a loan, the lender will check your credit record to ensure that you don't have any credit problems. If you have had a history of credit problems, you will probably want to get your credit report and be prepared to respond to any questions or problems on the report.

If haven't been late or missed any credit payments, you probably don't have to worry about getting a bad credit report. But mistakes do happen and sometimes your report may include something that is wrong or a problem that has been resolved. You may want to get a copy of your credit report just to double-check.

Getting a Credit Report

Federal law requires that you have access to any information in your credit files. You can obtain a credit report from a local credit report agency or a national credit bureau. Three of the best-known credit bureaus are Equifax, Trans Union, and TRW. (See Appendix B for a list of addresses and phone numbers.) The fee for a report ranges from $8 to $15. You must send them a letter including your full name, date of birth, social security number, and present and past addresses. You may also need to send in a copy of your driver's license and/or birth certificate.

If you have several credit cards, get rid of most of them before you apply for a loan. Having too many credit cards may be looked on unfavorably by lenders. With easy access to credit, you could get yourself into trouble.

Get the report two to three months before you apply for the loan so you'll have time to resolve any problems that turn up.

If you have been turned down for credit, the creditor has to furnish you a copy of the credit report, free of charge, if you ask for it.

Correcting a Mistake or Responding to Problems

If your credit report doesn't show any problems, you can rest assured that your loan won't be turned down because of your credit report. If your report does include a problem, you should correct it (if it is in error) or resolve it.

If you have an outstanding debt, resolve it by contacting the creditor. Be sure to send a letter to the creditor asking them to let all the reporting services and yourself know that the problem has been fixed. If you cannot resolve the problem, document your explanation. The credit agency must include your explanation of the problem in the credit report.

If your report has a mistake, you need to get the reporting agency to correct it. This is harder than actually clearing an outstanding debt! Write a complaint letter; call the local office. If you can't get resolution, call the bureau manager.

Slow pays are almost as bad as no pays. If you pay your bills, but pay them late, you may think that you don't have a bad record. Slow pays (late payments) reflect poorly on your credit record. You should document or explain any late payments, especially any late rent or mortgage payments.

WHOA! **Bad Debt, Bad Dreams**

How long will you be haunted by bad debt? Suppose that in the past you had some credit problems, but now they are all resolved. How long does bad debt stay on your record? Seven years. After that time, the unfavorable credit information should be dropped from your file. If you file for bankruptcy, this information stays on your record for 10 years.

The Least You Need to Know

Preparing financially to buy a home can be scary. If you don't figure out in advance how much you can afford, you may get your heart set on your dream house, and then not qualify for the loan, or you may get the loan but be unable to make payments. To figure out the maximum house you can afford, keep these things in mind.

➤ Lenders look at two ratios when deciding whether you qualify for a loan. The front or housing ratio requires that your mortgage payment not exceed a certain percentage (usually 28%) of your monthly income. The back or overall debt ratio requires that your mortgage payment plus your debt payments do not exceed a certain percentage (usually 36%) of your monthly income.

➤ Mortgage payments consist of the principal, interest, taxes, and insurance. You will see this abbreviated PITI.

➤ To find out how much you can borrow, you can talk with a lender and prequalify either formally or informally, or you can prequalify yourself.

➤ To prequalify yourself, divide your gross annual income by 12 to get your gross monthly income, then subtract your total monthly payments.

➤ It's a good idea to check your credit record to ensure you don't have any credit problems. If you do, resolve the problem or have your record corrected before you apply for a loan.

Chapter 4

Picking an Agent

> **In This Chapter**
>
> ➤ Your real estate scorecard—finding out who's who
>
> ➤ Who pays the agent?
>
> ➤ Do you need an agent?
>
> ➤ Selecting an agent
>
> ➤ Working with for-sale-by-owner homes

When you announce your desire to purchase a house, you may be surprised at the number of real estate people who want to represent you. Agents come out of the woodwork, calling you, sending you information, following you around at open houses, knocking on your door. It may seem like every other person you know turns out to be a real estate agent or knows an agent (maybe several). Your neighbor tells you "I only work at Pizza Hut part-time. I'm actually a real estate agent." Your mother calls and tells you that the Senior Citizen Center has sponsored a real estate class and your grandmother now has her real estate license.

You won't have to worry too much about finding an agent—you do need to worry about finding a good one. Because this person is going to play an integral role in helping you buy a home, you want to first understand the types of agents and then select an agent that you like to work with and that has the experience you need.

Types of Brokers

If you look at the terms used in the real estate business, you may think that you have wandered into the world of spies. There are agents and subagents, brokers and associates, and finally Realtors®—with a capital *R!* Understanding who does what in the process of buying a home can help you avoid any confusion.

Brokers

The principal broker is the big chief, the head honcho, the queen bee— the person licensed by the state to conduct a real estate business. All the other worker bees center around the principal broker. Having a broker's license means that the person can start and run a real estate office, but not all brokers do. The broker is more like an agent.

Sometimes the broker is associated with a franchise, such as Century 21. If you select a franchised broker, you have the advantage of national name recognition and usually a strong national advertising campaign. Keep in mind, though, how a franchise works. Each franchise is individually owned and operated. That means you aren't guaranteed a great agent just because you selected a well-known real estate franchise. You should select a firm based on that office's reputation—not the reputation of the national firm.

Agents

The person you will most likely deal with is the agent. This person handles the buying and selling of homes and may also be called a sales associate (or Bart or Betty). An agent is always associated with a broker, sometimes as an employee but more often as an independent contractor.

Remember that a broker can also be considered an agent, so to keep things straight, I'll use *broker* when I mean the principal broker (someone you are not likely to deal with) and *agent* for the person who will help you find your home.

The agent that puts the house on the market or lists the house is often called the listing agent. Your agent, the agent that shows the house and handles the buyer, is often called a *subagent.* (More on subagents later.)

Realtors®

If an agent is an agent, then who is a Realtor®? Are agents also Realtors®? Why the capital *R?* What's the penalty for not capitalizing the *R?* Realtor® is a trademark designation, hence the capitalization, and the penalty for not remembering to capitalize the *R* is death by beheading. Just kidding.

A Realtor® is a broker or agent who belongs to the local or state Board of Realtors® which has an affiliation with National Association of Realtors® (NAR). These members follow a code of ethics beyond state license laws. More importantly, Realtors® sponsor the Multiple Listing System (MLS) which is used to list houses for sale. More on this topic later in the chapter and in Chapter 6.

Who Pays the Agent, or Who's on My Side?

In the past when you bought a home, everyone worked for the seller— the broker, the agent, the Realtor®, the person showing you homes and working with you to find a home. All of these people represented the seller and were paid by the seller. This sometimes came as quite a shock to people buying a home.

The trend is changing, though, and now you can select how you're represented—with a subagent, a dual agent, or a buyer's agent.

Using a Subagent

A subagent has certain responsibilities to the seller. The agent must follow the seller's instruction (unless the instruction is illegal). The agent must be loyal to the seller. He must work to get the highest selling price (which is also in his interest because he gets a bigger commission).

The agent must keep confidential all seller information. The agent, for instance, cannot tell you that the sellers are desperate and that they are willing to accept a lower bid, unless doing so is in the seller's best interest.

37

The agent cannot tell you what to offer for a particular house and cannot point out defects of a house (unless they are hidden defects). However, the agent must pass along any information you say of interest. For example, if you say that you're going to offer $90,000 for the house but are willing to go to $100,000, your agent can pass along this information.

If you are both listing your house and looking for a new house, the sales commission may be negotiable. Ask your agent. Agents may be willing to lower the commission if they both list and sell the house.

The subagent is also paid by the seller. Here's how it works: When a house is put on the market, the seller agrees to pay a percent of the sales price to the agent(s) involved in selling the house. Seven percent is common. So suppose that a house sold for $100,000. The commission on the house would total $7,000. That money is divided into two parts. The agent that listed the house gets part of the money. (The amount will vary—sometimes half the money and sometimes a certain percentage.) This agent splits his pot with his principal broker. The agent that sold the house gets the other half and usually splits his commission with his principal broker. If the listing agent both listed and sold the house, the listing agent and his principal broker split the entire commission.

You may wonder why anyone would even use a subagent, but keep in mind that agents get other clients mostly by referrals.

Using a Buyer's Agent

The real estate practice of agency has evolved and now it is more common to find a different type of agent—a buyer's agent. This type of agent represents you, the buyer. The agent can make recommendations to you on what price and terms to offer. When the buyer's agent negotiates the deal, he negotiates it with only your interests in mind. Anything you tell the agent is confidential; he will not pass the information along to the seller.

How a buyer's agent is paid depends on the agreement you reach with the agent. Most get a flat fee or a commission based on the purchase price. Some require a retainer that may or may not be applied to the total fee. Some require a minimum fee. Sometimes you pay the fee, sometimes the seller pays the fee.

You need to know exactly what you will pay and how m~~...~~ ~~...~~ay also want to ha~~...~~ ~~...~~ost. Finall~~...~~ ~~...~~t the ~~...~~pplied ~~...~~imum

~~...~~rchase ~~...~~ays ~~...~~can ~~...~~mis- ~~...~~the ~~...~~price enough to ~~...~~fee. The seller ~~...~~vated to do this because ~~...~~r will only have to pay the listing agent's 3% commission. The listing agent will probably be amenable also, because he most likely will still get his 3%.

If you have a buyer's agent and she shows you a property listed by the same company, you have a *dual agency*. The buyer's agent should tell you when this occurs.

You will probably be asked to sign an exclusivity agreement, which says you will work only with that agent for the time specified (usually 60 to 90 days). The following two figures are examples of the contract a buyer must sign in procuring a buyer's agent (Buyer's Agency Selection Form), and the contract the buyer and seller must sign granting permission for an agent to act as a dual agent (Dual Agency Disclosure Agreement).

If you work with a subagent, you should not tell that agent how much you're willing to pay. Your agent must certainly know the price range you can afford, but don't tell the agent the highest you will pay for a property. Don't let on any special terms you would consider offering the seller. Don't tell your agent anything you wouldn't want the seller to know.

If you use a buyer's agent from a brokerage firm, be sure to ask how **conflicts of interest** are handled. The firm, remember, has both types of agents. Also, check into the disclosure rules. Will the firm tell you whether it is a *dual agency*, meaning it is representing both parties?

BUYER'S AGENCY SELECTION FORM

(Disclosure of A. H. M. Graves Company, Inc.'s policy on broker cooperation, compensation, and conflict of interest.)

A. H. M. GRAVES COMPANY, INC. (Graves) offers assistance to

Paul · Paula Pierce _____(Buyer) in locating property to purchase with

either of the following types of representation:

(Where the word "seller" appears, it shall also mean "lessor," "landlord" etc., if applicable. "Sale" or "sold" shall also mean "lease" or "leased." "Buyer" shall mean "lessee." The obligation of the broker shall also apply to any associated salesperson.)

_____ **Sub-Agent**
Sub-Agents are brokers and salespersons who procure buyers for the Seller's property and represent the interest of the Seller. A Sub-Agent is compensated from the sales transaction by the Seller and receives a portion of the commission Seller pays to listing broker.

OR

X **Buyer-Agent**
Buyer-Agents are brokers and salespersons who procure buyers for the Seller's property and who represent the interests of the Buyer. Representations which Buyer-Agents make about Seller's property are not made as the agent of the Seller. A Buyer-Agent is compensated from the sales transaction by the Seller and receives a portion of the commission Seller pays to listing broker. If Seller or Seller's listing broker elects to reduce compensation to Buyer's Agent, such reduction may limit the range of properties that Graves may show to Buyer.

BUYER CHOOSES TO HAVE GRAVES SERVE IN THE MANNER CHECK MARKED ABOVE.

Disclosure of Potential Dual Agency

Graves owes certain duties to Buyer when acting as Buyer's agent. Graves owes similar duties to a seller when acting as agent for the Seller under a Listing Contract. A Graves represented buyer may be interested in seeing a property listed by Graves. This situation creates a dual-agency and in such event Graves will have a potential conflict of interest. As such, Graves will not be able to represent both Seller and Buyer without the written consent of both parties. It is highly probable that Buyer will want to see a property listed by Graves. Buyer hereby consents to Graves acting as dual agent in such an event.

Paul Pierce	6/28/94	*Maris Bluester*	6/28/94
Buyer	Date	Agent/Salesperson	Date
Paula Pierce	6/28/94		
Buyer	Date		

Form P-227A 8/2/93

DUAL AGENCY DISCLOSURE AGREEMENT

1. This Dual Agency Disclosure Agreement ("Agreement") is entered into on *July 10* , 19 *94*.

2. by and between *Graves Realtors* ("Broker")

3. *Mr + Mrs Seller* ("Seller"). *Bess Manager* ("Listing Salesperson"),

4. *Mr + Mrs. Buyer* ("Buyer"), and *Newer Agent* ("Selling Salesperson").

5. A. The Broker has a Listing Contract with Seller dated *6/30/94*

6. whereby the Broker is appointed as the Seller's Agent to sell real estate commonly known as_____

7. *8169 Ashwood Ct* in *Andpls*

8. Indiana. *46268* Zip Code.

9. B. The Broker also has a Buyer/Broker Contract with Buyer whereby Broker is appointed as the Buyer's Agent to
10. assist in the purchase of real estate.

11. C. Seller wishes to sell said real estate to Buyer, and Buyer wishes to purchase Seller's real estate.

12. D. Seller and Buyer both wish to use the services of Broker who is a Dual Agent in this transaction.

13. E. Seller and Buyer understand that it can be unlawful for an agent to act as a Dual Agent, because (1) there is
14. an inherent possibility of a conflict of interest and/or breach of a fiduciary duty which (2) might cause damage
15. to a Seller or Buyer. A Dual Agent is not acting unlawfully if a Seller and Buyer agree that their agent can act
16. as a Dual Agent, and represent them both in a transaction.

17. F. The Broker/Dual Agent wishes to disclose to Seller and Buyer the nature of an agent's position when serving
18. two principals, so that Seller and Buyer can make an informed decision whether they want the Dual Agent to
19. serve them both in the aforesaid transaction. Since the Broker has agency duties to both the Buyer and Seller,
20. the Broker would represent both the Buyer and the Seller in the transaction only with consent.

21. In this dual agency relationship, the Broker's fiduciary duty will be limited by not disclosing confidential
22. information. Confidential information includes the possibility that the Seller will accept a price less than the
23. listing price, that the Buyer will pay a price greater than the price offered, or any other information that could
24. adversely affect either party's negotiating position. However, nothing would prevent the Broker from disclosing
25. to the Buyer any known material facts about the real estate.

26. G. Seller and Buyer agree that Broker is hereby empowered to act as their Dual Agent in this real estate
27. transaction; and that Seller and Buyer waive any claim they now have or may have in the future against
28. Broker for acting as a Dual Agent in said transaction.

29. This Agreement may be executed simultaneously or in two or more counterparts, each of which shall be
30. deemed an original, but all of which together shall constitute one and the same instrument. Delivery of this
31. document may be accomplished by electronic facsimile reproduction (FAX); if FAX delivery is utilized, the
32. original document shall be promptly executed and/or delivered, if requested.

33. **SELLER**

34. *John Seller* Dated: *7/10/94*
35. *Irma Seller* Dated: *7/10/94*

36. **BUYER**

37. *Diane Brooks* Dated: *7/10/94*
38. *Tom Brooks* Dated: *7/10/94*

39. **DUAL AGENT**

40. *Bess Manager* Dated: *7/11/94*
41. Listing Salesperson

42. *Newer Agent* Dated: *7/11/94*
43. Selling Salesperson

44. Accepted by: *Graves Realtor* Dated: *7/11/94*
45. REALTOR / BROKER

Using a Discount Broker

In recent years another type of broker has emerged—the discount broker. When you use this type of agent, you get access to the MLS listings and do most of the legwork yourself. You can view the houses alone (although in some states this isn't allowed), draw up your own contract, arrange for financing, and so on. In exchange for this, you don't pay the entire commission.

You want to be sure to completely understand what you can do, what break you will get on the commission, and what extras the broker charges for. For instance, the broker may charge you for making calls, arranging showings, and so on.

Do You Need an Agent?

Do you need an agent? Probably. The next sections explain some of the benefits you can expect to get from using an agent.

Financial Help

It would be great if by financial help I meant the agent was willing to lend or, better yet, give you the money to buy the house. That would make using an agent worthwhile! Unfortunately, I mean a different kind of financial help. A real estate agent can help you financially in these ways:

Analyzing your financial situation. Your agent can help you answer these questions: How much house can you afford? How much down payment can you afford? What can you do to be in a better situation to afford a home?

Estimating the costs of home ownership. In addition to analyzing your financial situation, your agent should also be able to prepare you for the costs of owning a home (mortgage, taxes, insurance, and so on). Also, the agent should be able to translate a mortgage amount into monthly payments. For example, if you purchase a $100,000 home, what (roughly) will your monthly payments be?

Educating you about the types of financing. An agent should be knowledgeable not only about real estate but also about financing. She should be able to explain the different types of financing available as well as what might be appropriate for your situation. If she can't answer all your financial questions, she should be able to put you in touch with someone who can.

Helping you get and work with a lender. Some agents can recommend a particular lender and tell you what to expect when you apply for a loan. Some agents may even go with you and help you through the loan application process. Some may help you shop for a loan with the best terms.

Finding the Right House

In addition to financial assistance, the agent's key role is in helping you find a house. Using an agent has several advantages over just looking yourself.

For example, an agent can help you define what type of house you want by asking you a lot of questions: How big a house do you need? Do you plan to resell the house? What's your family and job situation? Do you have children? Plan to have children? Will you be transferred to another job? By being nosy, an agent can help you get a good idea of what you want.

An agent has access to the Multiple Listing System (MLS), which lists detailed information about most homes for sale in your area. Without an agent, you cannot get access to this information. (However, times are changing! The automation of listing systems will make MLS information more accessible to the general public. This topic is discussed in Chapter 6.)

A good agent plays the role of matchmaker, listening to what you want and then helping you find the right house. An agent can search for houses within a particular area, within a particular price range, or with certain characteristics. A good agent will keep up-to-date on the current listings and show you new properties as they are listed.

An agent knows information about the community or city. If you're moving to a new city, an agent will be extremely valuable. The agent can recommend certain areas, give you an estimate of taxes, tell you about the local school system, community services, hospitals, police, and so on.

An agent will arrange appointments for you to visit houses and will tour them with you. From the listing, the agent can tell you a lot about the house—age, lot size, square footage of the entire house as well as each room, listing price, and more. The agent also has the experience of looking at many, many homes and can help you evaluate the quality of the home, compared to price.

Negotiating and Closing the Deal

An agent can be especially helpful in making an offer and negotiating the deal. She will help you prepare the sales agreement that lists the critical terms of the sale—selling price, terms, contingencies, and so on. She will represent your offer favorably, and will help you handle any counteroffers. Chapter 8 covers the details of making an offer.

The agent will be able to evaluate the property and has access to information about other similar properties. For instance, your agent can tell you the selling prices of other houses in the area. You can often use this knowledge as a bargaining tool.

Sellers take buyers represented by agents more seriously because they realize the agent has probably already prequalified them. The seller doesn't have to be nervous about wasting his time on a buyer who can't afford the home.

Even after the offer is accepted, the agent will help shepherd you through the rest of the process—getting the loan, having an inspection done, responding to any problems, and handling the closing. If any problems pop up during the process, your agent will help you through them.

Selecting a Good Agent

As with most sales jobs, the 80/20 rule applies to real estate. 20 percent of the agents sell 80 percent of the homes. When you're selecting an agent, you want one of the 20 percent. You want someone with experience. This section helps you find an agent you can be comfortable with.

Finding an Agent

If you've ever gone to an open house, you know how quickly you're besieged with offers to help you find your dream house. The open house agent may follow you around the house, trying to become your agent. Sometimes the agent is more interested in soliciting clients than in showing you the house. You may easily find yourself hooked up with an agent when you had no intention whatsoever of doing so. It's better to put some thought into selecting an agent. Don't necessarily sign up with the first person that promises you your dream home. Here are some strategies for finding a good agent:

Ask others for recommendations. The best sources of recommendations are family, friends, and co-workers who have recently purchased a house. If someone worked with an agent and had a good experience, chances are the agent is pretty good.

Ask the broker for recommendations. The broker should be knowledgeable about all his agents. Ask the broker for the agent who has sold the most in the office. Ask the broker to recommend an agent familiar with the area and price range you want.

Check the agent's background. What is the reputation of the firm? Has the firm sold a lot of houses? Does the firm have a lot of agents? Is the support staff friendly? Ask for the agent's résumé.

Check the agent's history. How long has he been in business? How long has he been working full-time selling real estate? (Some agents work only part-time.) How many properties has he listed? (The more, the better.) How many properties has he sold in the past few months? Be sure that the agent has access to the MLS listings.

Investigate problems. Ask the local real estate board whether there have been any problems with the agent.

Putting an Agent to the Test

Once you select an agent, be sure you enjoy working with that person. You're going to find that the more comfortable you are with your agent, the more pleasant the whole home-buying process is. Take this agent-comfort test to be sure you're working with an agent that you like.

Yes   No

❏   ❏   Does your agent return your calls? Is she pleasant and helpful when you call?

❏   ❏   Does the agent have time for you?

❏   ❏   Does your agent explain things so that you can understand? Does he explain different financing options? Implications of contracts? You want an agent that first knows the answers and second can explain the answers so that you can understand. You don't want an agent that glosses over the answers, explains things so that you end up more confused, or that tells you not to worry about the answers, he'll take care of it.

❏   ❏   Is your agent interested in your needs? Does she listen to you? You want an agent that listens—not one that is just interested in making a sale.

❏   ❏   Does the agent ask you personal questions about your financial situation? You may think the right answer is *no*, but the real right answer is *yes*. If you find your dream home and can't afford it, what good is it? An agent should first help you figure out what you can afford and second help you find houses within that range. If an agent doesn't first investigate your financial situation, you may find yourself in over your head.

❏   ❏   When the agent takes you to look at houses, do the houses seem to match what you're looking for? If you have stressed to the agent you want a one-story house, but all she shows you are two-story houses, the agent may not be listening.

❏   ❏   Does the agent know the area well? Some agents are more familiar with a certain area. You want an agent that knows the area—knows what houses have sold for in the area, knows the taxes, community, etc.

❏   ❏   Does the agent show only houses listed with his firm? If so, you might inquire whether the agent gets an incentive if he sells a house with his firm. You want an agent that isn't steering you to certain properties for his own benefit.

Getting Rid of an Agent

Just because you selected one agent doesn't mean you're stuck with that person for the rest of your house-buying life. You might have signed up with an agent spontaneously and then realized this person wasn't right for you. Maybe an agent is too busy? Or too pushy?

If you're uncomfortable with an agent, you should say so as soon as possible. You probably had to sign an exclusivity contract for 30–60 days, but if you make it apparent to the agent that he'll be wasting his time with you, he may let you out of the contract.

Working with For-Sale-By-Owner Homes

When you're looking for a house, you may see a lot of "For Sale By Owner" homes, abbreviated FSBO and pronounced, believe it or not, "fizz-bo." In this case, the seller is *not* using an agent, and has decided to sell the house direct to you. You and the seller, one-on-one.

Dealing with a FSBO can be tricky. You can decide to deal directly with the seller, or in some cases you can persuade the seller to accept your agent.

If you decide to deal directly, you will have to handle all the negotiations between you and the seller, and you will lack the experience of an agent in helping you write a good contract, get financing, negotiate, and close. Be careful. There are lots of *i*'s to dot and *t*'s to cross in the buying and selling of a house. You need to be sure not to forget something critical in the process. In fact, you should probably hire a lawyer to look over all the paperwork.

The seller should be prepared to help you with financing and should handle the closing. The seller may also have a sales contract you can use. But can you trust the seller? If he's handily prepared a contract for you, are you sure he's not salivating and stifling a giggle as you sign your first-born child away?

Be sure that you can handle the stress of dealing face to face with the seller. Sometimes you lose your leverage without a go-between. Face-to-face negotiating can be tough.

Finally, you have to know where your leverage is. For example, the seller, if he sells directly to you, is going to save seven percent of the sales price. On a $100,000 home, that's $7,000. Who's getting that savings? If the seller wants to pocket the entire savings, what's your benefit? You should be able to negotiate a lower selling price. Or you may want to insist on using your agent and having the seller pay the three percent commission fee, or you could negotiate to have your agent do the paperwork for a flat fee.

The Least You Need to Know

Selecting a good agent is another step along the way to owning a house. When you're selecting and working with an agent, keep these main points in mind:

➤ Most commonly, you will use a buyer's agent to represent you in your search for a house. This agent can assist you in every way a "regular" agent can, but will have *your* best interests in mind, not the seller's.

➤ An agent can help you prepare financially to buy a house, has access to house listings so that he can help you find a match, and can help you negotiate and close the deal.

➤ You want to select an agent that is active (sells and lists many homes) and knowledgeable. You also want an agent that you feel comfortable with and that listens to you.

➤ You shouldn't avoid FSBOs, but you should be prepared to handle some of the special situations that arise from them.

Chapter 5

Defining Your Dream Home

In This Chapter

➤ Understanding how your lifestyle affects your home selection

➤ Picking a good location

➤ Selecting a house style

➤ Deciding on a new home, existing home, or condominium

➤ Designing your ideal home

When you shop for anything, it's good to have a rough idea of what you want to buy. If you went out to buy a car, but had no idea what type of car you wanted, you could spend weeks or even months making a decision. Sports car? Van? Jeep? Luxury car? Station wagon? Truck? Minivan? Cart and horse?

It's the same way with buying a house. Before you start shopping, you should think about what you need and what you want in your ideal home.

A Few Cautions

Keep in mind that this chapter is intended to give you an idea of what elements to consider when you're searching for a home. You shouldn't use this chapter to narrow your house-hunting to a specific home—a split-level red brick home with 4 bedrooms, 2 baths (one with a hot tub), country kitchen with pot rack and blue-flowered wallpaper, dining room with chair rail, marble fireplace, entertainment room, two-car garage, asphalt driveway, swimming pool, and yard with privacy fence. If you do so, you may not find a home in your price range that matches exactly, and you could miss other homes that you may have liked better.

Instead, use this chapter to picture what you ideally would like. Try to keep in mind that you're probably going to have to compromise. What features are essential? What are extras?

When you go out looking at houses (as described in Chapters 6 and 7), do so with an open mind. Consider what you like and don't like about the house and compare how well it matches up to what you absolutely must have in a house.

Also, trust your agent. If you're working with a good agent (one that listens to what you need), she may recommend looking at houses that vary from your specs. But one of those homes could turn out to be your dream home.

This Is Your Life

The first aspect you should consider when shopping for a home is your lifestyle. A retired couple shopping for a home and a newlywed couple shopping for a home will have entirely different sets of needs. This section helps you consider how your family and job affect your housing decision.

Home to Stay or Home to Resell?

Ask yourself how long you plan to stay in the home. If you're buying your first home, will you stay in the house for just a while and then move on? If you're planning to move, you should consider the resale value of the home as you look at houses. (Most people stay in a home no more than seven years.)

On the other hand, if you're shopping for a home in which you plan to live for a long, long time, you want to first be sure that it will accommodate you for that long, long time. Also, you may not be as concerned about the resale of the house.

> **WHOA!**
>
> **A True Story ...**
>
> An artist in our neighborhood plans on staying in his house (which was his mother's house) forever. You can tell by looking at the house. For example, he has built a stone doorway with a large wooden owl on the top at the front of the walk. The rest of the yard isn't fenced in, so the doorway just opens up into the open yard. He also has mounted carousel animals (a giraffe and a swan) on the front porch and an 8-foot troll in the yard. If he planned to sell his house, he probably would have avoided such eccentricities. (I suspect his heirs will be cursing him sometime in the far future, though.)

Is This a Family Home?

Another aspect to consider is your family. Do you have children? Do you plan on having children? If so, you'll want to be sure you have a house large enough to accommodate them. Think not only about right now, but the future. That cute eight-year-old boy is going to be a teenager before you know it. Is the floor plan suitable for a teenage boy? Where will the kids park once they get that coveted/dreaded driver's license?

Also, consider the location and school district you want to live in. Checking out the neighborhood is covered in the next two chapters.

What Is Your Job Situation?

Take a look at your job situation. If you're planning to stay in the same job at the same location, consider how long a drive it will be from your new house to work. What's the maximum commute time you find acceptable? Do you have access to public transportation? Can you quickly get on the interstate?

If you're not planning to stay at the same job and location, how will purchasing a home affect your job situation? If you may be transferred soon, will you be able to resell the house quickly?

Also consider your income potential. Will your income go up? Down? Stay the same?

Location, Location, Location

Cover your eyes, because I'm about to use one of the most-often repeated cliches of the real estate market. The three most important factors in buying a home are: location, location, and location. This statement isn't very original, but it's true.

Suppose that you find a beautiful five-bedroom home with four baths, a three-car garage, a marble fireplace, a huge kitchen—everything you could want. What is that home worth? Now think about that same home smack dab next to a garbage dump or in the middle of a high-crime area. What's the home worth now?

The next two chapters give you some advice on how to scope out a neighborhood. Just keep in mind that selecting where you live is more important than selecting what type of house you want.

Style of House

As you drive down your street, you may look at houses and think "Who would want to live there?" There's a particular house in our city that is made of ceramic tile. The tile is yellow, has grout, and reminds me of a big bathroom. To top it off, the house has a rock garden decorated with bowling balls. I am not making this up. Every time I drive by that house, I wonder who would pick a house like that. My husband, who has spent the entire summer painting our frame house, finds the house appealing because of the low maintenance. I suppose you could just scrub it down with some Tilex.

As the saying goes, "To each his own." (OK. That's two cliches so far. I can think of a bunch more that would work here. Can you? "Different strokes . . .." I'll stop, though. One more cliche and you can thump me on the head.) What you like and what your best friend likes probably won't be the same.

How Many Stories?

When you look at houses, you will find many different styles: one-story, two-story, three-story, split-level, ranch, and so on and so on. What you want and like is up to you. For example, if you're a retired person, you may want a one-story home so that you don't have to worry about going up and down steps. If you have children, you may want a two-story house so that you can send the kids upstairs and you can hide out downstairs. Or you may want the children on the same level as you. You will have to weigh privacy versus safety.

I've been in a townhouse that had four stories, which was great if you wanted to get your daily exercise going from the laundry room (first floor) to the kitchen (second) to the office area (third) to the bedrooms (fourth). Forget about the Stairmaster!

To Paint or Not to Paint

Another element that defines the style of the home is what the home is made of. Is it a wood frame house? A combination brick and frame? Aluminum siding? Stucco? Hay? Sticks? Brick?

Again, selecting what you want will depend on what you like and how much maintenance you want to do. Also, consider the cost of maintenance. Frame houses will require painting; brick houses do not, but sometimes need to be "repointed" (bricks fixed), which can be expensive. Price will also be a factor. For example, a brick home may cost more than a similar frame house.

As long as the home has been well-maintained, you shouldn't have too many worries. You should inquire about the maintenance as well as keep in mind what you will have to do to keep up the exterior.

Age of the House

When you're shopping for homes, you will want to decide whether you want an existing home or a new home. You may also want to consider purchasing a condominium. Each type of dwelling has its advantages and disadvantages.

Existing Home

According to a 1994 publication of the *Fannie Mae Guide to Homeownership*, eight out of 10 home buyers purchase an existing home rather than a new home. There are many good reasons to purchase an existing home:

Most existing homes are in an **established neighborhood**, usually closer to the city. You can expect to find trees and sometimes larger yards.

An older home tends to have more **personality**. In a new subdivision, you may see several different house styles, but the houses may all look alike. (This will vary depending on the subdivision and the type of new homes.) In an older neighborhood, the style and size of the houses will vary. You might have a colonial brick house next to a frame Cape Cod next to a ranch. The older home may also have nice amenities such as hardwood floors or built-in cabinets, which, I can assure you, you'll pay dearly for in a new home.

You may get **more space for your money** in an older home. You'll usually find that the ceilings are higher and the rooms are bigger than in a new home. This won't be true in every case.

On the down side to buying an existing home, consider these factors:

Either women back then didn't have as many shoes as they do now or they had no say in the design of the home, because most older homes have **little, tiny closets** that will hold about three pairs of pants, three shirts, one coat, and three pairs of shoes. And that's for both you and your spouse. You may find that the bathrooms are small, too.

Times They Are A Changin'

A hundred years ago, most people had only a set of work clothes and a set of church clothes, so closets were understandably small. Luckily, they used the space they saved to build more bedrooms. A creative solution to the Tiny Closet Syndrome is to use one or more of the leftover bedrooms as a spacious, walk-in closet.

As the home gets older, it is going to require **more maintenance**. You may need to paint the house, fix the plumbing, do rewiring, and more.

Getting a good inspection (covered in Chapter 19) can help you be sure you aren't getting a house that will become a money pit. If repair work does need to be done, you will know about it ahead of time if you get an inspection.

Is A Fixer-Upper For You?

Should you buy a fixer-upper? You may think that's the ideal situation. You can buy the house cheaply and then make a bundle after you fix it up.

Beware!

If you intend to fix up a home, keep in mind that the repairs and renovations will always cost more and take longer than you anticipated. You should be sure that you can live with the mess. Do you want to take a shower in the basement for the next five years while your spouse redoes your master bathroom?

If you're handy, you may plan to do the work yourself. Most buyers do. Usually, they have to hire someone to finish the job. You should be sure you have the expertise and the time to do the repairs. The work is going to take longer than you think anyway and may end up being endless if you don't have the time to devote to it.

New Home

As your city expands, you will find that new subdivisions will pop up all over town with brand new homes and big closets. Consider the following benefits of owning a new home:

Because the heating, plumbing, wiring, air-conditioning, and so on are all new, you will have the advantage of **low maintenance costs**. Also, the home may be more energy efficient, and the builder will most likely offer a warranty for the major components.

Builders must have perked up and listened to what people want in a house because most new home designs include **big closets** and lots of cabinet space. New homes also usually include a well-designed floor plan—big kitchen, special amenities such as a master suite, and so on.

When you purchase an existing home, you either have to keep the red velvet wallpaper and black shag carpet or pay the price to redo them. With a new house, you have **more choices**. The builder will usually let you pick the color and type of floor coverings and wall coverings.

Many new subdivisions include **extra amenities for the community**, such as a clubhouse, swimming pool, tennis courts, and other fun things.

If you're thinking of purchasing a new home, you will also want to consider the disadvantages:

Although most builders just clear-cut all trees from the lot before you ever see it, if there are trees still standing when you pick your lot, you may want to discuss with your contractor the possibility of leaving some of them. You could negotiate to give up something else if you can keep some trees.

New homes are being built **farther out in the suburbs** than existing neighborhoods. They may also lack decent landscaping—at least until the trees and grass grow in. Most people are put off by this **barren look**.

If you have your home custom designed and custom built, you can select any type of house you want. But, most new homes are predesigned by the builders. You can select home **A**, **B**, or **C**. There will be several homes in your neighborhood that look exactly like yours—at least from the outside. This **lack of personality** has kept many people in the existing home market.

Land is expensive. Builders want to fit as big a house on as small a lot as possible. If you hate to mow your lawn, you're in luck. If you don't want to sit on your deck and stare directly into your neighbor's kitchen, you may be out of luck. **Small yards** are part of the bargain with a new house. Also, you may have to put some work into actually getting a yard. You may have to reseed and water until a decent lawn grows in.

In some cases, a new home costs more than an equivalent existing home. Also, you may have **less bargaining power** on the price when you buy a new home. The ins and outs of making an offer on a new home are covered in Chapter 10.

Condominium

Another type of home you may want to consider is a condominium. When you purchase a condominium, you own the actual living unit, which may be similar to an apartment. You also own a percentage of the common area—building and land. You get a tax break, like other homeowners, but you don't have to worry about home maintenance. Usually, you pay a condo fee for the upkeep of the grounds and the building. Some condominiums include extra amenities such as a swimming pool, clubhouse, and so on. Purchasing a condominium is covered in detail in Chapter 11.

The Home Itself

So far you should have thought about how long you want to live in the house, who's going to live in the house with you, where you want to live, and what type of house you want. Finally, it's time to think about the house itself.

Eating

The most important area of the house is probably the kitchen. Everybody has to eat. If you like to cook or entertain, you may want to put a big kitchen on the top of your "have to have list." (I don't know what it is about a kitchen, but at parties people are drawn to it. Maybe the appliances are magnetized or something.)

If you have children, you may also want to have an eat-in kitchen—where Junior can throw his Spaghettios as far and as often as he wants without ruining the dining room carpet and table.

In addition to a kitchen, you may want a dining room. (Sometimes the kitchen is both.) The size and style of the dining room will depend on what you like.

Sleeping

What's the first thing you want to do after eating a big meal? Take a nap. The number and size of bedrooms is next on the list of things to consider in a home.

Bedrooms are for more than just sleeping. They can provide office space, storage space, hobby rooms, whatever.

How many bedrooms do you want? How big do you want them? I've been in a "four-bedroom" house where the fourth bedroom was so small you'd have to sleep standing up. When you consider the number of bedrooms, remember your family situation. Do you have children? *Will* you have children? Will you have *more* children? Will you need to take in an aging parent sometime down the road? Do you have guests frequently?

Getting Clean

The big three for home selection are kitchen, bedrooms, and bathrooms. The more bathrooms the better! You will want to decide on the minimum number of bathrooms you need. One? (Good luck!) One and a half? (Be sure the half is big enough for a person. Sometimes people convert a closet into a bathroom. If you can barely fit four outfits in the closet, how do you expect to fit a 5-foot, 11-inch person?) Two? (Two is the recommended minimum.) Three or more? (You're living like a king.)

Relaxing

OK. You eat, you sleep, and you go to the bathroom. What else do you do in your home? You will want to be sure you have an area to relax, entertain, work, workout, and so on.

Most homes have a living room. Sometimes this is a formal room where no one actually does any living and the furniture is covered with plastic. It looks good, but no one is actually allowed in the living room. Sometimes the living room is a living/family room where you watch TV, entertain, and lay on the couch.

Some homes have both a living room and a family room or a combination living/family or living/dining room. The family room may be called different names—great room, rec room, den, "pig" room (that's what my aunt calls it—she has two teenagers). The family room may be used for watching TV, or it may be used as an office. (Sometimes a spare bedroom is converted into an office.) You will want to consider the number and size of the living rooms you need.

Storing Stuff

I often wonder, if I didn't have a basement or an attic, would I keep so much stuff? In my parent's basement, for instance, you'll find cabinets of dusty games including a broken EZ-Bake Oven, a toy chest full of mildewy old dolls, all my old term papers, trunks of clothes including my Catholic high school uniform, and much, much more. Do we need any of this stuff? No. But every time my dad threatens to throw it out, my mom and I have a fit. (Plus, we threaten to get rid of his train set, which is also down in the basement.)

When you're thinking about your dream house, think about where you're going to put all your stuff. Do you need a basement? Basements add up to 50 percent more room to a two-story and 100 percent more room to a ranch. The basement can serve as a storage area, a place to put your washer and dryer, or a place to stick your teenager until he outgrows puberty. Many people move only because they lack a basement. And a basement can add to the resale value of the house.

Your house may also include extra storage space in an attic or storage shed. (Garages are covered in the next section.) Of course, don't forget closets.

Outside the House

By now, you should have a good idea of what the inside of the house should look like. Now let's take a walk around the outside of the house. What's important to you here? Consider these questions:

Do you want a little yard, big yard, no yard?
I've been in houses with no backyards, with the backyard on the side of the house (it was very hard to get your bearings in the house), and with a backyard as big as a football field. My husband liked the football field-sized yard until he thought about mowing it.

Does the house have a nice view?
A good view can provide you and your family with many years of
pleasure, as well as increase the sales value of the home.

Is the yard fenced in?
Do you need a fence to keep Falstaff, your bulldog, in the yard? Your
kids in the yard? Do you want a fence just for decoration, such as a
split-rail fence, or for privacy, such as a ten-foot fence around your
swimming pool? Can you add a fence? Is it against local zoning laws?
Neighborhood covenants or ordinances?

Is there room for the kids to play?
Will there be room for their swing set, tree house, and umpteen bicycles and scooters?

Do you like to garden?
If so, is there room for one? Is the terrain right for a garden? Is it too
rocky? Too sloped?

Where will you park?
On the street? In a driveway? In a garage? How big is the garage? Can
you use the garage to store all the stuff that won't fit in your basement:
bicycles, sports equipment, yard and gardening tools?

Does it have a driveway?
Is it gravel? Paved? Does it need to be paved? Is it flat, or on a hill?
Think about driving down or up the driveway after an ice storm. Can
you add a basketball hoop?

Heating, Cooling, and More

You will also want to think about heating and cooling. Is it important
to you whether it's gas heat or electric, radiators or steam? Do you
want air-conditioning? How expensive would it be to add central air?
Can you rely on window air conditioners? Is the house on city water or
well water? Who picks up the trash?

Amenities

This section covers some of the other "goodies" you may want your
house to have. Make a separate list of "Must haves," and "Would love
to haves." Here are some ideas:

➤ Does it have a deck? Can you build a deck?

➤ How about a hot tub? Swimming pool? Tennis court?

➤ Do you want a fireplace? Hardwood floors? Built-in cabinets?

Definite No's

In addition to thinking about what you want, also think about what you don't want. For example, I hate a house where a cat has lived because I am allergic to cats. Even if the carpet is shampooed, I can smell the cat, and I sneeze and sneeze and sneeze.

Also, remember that some of the things you hate can be changed. Just because you hate the living room wallpaper doesn't mean you shouldn't buy a house that you otherwise like. On the other hand, it is usually not wise to buy a three-bedroom house when you need a four-bedroom, thinking it will be easy to "knock this wall out and add another room right here." Be sure to consider the difficulty and expense of the changes you'll want to make.

Use the checklist on the following page to help you define what you do and don't want in your dream home.

A Dream House New Home Checklist

Style of House

- ❏ One story
- ❏ Two story
- ❏ Ranch
- ❏ Split level
- ❏ Doesn't matter
- ❏ Other_____

Construction

- ❏ Wood Frame
- ❏ Brick
- ❏ Concrete, Brick, or Stucco (CBS)
- ❏ Aluminum Siding
- ❏ Brick and Frame
- ❏ Stone
- ❏ Doesn't matter
- ❏ Other_____

Type of Kitchen

- ❏ Eat-in
- ❏ Country
- ❏ Doesn't matter

Features

- ❏ Pantry
- ❏ Appliances

Number of Bedrooms

- ❏ One
- ❏ Two
- ❏ Three
- ❏ Four
- ❏ Five or more
- ❏ Doesn't matter

Number of Bathrooms

- ❏ 1
- ❏ 1 ½
- ❏ 2
- ❏ 2 ½
- ❏ 3 or more

Features	Really Need	Really Want	Would Trade	Definitely Don't Want
Living room	❏	❏	❏	❏
Dining room	❏	❏	❏	❏
Family room	❏	❏	❏	❏
Basement	❏	❏	❏	❏
Finished basement	❏	❏	❏	❏
Workout room	❏	❏	❏	❏
Office	❏	❏	❏	❏
Screened porch	❏	❏	❏	❏
Big closets	❏	❏	❏	❏
Fireplace	❏	❏	❏	❏
Built-in cabinets	❏	❏	❏	❏
Big yard	❏	❏	❏	❏
Room for a garden	❏	❏	❏	❏
Garage	❏	❏	❏	❏
Paved driveway	❏	❏	❏	❏
Swimming pool	❏	❏	❏	❏
Hot tub	❏	❏	❏	❏
Other_____	❏	❏	❏	❏

The Least You Need to Know

Before you go house hunting, you should have in mind a general idea of the type of house you want. This chapter helped you define your dream home by focusing your attention in these areas:

➤ Think about your lifestyle now and in the future. Factors such as whether you may be transferred to another job or whether you plan to have children will affect your housing decisions.

➤ Buying an existing home usually means a more established neighborhood and unique home design. On the down side, expect to have less closet space and higher maintenance costs.

➤ When you buy a new home, you can expect lower maintenance and a better floor plan. The location and lack of personality and yard are drawbacks.

➤ The three most important rooms to consider are the kitchen, bedrooms, and bathrooms.

A man travels the world over in search of what he needs, and returns home to find it.

—George Moore

Chapter 6

Finding Houses on the Market

> **In This Chapter**
>
> ➤ Knowing what to expect when you're looking for a house
>
> ➤ Finding a house
>
> ➤ Finding a good neighborhood

"For Sale" signs are like wildflowers; they crop up all over the place every spring. You can almost hear them as you drive through the neighborhoods in your city: *pop, pop, pop.*

Why do a lot of homes go on the market in the spring? Is that the best time to shop? Find out the answers to these questions and more right here.

What to Expect When Looking for a Home

What should you expect when you begin to look for a home? How long will the process take? When is the best time to shop? This section covers these questions, and more.

How Long Does It Take?

Finding the right house is a lot like dating. The first one could be your dream house. Or you could have to go through a lot of duds before you find your princely estate. The entire process of looking, making an offer, financing, and moving can take anywhere from a couple of months to over a year.

Here's a rough timeline of the homebuying process:

1. You begin by looking for a house that you like. This process can take a few weeks to several months. A 1991 survey by the National Association of Realtors found that the average buyer spent 16 weeks looking for a home. You will want to start looking as soon as you think you want to purchase a house. If you have to move because of a job situation or because you have sold your house, you could be in a weak bargaining position if you need a house right away.

2. After you've found the house, you make an offer. The offer is accepted either right away or after a series of counteroffers. Plan on a couple of days for this process. If the offer isn't accepted, go back to the first step.

3. You secure financing for the house. Your contract will probably stipulate that you must apply for a loan application within a couple of days. Then the lender must approve or underwrite the loan. Count on 30 to 60 days for this step.

   During the financing phase, other key steps occur. The house may be inspected and appraised. If the seller agrees to make repairs, these must be made before closing. A title search will be done.

4. Your loan is approved, you close on the house, and finally get the keys. Count on a week for this step.

If you're selling your house, you should probably put it on the market before you start looking. If you find a house you want, the seller might not take you seriously if your house is not already on the market or already sold. It's a balancing act. It's nice to sell your house and buy your new house at the same time so you can move from your old house to your new house. If you find a house before you sell yours, you may lose it to a buyer who can close immediately. On the other hand, if you sell your house before you find a house and the buyers want to move in right away, you'll have to arrange for temporary housing.

Buyer's Market Versus Seller's Market

Depending on the economy, you may find yourself in a buyer's market in which the buyers get the best deals, or you may find yourself in a seller's market in which the sellers get the upper hand. Sometimes, you'll find yourself somewhere in between.

In a buyer's market, there are a lot of homes on the market, and they may take a while to sell. To sell a house, the seller might need to offer a really good price, plus additional incentives such as help with financing. If you're buying a home in this type of market, you can take your time looking and can usually strike a pretty good deal.

In a seller's market, houses aren't on the market for long. In fact, they may sell before they are even listed. Because the market is so strong, many owners will decide to sell their homes themselves; you'll see a lot of for-sale-by-owner homes. If you're selling a house in this market, you're lucky. You'll probably get many good offers and not need to offer any additional incentives. If you're buying a house in this market, you may have to work hard to find a house that you like and can make an offer on before it is sold (see "Finding a House," later in this chapter). To get your offer accepted, you should be financially ready (prequalified). Also, don't expect to submit and have accepted a contract with a lot of contingencies.

Seasonal Sales

If you charted the sales of homes for the months of January to December, you would probably find that it followed the traditional bell pattern. Sales are slow at the start and end (January and December) and peak in the middle (May and June).

If you think about these seasonal peaks, you will see they make sense. Most people don't want to move or be bothered with moving around the holidays (November to January), so there may not be a lot of homes on the market during this time. Plus, houses don't look as appealing in the dreary days of winter. The trees are bare and the skies are dark.

If you're looking for a bargain, consider shopping during the down time. You may find that homes on the market in this season have to be sold. Otherwise, why wouldn't the sellers wait for a better time?

Homes look nice in the spring, and it's easy to work on repairs at this time. So you'll see lots of folks out on ladders and lots of homes for sale from March through April. The peak of home buying occurs somewhere around May and June—that's a good time to move if you have children in school, but also may be the worst time to buy. You have a good selection, but the market moves fast.

Sales tend to drop off at the end of the summer—again, children are heading back to school, and parents may not want to uproot them. You may see an increase in September and October, but once the holidays come up, sales drop.

If you have the luxury of shopping when you want, you may be able to use these sale seasons to your advantage.

Finding the Right Place

You already know that the most important decision you make about where to live is where to live. This section starts by moving from the bigger area (the community) to the smaller area (the neighborhood). The dictionary defines community as "a social group of any size whose members reside in a specific locality, share government, and have a cultural and historical heritage." The concept of community, then, encompasses what services are offered in the area (hospital, fire department, and so on) as well as social aspects (shopping, community entertainment centers, and so on).

A neighborhood is more loosely defined as "a number of persons living near one another or in a particular locality." Often the character of the district defines the area, and neighborhoods tend to retain their basic character over long periods of time. If you think of your town, you can probably think of several neighborhoods and their associated character. For instance, one neighborhood may call to mind local artists and little boutiques and restaurants. Another may call to mind the theme to *Deliverance*.

Finding the Right Community

What's the right community? Depends on who you are and what you want.

If you're most interested in living in the "hot" community, you may want to look for a community that is about to have a growth spurt—one where the resale value of the home is likely to go up. You can spot promising growth by looking for the construction of new homes, new roads, new community services, new businesses.

If you are moving from another town or state, you will have to rely on your agent to provide you with information about different communities and neighborhoods.

If you're more interested in the social aspects of the community, you may want to check out the local shopping malls, libraries, houses of worship, and community centers.

If you have children, you will probably want to consider the school district. (Even if you don't have children, you may want to look at the school district. Living in a good district can improve the resale value of your house. The school district is one of the most significant factors for evaluating a community.)

No matter what your situation, you will want a community that has good police and fire departments. You will also want to consider the commuting distance to work.

If you don't want to finance the new school gymnasium or end up living next to a Taco Bell, you will want to investigate any plans for the community. What improvements are planned? How will they be financed? Are any zoning changes coming up?

To get a feel for a particular community, try subscribing to a local newspaper. What types of stories are covered? What is the attitude of the paper? What about the Letters to the Editor? What are the views of the community leaders? Finding out this information can help you decide whether you will feel comfortable in a particular community. Visit the community and stop by local stores, libraries, and community centers. Are the stores prosperous? Inviting? Are the people pleasant?

Agents have to be careful when characterizing a neighborhood. Steering you to a particular neighborhood based on race, color, religion, country of origin, age, or sex is discriminatory and is against the law. If you think you have encountered discrimination, see Appendix B for the HUD discrimination hotline.

Talk to local residents. Do the residents work in the area? Or do they commute to another location? What do they like about the community? What do they dislike? How long have they lived in the area? The community is really a reflection of its residents, so the more you know about the residents, the better sense you will get of the community.

Ask your agent. Your agent should be able to give you information about particular communities—statistics about home sales, crime rate, schools, taxes, and more.

Check with the chamber of commerce and other associations. You may be able to find information about population and income trends. For instance, you can check with the Homebuilder's Association to find out which areas of the town have seen the most growth.

Finding the Right Neighborhood

Within each community, you may find several different neighborhoods. (Sometimes the community and neighborhood are one and the same. Sometimes the town, community, and neighborhood are the same. It depends on the size of the town.) Just as you check out the community, you will want to check out the neighborhood. Drive around the neighborhood, and ask yourself the following questions:

Are there a lot of homes for sale in the neighborhood? A lot of homes could be a good sign—a hot market. Or it could be a bad sign—people trying to get out.

Are the homes well-kept, well-maintained? Or are the homes in need of repair?

Is the neighborhood close enough to your relatives? Or, depending on your family situation, far enough away? Do you have access to public transportation?

Can you characterize the lifestyle of the neighborhood? And if so, do you fit in? If you have children, for instance, you may want to select a neighborhood with other young families. Are there a lot of swing sets or bicycles? If you're a swinging single, you may want to find a neighborhood where the singles swing.

> Be sure to check for toxic waste and radiation. You can have some of these tests done as part of the home inspection.

Do you see any problems in the neighborhood? Check the local police station for information about the crime rate. Look for any negative aspects of the neighborhood—heavy traffic, graffiti, unkept houses, pollution.

Ask your real estate agent for information about home sales in the neighborhood. How many homes have been sold in the past year? How long did it take the homes to sell? What was the swing (difference between listing price and sales price) for the homes?

Finding a House

You've narrowed down the community and neighborhood to a few choices. Now you can begin to look for a house in one of those areas. How do you find a house? There are many ways, as described here:

Drive-Bys

As you take a look at the community and neighborhoods you like, you should keep your eyes open for homes for sale. Most homes on the market include a for-sale sign in the yard. You can watch for these signs as you search for the neighborhood you want. Jot down the address and listing Realtor of any homes that catch your eye. Write down the numbers of any for-sale-by-owner properties.

Local Papers

You can also find homes by reading your local paper, which probably has a section advertising homes for sale. Because many sellers hold open houses on Sunday, the Sunday paper usually has an entire section devoted to real estate. You can read through the paper and mark homes that sound interesting. If you're just starting to look, you may want to visit a few open houses in the area you think you want to live. The following figure shows how cryptic some ads can be. Refer to the following table for help in deciphering the codes.

House For Sale

Cute 2 BR w/hardwood throughout. Finished bsmt. Bonus rm. First flr family rm w/new carpet & paneling. Sep DR w/Corner Hutch. Super backyard. Great curb appeal!

A typical ad.

The first few times you read an advertisement for a home, you may think you're playing a round of *Wheel of Fortune*. What happened to all the vowels? Pretty soon you'll recognize the terms and abbreviations used.

Abbreviation	What it means
BA	Bath
BR	Bedroom
MBR	Master bedroom
LR	Living room
DR	Dining room
GR	Great room
FR	Family room
CA or C/A	Central Air
2 C GAR	Two-car garage
BSMT	Basement
FP or FRPLC	Fireplace

If you're searching for a bargain, look for words such as *reduced*, or *motivated sellers*. These terms may indicate the house has been on the market for a while.

Words and phrases such as *fixer-upper, TLC needed, handyman special, needs updating* should clue you into the fact that the home isn't in the best condition. If you're looking for a fixer-upper, then watch for these phrases. If you don't want to worry about repairs and redecorating, look for houses described as *move-in condition*.

MLS Listings

Ninety-five percent of all homes on the market are listed with an agent. And when a home is listed with an agent, information about the home is entered into a computer system known as the *multiple listing system* or *MLS* (see the following figure of a sample MLS listing).

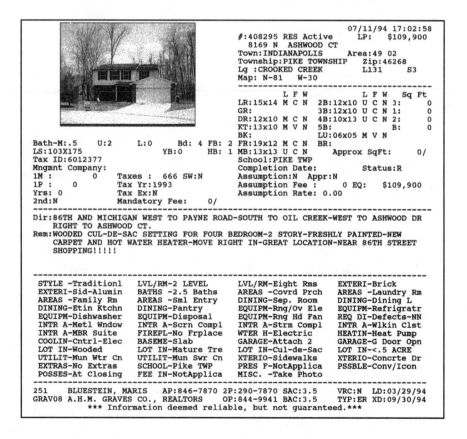

A sample MLS listing.

Your agent will use the listing to tell you key aspects about the home. She will understand the format, abbreviations, and information included. Basically, the MLS listing includes the following information:

➤ The top section includes the two most important pieces of information—the address and listing price. This section also includes information about the location of the property: town, area, township, lot number, and map coordinates.

➤ The next section includes information about the type and size of the rooms—living room (LR), great room (GR), dining room (DR), kitchen (KT), family room (FR), bedrooms (MB, 2B, 3B, 4B, 5B). This section also includes information about the first mortgage (1M), first mortgage payment (1P), taxes, tax year, assumption information, and school district.

➤ The next section includes directions to the home as well as a short summary of the property.

➤ The next section includes a description of the property—style of house, number of rooms, type of exterior, and so on.

➤ The last area includes information about the listing agent—name, phone number, listing date, expiration date of listing, commission.

If you're working with an agent, she should be able to provide you with lists of homes in a particular price range and in a particular area. Most likely your agent will pull several listings from the system and take you by the homes. If you're interested in a home, the agent will set up an appointment to tour it.

Most often, the agent will want to accompany you—even when you're just driving by the houses. Sometimes you can convince the agent to give you the listings so that you can drive by yourself.

Word of Mouth

In a seller's market, houses may sell even before they are listed in the computer system. In this type of market, you may have to be more aggressive in finding a house. Also, the best time to purchase a home is before it is put on the market—when the seller is thinking about selling. If you can catch the seller at this critical point, you may be able to negotiate a good deal. The seller will avoid the hassle of putting the house on the market, and you will get a house you want.

To find houses about to be put on the market, tell family, friends, co-workers, and acquaintances that you're looking. Any one of these people may know of a house about to be sold. For instance, your friend Pam might know that your mutual friend Steve is getting a divorce and will be selling his house soon. Your mother might know that Cousin Billy is about to be transferred to Akron, Ohio and will be putting his house on the market.

> You can get the best deal when the seller is highly motivated to sell—for instance, in special situations such as transfers, divorce, and so on.

Auctions and Foreclosures

If you're really in a hunt for a bargain, you may want to actively search for an "as-is" or foreclosed property. Usually this type of home is sold directly by the lender. Look for advertisements in the paper or call some local lenders and ask whether they handle foreclosed properties and if so, how you can get information about the homes. Foreclosure notices are also posted in the county courthouse.

Another source of foreclosed properties is the Resolution Trust Corporation (RTC). This agency helps the government auction off properties that came into the government's possession with all the failed savings and loans. You can get a list of RTC properties by calling the RTC hotline (1-800-624-HOME). You may also be able to find a good property in a private auction. Again, look for advertisements.

If you're thinking about buying this type of property, you will want to be sure to do a title search. Find out before you close if any back taxes are due or there are any liens against the property.

> Buying a home from an auction is not for the novice. This process requires great care and caution. You need to be experienced in the home-buying process—know what to pay for a certain property and how the process works. You could ask your agent to act as a bidder for you in an auction.

Foreclosed properties may not have been well-maintained; therefore, be sure to have a careful, professional inspection done so that you know about any problems or costly repairs that are needed.

When you're at an auction, be sure that you understand the rules. You may be required to have a certified check ready for the deposit, and you will most likely need to be prequalified for a loan. Your bidding card may include information about the maximum financing for which you're qualified. Also, be sure you understand when the sale is final. Some auctions take the highest bid—no matter what. Other auctions have a minimum bid. Some auctions require for the sale to be confirmed by the seller before it is final.

Be careful not to overbid. Do your homework and decide on the market value for the house as well as how high you will bid. If you get into a bidding war, stop at your maximum price. Otherwise, you may end up paying far more for the house than you intend.

What to Expect in the Near Future

In the past, agents have had a stranglehold on the MLS listings. A person working on his own could not get access to the listings without the help of an agent. With the advent of new technology—computers and computerized phone systems—this information is becoming more readily available to the public.

Some Realtors (for example, the Greater Dallas Association of Realtors) allow househunters to use a modem and a computer and gain access to its database of homes for sale (the MLS). Some firms provide access to a computer bulletin board of homes for sale. A Kansas firm uploads information about homes for sale in that region to Prodigy (an online information service).

Some agencies have access to a computer and on-line information about the homes. For instance, your agent may be able to show you six to eight different color pictures of the home right on your PC screen. You can view 50 to 100 homes in about an hour and narrow your choices considerably before venturing out. If you don't have access to a computer and a modem, you may be able to use your touch-tone phone to dial in and get information about homes for sale.

In the future, virtual reality systems will enable you to "visit" a home without actually going there. For example, you could view the home on the computer screen and then tour the home by walking through it on-screen. You could visit the rooms, check the closets, see the outside—without ever leaving the real estate office.

The Least You Need to Know

House-hunting is like searching for a lost treasure. You will need to follow maps, decode secret messages, and use your best sense to find the treasure. On your search, keep these things in mind:

➤ To buy a house, you need to go through four steps: find the house, have an offer accepted, finance the purchase, and close. There's no set time limit for these steps—it varies wildly.

➤ Check out the community by reading the local paper, visiting community stores, talking with residents, and driving around.

➤ Neighborhoods come with their own unique characters. You will most likely want to move to a neighborhood in which you feel comfortable.

➤ You can find houses on the market through your agent, by reading the local paper, by driving through neighborhoods you like, and by word of mouth.

**We must be the worst family in town.
Maybe we should move to a larger
community.**

**—Bart Simpson
(Matt Groening)**

Chapter 7

Looking at a House

In This Chapter

➤ Touring the house

➤ Deciding whether the house fits you

➤ Ensuring the house meets your needs

➤ Making sure the house is well-maintained

➤ Checking the neighborhood

➤ Keeping notes

A recent survey showed that the typical homebuyer looks at 15–19 homes before making a decision. When you're looking, how can you keep all the homes straight? What are you looking at in each of these homes? This chapter gives you some strategies for taking a good look at a house, for checking the neighborhood, and for keeping all the houses straight.

What to Expect

Your agent will do her best to match your needs to houses currently on the market. She may drive you by some homes and then set up appointments for the ones you find appealing. Or she may set up

Tips on Remembering...

It's a good idea to view just a few houses at a time. If you view 10 or more, the homes will quickly become a blur.

Pick a nickname for the house you want to remember. Maybe it's the "baby blue," the "cat house," the "new baby home."

If you have a video camera, take it along and videotape the home. Be sure to get permission to do so first.

appointments for houses she thinks you will like. You could have several appointments in one evening or day.

When you tour a home, the agent will accompany you, but the homeowners may or may not be in the house. Your agent will also most likely give you an information sheet that tells you the age of the house, square footage, size of rooms, property taxes, utility bills, and so on. The information sheet may also include a picture. (An example of an MLS listing is shown in Chapter 6. The information sheet may be the same as this listing.)

As you tour the house, you may want to jot down notes to yourself. You can use the checklist at the end of this chapter to record your impressions of the house. Or you may want to jot down notes on the information sheet.

If you have any questions, ask your agent. If she does not know, she can usually find out. For instance, you might ask when the roof was replaced or what type of plumbing is in the house.

If you can easily revisit the house, you may not need to worry about remembering exactly how the house looked. If you're moving from another town and cannot easily return, you may want to take a camera and snap pictures or sketch floor plans.

As you look at more and more houses, you may find it hard to keep track of them, and you may not want to keep notes. Instead, you might want to pick one house that is the house to beat—the best house you have seen so far. If you compare a house to this house, and it doesn't hold up, forget about it. If you compare a house and it is better, forget about the first one.

After you look at several houses, you may find that there's one you want to return to. You can set up an appointment to see a house a second time. You can set up more appointments, but keep in mind that you don't want to waste the seller's time. With each visit, the seller thinks you're more and more interested in the house. If you don't make an offer, they may be miffed.

The rest of this chapter gives you some suggestions on what to look for as you tour.

Do You Like the House?

If everyone had the same tastes, all the homes on your street would look the same. Instead, all homes are different, and each person has different likes and dislikes. The first thing you have to decide about a house is if you like it.

Sometimes you will have an immediate reaction to the house. It just *feels* right. "This is my house," you may think. Sometimes you may take awhile to warm up to the house. As you go through it, you may hear a little voice saying "Yeah, yeah." Other times you will immediately hate a house.

Why the intense emotions? Because your home is a reflection of you. Some houses will fit, some won't. There's no way to predict any individual's reaction. You just have to gauge yours.

You may think that there's just one home that is perfect for you, but there are probably several. Keep your perspective. If a deal doesn't go through on that perfect home, rest assured that you will find another one that yo will like just as well.

Does the House Have Everything You Need?

After noting the emotional appeal of the house, you need to check out what the house has and what it lacks. Walk through each of the rooms and compare the features to the "dream home wish list" you created in Chapter 5. Keep in mind that you're going to have to be flexible and compromise on some features. Here are some questions to consider:

Does the house have enough bedrooms to accommodate your family now? Five years from now? Can you add on?

Does the house have enough bathrooms? Are the bathrooms big enough? Can you add a bathroom? If so, what would be the cost?

81

Is the kitchen adequate for your needs? Is there enough counter space? Cupboard space? Are the range and refrigerator included in the sale of the home? If so, are they in good condition? All built-in appliances are usually included; others are negotiable.

Does the house have enough living space? Room to work? Watch TV? Relax? Can the living space be adapted to meet your needs in the next five years? For instance, if you're planning on having a child, will there be room for the child to play?

Does the house have enough storage space? Check the attic, basement, garage, and closets.

Are the yard and landscaping acceptable? Is the lawn overgrown or bare? Will it require work? Do you care how the lawn looks?

Does the home have the amenities that you want? Hardwood floors? Built-in cabinets? Fireplace? Deck? Patio?

What personal property is included with the house? The washer? Dryer? Dishwasher? If these items are included, are they in good shape? If they aren't included, keep in mind that you may need to purchase the items separately.

Can You Live in the House?

The best home isn't necessarily the home equipped with everything you want; the best home is the one you like living in. Once you are sure the home has the basic features you need, imagine living in the house. For example, you might think the house is okay because it has four bedrooms, and you need four. But how are the four bedrooms situated? Are they all right next to each other so that you can hear your 14-year-old's headbanger music from your room? Are the bedrooms big enough? Can your 8-year-old fit her entire Barbie collection in her room? As you walk through the home, imagine it's *your* home. Think about the things you'll do in the home:

Imagine your daily routine. Where will you sleep? Watch TV? Cook? Eat?

Imagine your entire family in the house. Where will your children sleep? Are their rooms close enough to yours that they feel safe, but far enough away to have some quiet? Where will your children do their homework? Watch TV? Where will your spouse or you work?

Walk through the house and check the traffic pattern. Do you have to walk through 5 rooms to get to the family room? Are the bathrooms easily accessible for you and any guests you may have over? Or will your guests have to traipse through your bedroom to get to the bathroom?

Think about your lifestyle. Will you have enough privacy? Do you like to entertain? If so, where will you entertain? If you have guests over, where will they sleep?

Think about all your possessions. Where will they fit? Where will you keep your 50-plus pairs of shoes? Your tool collection?

Think about your household chores. What work will need to be done routinely around the house? Where will you do laundry? Where will you put the groceries when you come in? Where will you put mops, brooms, vacuum cleaner?

Imagine your furniture in this house. Do you prefer this home with your old furniture or your old home with new furniture? You may dislike your current home for reasons you don't realize.

WHOA!

Try It On for Size

Taste the water, and stand in the shower. These are two things I routinely do when I visit a house. First, water tastes different depending on whether it's city water or well water. And water varies from city to city. You probably don't want to buy a house where you hate the water.

Also, I stand in the shower. Why? Because my sister lives in a house where the shower nozzle is right about chin level. When I have to take a shower there, I have to do a back bend to get the shampoo out of my hair. Which reminds me of another thing: check the water pressure. There's nothing worse than taking a shower where the water drip drip drips out.

If You Don't Like Something, Can You Change It?

Keep in mind that certain aspects of the house are unchangeable. You can't move the garage to the other side of the house. You can't change where the house is located. (Well, I suppose you can if you want to go to the trouble of moving the house, but it's not likely.) You can't change the shape of the attic.

Other things are changeable. If you don't like the carpeting, for instance, you can have it replaced. Wall papering, paint, curtains can all be changed. Sometimes when you're looking at a home, you have to look past the decorating to see the actual home underneath. When you're redoing the house in your mind, also keep in mind the cost of any redecorating or remodeling. Sure, you can redo the kitchen so that it has just the layout, cabinets, and flooring you want, but at what price?

Is the House Well-Maintained?

You love the house. It has charm, character, and all the features you could want. Are you ready to make an offer? Better wait. Behind that beautiful facade could be a cracking, leaking, sinking mess.

Checking Out the Structure

When you look at the house, you will also want to consider its structure—the exterior, electricity, plumbing, and so on. Here are some points to consider:

If you find yourself in love with a house that has a shower head positioned for a munchkin, you can always install a shower head on a hose (takes about 15 minutes). If you're really ambitious, you can even raise the position of the pipe.

Check the exterior of the home to see whether it is well-maintained. Do you see peeling paint? Missing shingles? What will you need to do to maintain the house?

Check the roof. An inspector will check the roof more carefully, but you may be able to spot problems right away. Moss on the roof usually indicates moisture. Cracked, curled, or missing shingles may indicate that the roof needs repair. If it's winter and all the other houses have snow on the roof and yours doesn't, you probably are looking at a poorly insulated house.

Check the gutters to be sure they are intact and attached.

Check the electricity. Again, an inspector will carefully check the electricity, but you may want to be sure there are outlets placed conveniently in all the rooms. Also find out what the electric bill runs each month. You can usually get this information from the agent or directly from the electric company with just the address of the house.

If you see a tangle of extension cords in a room, it probably means that the room doesn't have adequate wall outlets

Check the interior walls and ceilings. Are they drywall? Plaster? Are the interior walls in good shape? Any cracks? Keep in mind that some cracks will appear as a normal result of the house settling—it doesn't mean the house is going to fall in, but you will want the inspector to take a close look at structure.

Check the condition of flooring. Is the carpet in good shape? Are the floors level? Is the tile or linoleum cracked or dirty? Do the floors creak? There are remedies for these problems, but it is best to know about them ahead of time.

Check the basement. Is it dry? Any indication of water damage? If the homeowners store a lot of stuff on the basement floor, it probably means it's dry.

Check the insulation. Check the attic to see if the home is properly insulated. Make sure the storm windows are in good shape. Are they broken or bent?

Check the local utilities. Is trash collection included as part of the taxes? Do you use city water and city sewers? If so, what's the fee?

Check the heating. How is the house heated? Is the house air-conditioned? If so, how—central air or window units? Is the air conditioning sufficient? What's the monthly heating bill?

Ask the seller for any disclosure information. The laws about seller disclosure are changing. Some states require the seller to disclose any defects in the property. In some states, a seller disclosure form is mandatory. Even if the form is not required by law, you may ask the seller to provide this form anyway.

Is the Neighborhood Acceptable?

Chapter 6 explained how to pinpoint a neighborhood that you liked, then find a house. Here you're doing the opposite—finding the house and then double-checking the neighborhood. Of course, if you're only looking for houses in neighborhoods you've already checked out, then you're in good shape. You can skip this step.

What Are the Taxes?

Your agent or the homeowners should provide you with the general taxes for the area. Remember that your house payment is PITI (principal, interest, taxes, and insurance). The amount of the taxes will have an effect on what you pay each month. The lender will also consider the tax amount in determining what you can afford to pay each month.

Find out when taxes are reassessed. In some places, taxes are reassessed every so many years. If you're due for a reassessment, you may want to keep in mind that the taxes may be raised. In other places, taxes are reassessed when a property is sold. In this case, you might have to come up with more money for the closing as well as for the taxes. Ask your agent.

Your House and the Neighborhood

Take a look at your house and the surrounding neighborhood. Does it fit in? A modest house in a more expensive area has the highest resale value. The most expensive house in a modest area has the lowest resale value.

Checking the Area

Even if you find your dream home, you aren't going to be happy if your next-door neighbors have a garage band called Ear Drum Explosions who practice every night. You will want to take a close look at your neighbors, your neighborhood, and your community. Here are some avenues to explore:

Drive around the immediate area. Do you notice any "bad" neighbors? Loud dogs? Unsightly homes? Are there a lot of rental properties?

You will have to define for yourself the type of neighbor you'll be comfortable with. Once when we were looking at a house, the next-door neighbor came over and told us how his brother, who also lived there, was arrested the night before for beating his wife. Not my idea of someone I'd borrow a cup of sugar from.

Consider your routine. Where will you shop? How far a drive is it if you have to run out for a six-pack of Cokes? How far is it to your office? What's the traffic like?

Drive around the city. What's downtown like? Are the businesses well-kept or is it a ghost town? Are the people friendly?

What Are the Schools Like?

Investigating the school district will be important if you have children. Even if you don't have children, living in a good district can increase the resale value of your home. Here are some strategies for making sure the schools make the grade:

Figure out which school district you are in and which schools are available. Are there private as well as public schools in the area? Find out how the children get to school. Do they walk? Ride a bus?

Visit the schools. Examine curriculum, class load, school policies. Talk to the principal. Talk to the teachers. Do they welcome your visit? Are they open?

Ask a lot of questions. What is the average class size? How do students rate on the standardized tests? How many students graduate? How many go on to college? What is the per-pupil expenditure? What extracurricular activities are supported?

Talk to other parents in the area. How involved are they? What do the parents like and dislike about the school? What is the general reputation of the school? You might want to attend a parent-teacher meeting, if possible.

Property insurance is cheaper if your property is close to a fire hydrant, you have a burglar alarm, or you live in a newer home.

What About Emergencies?

You may not want to live right next door to a hospital unless you like the sounds of screaming sirens, but you will probably want to know where the closest medical facility is and make sure it is up to your standards.

You will also want to find out where the nearest fire and police stations are. What is the crime rate in the area? You can check with the local police station for crime statistics, or you might check out the "Police Blotter" section of the local paper, which can tell you more about the types of crimes—vandalism, public intoxication, versus burglary or assault.

What About Fun?

In addition to looking into the public services provided in a community, you may also want to see what recreational facilities are available. Think about what you like to do and then be sure you will have the means to do it. Does the community have a local library? Is there a swimming pool nearby? Golf courses? Tennis courts? Does the area have well-kept parks? Are the facilities easy to get to? Are they over-crowded?

Checklist

Make copies of the following checklist to carry with you as you view homes. Use it to make notes about the homes you have seen and liked.

Address: _____

Price: $ _____

Type of house: _____

    Construction (frame, brick, etc.): _____

    Style: _____

    Condition of house: _____

INSIDE

❏ Kitchen
    Notes: _____

❏ Bedrooms. No.:_____
    Notes: _____

❏ Bathrooms. No.: _____
    Notes: _____

❏ Dining Room
    Notes: _____

❏ Family Room
    Notes: _____

❏ Basement

❏ Finished ❏ Unfinished

OUTSIDE

Lot Size: _____

❏ Fence

❏ Landscaping

❏ Garage

❏ Driveway

Notes: _____

AMENITIES

❏ Deck

❏ Screened-in patio

❏ Ceramic tile

❏ Built-in cabinets

❏ Hardwood floors

❏ Fireplace

❏ Crown moldings

Other: _____

UTILITIES

❏ Heating

❏ Air-conditioning

❏ Plumbing

❏ Electricity

❏ Water

Notes: _____

PERSONAL PROPERTY

❏ Refrigerator

❏ Washer

❏ Dryer

❏ Dishwasher

Other: _____

The Least You Need to Know

Finding a house you like is 20% research and 80% gut instinct. As you're looking, keep these points in mind:

➤ Your agent will set up appointments for you to tour different homes and will accompany you on the tour. You should ask your agent a lot of questions; after all, she is the expert. Ask her opinion of the home.

➤ When you tour the home, ask yourself these questions: *Do you like the house? Does the house meet your needs? Can you live in the house?*

➤ Keep in mind that some things cannot be changed, and some things can. For example, don't rule out a house just because you hate the wallpaper.

➤ You will want to have the house thoroughly inspected by a professional, but as you tour the home, be sure to look at the structure—plumbing, wiring, heating, exterior, interior, and so on.

➤ Find out information about the taxes on the home, the school district, the neighborhood, and community services.

Part II
Make an Offer

After you find your dream house, you have to enter into the negotiation process to buy that dream house. Doing so can be pretty tense. What's a good price to offer? Will the sellers take your offer? Will you have to counteroffer? Your agent can help you with the negotiations. If all goes well, at the end of the process, you'll own a home!

Chapter 8

Making an Offer

In This Chapter

➤ Understanding the sales contract

➤ Deciding on a price

➤ Deciding on terms

➤ Making a deposit

I personally hate buying anything where negotiation is involved—for instance, a car. Why can't there just be a price for the car and either you pay it or you don't? No, instead, you have to play an elaborate game. You make an offer, and the salesperson takes it to his manager and comes back with a story about how the manager really wants you to have the car, but can't accept the offer. The salesperson asks you to make another offer. You make another offer, she goes to the elusive manager, comes back. Same story, slight variation. Sometime near the end of the process the manager himself makes an appearance, explaining what a nice guy he is, and so on and so on. I hate that dance. When you buy, say, a shirt, you don't have to think, "Is the shirt really $20 or can I get it for $15? Or is the salesguy going to split the difference with me and make it $17.50?"

Others love the game of negotiation, though, and to these people, bargaining is part of the fun. If you like negotiation, you'll like the process of making an offer on a home. If you don't like to negotiate, don't worry. That's what agents are for. This chapter covers the art of making an offer.

Understanding the Sales or Purchase Contract

When you have found the house that you want, you make a formal offer on the house. Real estate laws differ from state to state. What the contract looks like and what it includes will vary. This section gives an overview of what's included in the offer; later sections explain the components of an offer in more detail. This section also includes some tips on making a successful offer. Flip to the back of this chapter to see a sample "Purchase Agreement."

What's Included in the Offer

Your agent should help you decide what to include in the offer and then help you write the offer. Usually, the agent will use a preprinted offer form, which is modified to match what you want to offer. All offers should be submitted in written form and should include the following:

➤ The address and legal description of the property (lot, block, and square recorded in government records).

➤ The names of the brokers involved.

➤ The price, down payment, loan amount, and the amount of the deposit. Deciding on the price to offer is covered in "How Much Do You Offer?," later in this chapter. Handling the deposit is covered in "Making a Deposit."

➤ A time limit for the response to the offer, for getting financing and closing on the house, and for moving in.

➤ Certain conditions or contingencies that must be met. For example, the offer will probably be contingent on your being able to obtain financing. Contingencies are covered in "What Terms?"

There may be other provisions, such as what personal property is included, whether certain payments are prorated, how assumptions, damages, and other special circumstances are handled, and so on. See the sample "Purchase Agreement" at the back of this chapter.

Tips on Making an Offer

When you are working up an offer, consider that all offers are a combination of price and terms. If you give something on price, you can expect to take something on terms. For instance, you might offer close to the selling price, but ask for help on closing costs or other beneficial terms. Or, for instance, if you see that the roof needs to be replaced, you might want to tell the seller to fix the roof or offer a lower price in exchange for fixing the roof yourself. Any obvious repairs should be addressed in the initial offer.

When you make an offer on a house, everything is negotiable—the price, the terms, the occupancy date, what personal property is included, everything. You can ask for what you want. You may not get it, but you can ask. Unless you are in a very competitive seller's market, don't offer your best price first. Leave room for negotiating.

In the contract, be specific and include everything in writing. You may have a verbal agreement that the washer and dryer stays, but without a written contract, you will have no recourse if suddenly the washer and dryer aren't part of the deal. Being specific is especially important when it comes to personal property, because what *you* consider personal property and what the *seller* considers personal property may differ. When in doubt, put it in writing.

The more contingencies you include in the offer, the less attractive the offer will be to the seller. That's okay if you're working in a buyer's market. In a seller's market, though, if you really want the house, consider making an offer close to or at the asking price, and leave off any contingencies.

Keep in mind that the contract will become a legal document if it is accepted. Consider having an attorney look over the contract before you submit it.

How Much Do You Offer?

Remember that when buying a home you are in a bartering situation. You have to decide how much to pay for the home. Do you offer less than the listing price? If so, how much less? Do you offer the exact listing price? Or do you offer more than the listing price? In deciding on how much to offer, you need to consider the sales prices of comparable homes, the motivation of the seller, the price you can afford to pay, and how motivated you are to buy.

Comparing Other Sales Prices

You probably don't want to pay more for the home than it is worth, but how can you figure out what a particular home is worth? One way is to ask your agent what he would consider a fair offer. Your agent has lots of experience in selling homes, so he should be able to give you his opinion of a fair price.

 If you are working with a subagent, keep in mind that the agent is actually working for the seller. She probably wouldn't (or shouldn't) give you an inaccurate price range, but she is motivated to make the sale. If you are working with a buyer's agent, you can rest assured that this agent is working for you only.

Another strategy is to find out the selling price of comparable homes in the area. Ask for statistics of list price versus sales price. As you look at several homes, you will know what the home is listed for, and you can compare the home you want to purchase to these other listings. But what a home lists for and what it sells for can be quite different. Therefore, you need to ask your agent to investigate the selling prices of comparable homes. If similar homes in the area sold for $100,000, and the listing price of the home you want is $120,000, you may want to offer less. Most homes sell for about six percent less than list price, but that's just an average. The actual difference will vary depending on the location and the current market.

Another way to determine the market value of a home is to have an appraisal done before you make an offer. As part of the loan process, the house will be appraised, but this appraisal occurs after the deal has been made. If the house appraises for lower than the offered price and if you make the offer contingent upon the appraisal, you may be able to negotiate a lower price. See the section "What Terms?" later in this chapter. You may choose to pay to have an appraisal done before hand. If the sellers sell it to someone else, though, you will have lost the money you spent.

How Motivated Is the Seller?

When you are deciding on a fair price, you should also take into consideration the mindset of the sellers. The sellers probably aren't going to come right out and say they are desperate, but certain clues can give away the sellers' thinking. For instance, find out how long the house has been on the market. If the house was just put on the market, the sellers might not be too anxious to take the first offer. If the house has been on the market for several months, the sellers may be more ready to accept an offer.

Find out whether the price has been reduced and if so, how many times. A house that has been reduced several times may be ripe for an offer. Ask your agent to also tell you when the sellers originally bought the house, what they paid for it, and what their equity is.

A buyer's agent also may be able to ferret out other information from the listing agent. For instance, are the sellers being transferred? Is the couple divorcing? Have they had other offers?

Can You Afford the House?

You may think that this is the first question you should ask when you are considering a house. Certainly, being able to afford a house is a critical part of deciding what to offer—even in deciding whether to make an offer.

Your agent will probably keep you focused on homes in your price range, so you shouldn't have to fret too much about whether you can afford the home. If you find yourself looking at houses slightly out of your range, you may decide you can—somehow—spend a little more. For example, suppose that you feel you can afford a $150,000 house, but find the perfect house for $160,000. You may find a way to come up with a little more money. For instance, perhaps you can sell off some assets. Or perhaps you can consider a different type of financing that will enable you to qualify for a larger loan amount.

If the agent leads you to homes way out of your range, you should probably get another agent.

What Terms?

In addition to including the price of the house, you will also want to specify the terms of the sale. The terms can include any of the following:

What else you want the seller to provide. For instance, you may ask the seller to help pay for the closing costs or provide a warranty.

What else has to happen for the deal to go through (in other words, contingencies). For example, you will probably want to make the offer contingent upon getting financing.

Sellers often focus on the price. If you offer the sellers full price, you may be able to get very favorable terms.

A response time, settlement time, and occupancy time. For example, you may give the seller two days to respond to the offer. You may ask for 60 days to secure financing and then require the seller to be out of the house on the day of the closing. The custom varies depending on the area.

What else is included with the house, such as appliances, window treatments, Porsche in the garage (you wish!)

The required condition of the house at settlement. For example, you may want to request that certain repairs be made.

Other provisions, such as the proration of taxes, club dues, and so on.

What Else from the Seller?

Keep in mind that everything is negotiable. You can ask the seller to do or include anything you want. For example, you may ask the seller to pay for some or all allowable closing costs. Suppose that your loan has three discount points. On a $100,000 house, that's $3,000 you have to come up with at closing. You may ask your seller to pay all or some of the points.

You can also ask the seller to pay for other closing costs, such as the inspection, appraisal, title search, document fees, and so on.

In addition to monetary requests, you can ask the seller to make changes to the house. For instance, you may ask for the seller to have the roof repaired. You may ask the seller to replace the carpeting (or allow for a redecorating fee).

Contingencies

Suppose that you agree to purchase a house, but can't get a loan. Or suppose that you agree to purchase a house, but find out in the meantime that the house is riddled with termites. If you didn't include any contingency clauses in your contract, you would be stuck with buying the house anyway. A contingency clause says "Sure, I'll buy this house, if ...."

This section covers some common contingencies that are included in sales agreements.

Financing

If you can't get financing for the home, you will want to be able to bow out of the deal. You will also want to specify exactly what financing is acceptable. For instance, you could get a loan from Eddie the Armbreaker at 20% interest, but would you want to?

You should specifically state the following:

➤ The amount of time you have to get financing

➤ The loan amount

➤ The down payment amount

➤ The maximum interest rate you will pay

➤ The type and term of loan

The Deed and Title

You will want to ensure that you get a clear deed and title to the house. The lender will require a title search. Who pays for this search and what happens if problems pop up should be stated in the contract. Title searches and insurance are covered in detail in Chapter 18.

The Inspection

You may want to make the sale conditional on a professional inspection of the home. (Inspections are covered in Chapter 19.) You will want to specify who pays for the inspection and what happens if a problem is reported in the inspection. For example, just having the sale contingent on an inspection doesn't ensure that the seller has to fix the broken toilet. Is the seller required to fix any problem? All problems? Can you withdraw the offer if the inspection is not acceptable? You will want to work out these terms with your agent.

You may also want to have the house inspected for termites, radon, lead paint, asbestos, or other hazards. Your lender may require some of these tests before approving the loan.

The Appraisal

Your lender will require an appraisal of the property before the loan is approved. You will probably want to make your offer contingent on an appraisal, and you may want to spell out what to do if the appraisal comes back lower than the selling price. Can you renegotiate the price? Can you withdraw from the deal?

Other Contingencies

You may want to include other contingencies as well. For instance, if you own a home, you may want to make the sale contingent upon selling your current home. In order to secure financing, some lenders will make the financing contingent upon the sale of your home.

Sometimes a contingency is countered with an escape clause, or *kickout.* For example, the seller may want to continue to show the house. If the seller receives another offer, you will have the option of removing the contingency or backing out.

Keep in mind that the more contingencies, the less attractive the offer. Also, it's usually not a good idea to include frivolous contingencies: "I won't buy the house unless the sellers paint it pink."

Setting Time Limits

Buying a home is a waiting game. You will want to specify how long you are willing to wait. How long do the sellers have to respond to the offer? You should require a written response within a certain time limit—for instance, 48 hours. If you don't require a response, the seller can sit on your offer, perhaps until a better offer comes along. But remember, you can cancel an offer any time before it has been accepted.

How long until you close on the house—that is, when is the settlement date? In setting this date, you will want to allow enough time for your loan application and approval (usually around 45 to 60 days).

How long until you move in or take occupancy? You will usually want to move in immediately after closing or settlement. It's a good idea to ensure the sellers are out before settlement; otherwise, how are you going to get Mr. and Mrs. McCrocklin, their three kids, two dogs, three fish, and Aunt Hattie out? In some cases, you may make a special arrangement for the sellers to remain in the house after closing and pay you rent. If this is the case, the exact terms should be spelled out in the contract.

Personal Property

Personal property is defined as anything that can be picked up and moved. Anything that is attached is real property. The sellers are entitled to take the personal property, but must leave the real property. Seems clear enough. That is until you move into your house and find that the sellers took the wall-to-wall carpeting, curtains, stove, refrigerator, dishwasher, cabinets, and anything else that wasn't nailed down tight.

To avoid a situation such as this, you should explicitly state which items you want the sellers to leave. Do you want all the window treatments? Ceiling fans? What about the pot rack hanging in the kitchen? The chandelier in the dining room? What appliances are included? The washer, dryer, dishwasher, refrigerator, stove? What about any rugs? Mirrors? Stained glass?

If a certain possession is key to the house layout, you may ask for it to be included. For example, suppose that the kitchen includes a bar and stools for dining at the counter. You may want to ask for the sellers to leave the stools; they may not have any need for them in their new house anyway.

Condition of House at Settlement

In the contract, you will also want to state in what condition you expect to receive the house. For instance, you may state that the plumbing, heating, mechanical and electrical systems are in working order at closing. You may want to be sure that the house is left empty and "broom clean."

You should request a walk-through inspection right before settlement to ensure that the house is in the same condition as when you made the offer. If you want a walk-through, put it in the offer. If you take one, check for any damage to the property—holes in the wall, broken windows, marks in the flooring, spots on the carpet. Check to be sure the heating, air conditioning, plumbing, and other components are working. See Chapter 20 for information on how to handle problems found at the walk-through.

Prorations

The contract should state which items will be prorated and how they will be prorated. For example, the sellers may have already paid taxes on the house for the next three months. Are they entitled to a portion of the money back? Or taxes may be due, and you may want to have the sellers pay a prorated amount for the due taxes. Depending on the type of loan and the situation, different items will be handled differently.

Other Provisions

The contract may include other provisions such as confirmation of the type of zoning, explanation of what happens if the house burns down in the mean time, statement of what type of sewer and water, statement of assignability, and so on. Your agent should explain any other provisions included in the contract.

Making a Deposit

When you make an offer on a house, the seller will want to see that you are committed to making the purchase and will usually require a deposit or earnest money. The amount of the deposit varies, but should be specified in the contract. The contract should also state who holds the deposit until closing. (You will want to have a neutral party hold the money—the real estate agent should put the money into escrow. Keep in mind that escrow accounts do not pay interest.)

Finally, be sure to state what happens to the deposit if the deal doesn't go through. If the seller doesn't accept your offer or if the deal falls through because of the seller's fault, you will want the money returned within a reasonable time period.

The Least You Need to Know

Making an offer on a house can be scary. You are making a big commitment—to living in a certain location, to making payments for a long time. Take your time and be sure you understand any offers you do make.

➤ The sales contract, once signed by both parties, is a legally binding contract. Your agent should help you prepare the contract. You may also want to have your attorney look it over. In this case, have the attorney look over the contract before you sign, or make the offer contingent upon attorney approval within 24 hours of acceptance.

➤ Critical items to cover in the sales agreement include a description of the property, the price, financing terms, response time, settlement date, and any contingencies.

➤ You can decide on a fair price to offer by seeing what comparable homes have sold for in the area. Also take into consideration your motivation and the seller's motivation.

➤ Common contingencies include getting financing and having the home inspected.

➤ In the sales agreement, spell out any personal property you want included as part of the sale.

GRAVES REALTORS®

Selling Broker *Graves Realtors* (#*Grv8*) By *Maris Bluestein* (#*251*)
Listing Broker *Otry Real Estate Co* (#*OTR1*) By *Charles Chuck* (#*127*)

PURCHASE AGREEMENT

1. Date: *July 12, 1994*
2. Buyer offers to buy real estate (the "Property") known as *3569 Camelot Lane*
3. in *Clay* Township, *Hamilton* County, *Carmel* Indiana *46033* Zip Code, which is
4. legally described as: *#60 23 Brookstone Village Section 2*
5. in accordance with the terms and conditions set forth below:
6. **A. PURCHASE PRICE:** Buyer agrees to pay $*103,000* for above Property.
7. **B. IMPROVEMENTS AND FIXTURES:** The above price includes all improvements permanently installed and affixed, such as, but not limited
8. to, electrical and/or gas fixtures, heating equipment and all attachments thereto, gas grills, incinerators, window shades, curtain rods,
9. drapery poles and fixtures, awnings, TV antennas, all landscaping, mailbox, garage door opener with control(s), ceiling fans, smoke alarms,
10. mini barns/storage sheds, satellite dish with control(s) and the following:
11. *all items as listed in MLS #418369 also include refrigerator in*
12. *kitchen, fireplace screen and tools*
13.
14. All items sold shall be fully paid for by Seller at time of closing the transaction.
15. **C. METHOD OF PAYMENT:** *(Circle appropriate paragraph number)*
16. 1. **CASH:** The entire purchase price in cash and no financing is required.
17. 2. **NEW MORTGAGE:** Completion of this transaction shall be contingent upon the Buyer's ability to obtain a (Conventional) (Insured
18. Conventional) (FHA) (VA) (Other _____) first mortgage loan
19. for $ *90% of sale price*, payable in not less than *30* years, with an original rate of interest not to exceed *9%* %
20. per annum. Buyer shall pay all costs of obtaining financing, except *seller shall pay 2 discount*
21. *points for buyer*
22. 3. **ASSUMPTION:** Buyer shall pay (approximately) (exactly) $ _____ in cash and agrees to pay the unpaid balance of
23. the note and to perform the provisions of the existing mortgage on the Property held by _____
24. Seller represents that the unpaid principal balance is [approximately] [exactly] $ _____ as of _____
25. 19 _____, payable at $ _____ per month including interest at a rate of _____% per annum, and also
26. including: (taxes) (insurance) (mortgage insurance). The exact balance including interest shall be computed through day of closing.
27. Buyer shall pay the next payment due after closing. If the existing mortgage cannot be assumed by Buyer at the interest rate shown
28. above, Buyer hereby agrees to accept an interest rate not to exceed _____% per annum and if this is not available, at Buyer's
29. option, this Agreement may be terminated. Seller agrees to pay any shortage in escrow account. Buyer agrees to pay all fees charged
30. by mortgagee for assumption. The parties agree to (reimburse the Seller) (assign at no cost to Buyer) any escrow account balance on
31. day of closing.
32. 4. **CONDITIONAL SALES CONTRACT:** Within _____ days after acceptance of this Agreement the parties hereto shall approve
33. the Metropolitan Indianapolis Board of REALTORS Conditional Sales Contract form or another acceptable form embodying the terms
34. contained herein:
35. Cash down payment $ _____, interest rate on the unpaid balance _____% per annum calculated monthly and paid monthly
36. in arrears: monthly principal and interest payment $ _____; first payment shall be due on _____, 19 _____;
37. interest shall commence the day after closing. Property taxes and insurance are to be paid (separately) (monthly) in addition
38. to the monthly principal and interest payment; no prepayment penalty for early pay-off; a _____ day default period for any
39. time provisions; forfeiture provisions are to be released by Seller when Buyer has paid more than $ _____ or (_____%)
40. of the purchase price. Contract shall be paid in full on or before _____, 19 _____.
41. Special provisions: _____
42.
43.
44. The Conditional Sales Contract is to be prepared by _____
45. at _____ expense. Buyer shall only use the Property for _____
46. **D. TIME FOR OBTAINING FINANCING:** Buyer agrees to make application for any financing necessary to complete this transaction, or for
47. approval to assume the unpaid balance of the existing mortgage within *5* days after the acceptance of this Purchase
48. Agreement and to make a diligent effort to obtain financing in cooperation with the Broker and Seller. No more than *30* days
49. after the acceptance of the Purchase Agreement shall be allowed for obtaining favorable commitment(s) or mortgage assumption approval.
50. If a commitment or approval is not obtained within the time specified above, this Agreement shall terminate unless an extension of time for
51. this purpose is mutually agreed to in writing.
52. **E. CLOSING DATE:** Closing date shall be on or before *August 15*, 19 *94* or within *3* days
53. after *loan approval*, whichever is later.
54. **F. POSSESSION:** Seller may retain possession of the Property up to 12 o'clock midnight on *August 18*, 19 *94*
55. or 12 o'clock midnight *3* days after closing the transaction, whichever is later, and Seller's possession until that date shall be
56. free of rent. If Seller does not deliver possession by that date, Seller shall pay Buyer $ *100.* per day as liquidated damages
57. until possession is delivered to Buyer; and Buyer shall have all other legal and equitable remedies available against the Seller.
58. **G. INSPECTIONS:** *(#1 OR #2 MUST BE CIRCLED AND INITIALED.)*
59. 1. Buyer reserves the right to have the Property inspected. All inspections shall be made within *10* days after *acceptance*,
60. with written reports delivered within SEVEN days thereafter to Buyer, Buyer Agent and/or Sub-Agent and Seller and/or Listing agent.
61. Inspections are to be at Buyer's expense by qualified inspectors or contractors, selected by Buyer.
62. If the Buyer does not make a written response to a report within FIVE days of its receipt, the Property shall be deemed to be acceptable.
63. Inspections include, but are not limited to, heating, cooling, electrical, plumbing, roof, walls, ceilings, floors, foundation, basement, crawl
64. space, well, septic, water analysis, wood eating insect infestation and radon. Other _____
65. If the inspection report reveals a major problem affecting the Property, and the Seller is unable or unwilling to remedy the problem, then
66. this Agreement may be terminated by the Buyer.
67. It is agreed that any Property defect previously disclosed to Buyer, shall not be a basis for cancellation of this Purchase Agreement.
68. Inspections required by FHA, VA or lender do not necessarily eliminate the need for other inspections.
69. 2. BUYER HAS BEEN MADE AWARE THAT INDEPENDENT INSPECTIONS DISCLOSING THE CONDITION OF THE PROPERTY ARE
70. AVAILABLE AND HAS BEEN AFFORDED THE OPPORTUNITY TO REQUIRE AS A CONDITION OF THE AGREEMENT THE ABOVE
71. MENTIONED INSPECTIONS. HOWEVER, BUYER HEREBY WAIVES INSPECTIONS AND RELIES UPON THE CONDITION OF THE
72. PROPERTY BASED UPON BUYER'S OWN EXAMINATION AND RELEASES THE SELLER, BROKER, AND LISTING AGENT,
73. BUYER AGENT AND/OR SUB-AGENT FROM ANY AND ALL LIABILITY RELATING TO ANY DEFECT OR DEFICIENCY AFFECTING
74. THE PROPERTY, WHICH WAIVER SHALL SURVIVE THE CLOSING.
75. **H. REAL ESTATE TAX:** BUYER shall pay all real estate property taxes, beginning with the installment due and payable in
76. *May*, 19 *95*, and SELLER shall pay all real estate property taxes due prior thereto. In the event real
77. estate taxes are unknown at time of closing, then the last installment of such taxes shall be used as a basis for any credits due Buyer. Buyer
78. agrees that any variance between actual tax liability and the amount credited at closing shall be their sole responsibility, and Buyer agrees,
79. if necessary, to escrow an amount necessary to satisfy the first installment of taxes due after closing. ("Real Estate Taxes" shall include all
80. charges placed on Tax Bill for collection.)

1-94/P-200

81   **I.**   **TITLE EVIDENCE:** Prior to closing. Buyer shall be furnished at Seller's expense, a commitment for title insurance in the amount of purchase
82   price. Any encumbrances or defects in title must be removed from said commitment and subsequent title insurance policy issued free and
83   clear of said encumbrances and title defects, with the exception of any mortgage assumed by Buyer. The final policy shall be subject only to
84   taxes; easements and restrictive covenants of record, encumbrances of Buyer; and rights or claims of parties in possession, boundary line
85   disputes, overlaps, encroachments and any other matters not shown by the public records which would be disclosed by an accurate survey
86   and inspection of this Property. The commitment shall be ordered (immediately) (after mortgage approval) (other _____
87   _____).
88   **J.**   **SETTLEMENT/CLOSING FEE:** If the method of payment for this transaction is cash, assumption, or conditional sales contract, the
89   settlement/closing fee shall be paid by _____
90   **K.**   **SURVEY/SURVEYOR LOCATION REPORT:** At Buyer's expense a (staked survey) (improvement location report) of the Property is
91   required, which shall (1) be received prior to closing, (2) be reasonably satisfactory to Buyer, (3) be certified as of a current date, and (4)
92   show the location of all improvements and easements.
93   **L.**   **UTILITIES/MUNICIPAL SERVICES:** Seller shall pay for all municipal services and public utility charges through the day of possession.
94   **M.**   **PUBLIC IMPROVEMENT ASSESSMENTS:** Seller warrants that Seller has no knowledge of any planned improvements which may result
95   in assessments and that no governmental or private agency has served notice requiring repairs, alterations or corrections of any existing
96   conditions. Public or municipal improvements which are not completed as of the date hereof but which will result in a lien or charge shall be
97   paid by Buyer.
98   **N.**   **RISK OF LOSS:** Seller shall be responsible for risk of loss and/or damage to the improvements on the Property until time of closing when
99   title to or an interest in the Property is transferred to the Buyer.
100   **O.**   **MAINTENANCE OF PROPERTY:** Seller agrees that maintaining the condition of the Property and related equipment is his responsibility
101   during the period of this Contract and/or until time of possession, whichever is later.
102   **P.**   **TIME IS OF THE ESSENCE:** Time periods specified in this Agreement shall expire at midnight on the date stated unless the parties agree
103   in writing to a different date and/or time.
104   **Q.**   **EARNEST MONEY:** Buyer submits herewith $ *2 500.00* _____ as earnest money which shall be applied to the purchase
105   price. Earnest money shall be deposited in the listing REALTOR's Escrow Account, immediately upon acceptance of the Purchase
106   Agreement, and held until time of closing the transaction or termination of this Purchase Agreement. Earnest money shall be returned
107   promptly in the event this offer is not accepted. If this offer is accepted and Buyer shall fail or refuse to close the transaction, without legal
108   cause, the earnest money shall be forfeited by Buyer to Seller as liquidated damages, or Seller may pursue any other legal and equitable
109   remedies. The Broker holding any earnest money is absolved from any responsibility to make payment to the Seller or Buyer, unless the
110   parties enter into a Mutual Release or a Court of competent jurisdiction issues an Order for payment.
111   **R.**   **HOMEOWNERS ASSOCIATION/CONDOMINIUM ASSOCIATION:** Documents for a MANDATORY membership association shall be
112   delivered by the Seller to Buyer within ___7___ days after acceptance of this Agreement. If the Buyer does not make a written response
113   to the documents within ___7___ days after receipt, the documents shall be deemed acceptable. In the event the Buyer does not accept
114   the provisions in the documents and such provisions cannot be waived, this Agreement may be terminated by the Buyer and the earnest
115   money deposit shall be refunded to Buyer without delay. Any approval of sale required by the Association shall be obtained by the Seller, in
116   writing, within ___7___ days after Buyer's approval of the documents.
117   **S.**   **MISCELLANEOUS PROVISIONS:** The transaction shall be closed in accordance with the following:
118   1. Prorations for rent, association dues/assessments, or any other items shall be made and computed through the date of closing.
119   2. Notwithstanding any other provisions of this Agreement, any inspections and charges, which are required to be made and charged to
120   Buyer or Seller by the lender, FHA, VA, Mortgage Insurer or closing agent, shall be made and charged in accordance with their
121   prevailing rules or regulations and shall supersede any provisions of this Agreement.
122   3. Conveyance of this Property shall be by general Warranty Deed, or by _____
123   subject to taxes, easements, restrictive covenants and encumbrances of record, unless otherwise agreed to herein.
124   4. Seller agrees to pay the cost of obtaining all documents necessary to perfect title, so that marketable title can be conveyed.
125   5. If said title insurance is not available, Buyer shall be furnished, at SELLER'S expense, an abstract of title continued to date, showing a
126   marketable title to said Property in OWNER'S name.
127   6. The price and terms of financing on a closed sale shall be disseminated to members of the Metropolitan Indianapolis Board of
128   REALTORS', to other Brokers upon request, and shall be published in the MIBOR'S Multiple Listing Service.
129   7. The Professional Service fee payable to the Listing Broker is the obligation of Seller.
130   8. Seller represents and warrants that Seller is not a "Foreign Person" (individual or entity) and therefore is not subject to the Foreign
131   Investment In Real Property Tax Act.
132   9. Any amounts payable by one party to the other, or by one party on behalf of the other party, shall not be payable until this transaction is
133   closed.
134   10. Buyer hereby discloses to Seller that Buyer is licensed under the Indiana Real Estate Broker and Salesperson Licensing Act and holds
135   License # _____
136   **T.**   **FURTHER CONDITIONS:** *This offer is contingent upon the closing of*
137   *purchasers, house at 1024 Hampton Rd, Indianapolis In*
138   *for which an offer has been accepted and is expected to close*
139   *no later than 8/15/94*
140
141   **U.**   **EXPIRATION AND APPROVAL:** This Purchase Agreement is void if not accepted in writing on or before ___*12*___ (AM) (PM)
142   (Noon) (Midnight) *July 13* , 19 *94*
143   **V.**   **TERMS BINDING:** All terms and conditions are included herein and no verbal agreements shall be binding.
144   **W.**   **ACKNOWLEDGEMENTS:** Buyer and Seller acknowledge that each has received agency disclosure forms, have had their agency options
145   explained, and now confirm their respective agency relations. They further acknowledge that they understand and accept agency
146   relationships involved in this transaction. By signature below the parties verify that they understand and approve this Purchase Agreement
147   and acknowledge receipt of a signed copy.

148   This Agreement may be executed simultaneously or in two or more counterparts, each of which shall be deemed an original, but all of which
149   together shall constitute one and the same instrument. Delivery of this document may be accomplished by electronic facsimile reproduction
150   (FAX); if FAX delivery is utilized, the original document shall be promptly executed and/or delivered, if requested.

151   *Paul Pierce*   *7/8/94*   *Paula Pierce*   *7/8/94*
152   BUYER'S SIGNATURE   DATE   BUYER'S SIGNATURE   DATE
153   *PAUL PIERCE*   *PAULA PIERCE*
154   PRINTED   PRINTED
155   *108-03-4153*   *116-32-6498*
156   BUYER'S SOCIAL SECURITY # / FEDERAL I.D. #   BUYER'S SOCIAL SECURITY # / FEDERAL I.D. #

157   **ACCEPTANCE OF PURCHASE AGREEMENT**
158   The above terms and conditions are accepted this _____ day of _____, 19 _____
159   at _____ (AM) (PM) (Noon) (Midnight).
160
161   SELLER'S SIGNATURE   SELLER'S SIGNATURE
162
163   PRINTED   PRINTED
164
165   SELLER'S SOCIAL SECURITY # / FEDERAL I.D. #   SELLER'S SOCIAL SECURITY # / FEDERAL I.D. #

Approved by and restricted to use by members of the Metropolitan Indianapolis Board Of REALTORS.
This is a legally binding contract if not understood seek legal advice   ©MIBOR 1992   (Form No. 310-01/94)

If at first you don't succeed, find out if the loser gets anything.

—Bill Lyon

Negotiating

The tennis game begins when you make the first serve. The ball goes to the seller. The seller may decide not to play or may return the offer to you. If he returns the offer, the ball is back in your court. You may decide to quit, or you may return the offer. The ball goes back to the seller. This back-and-forth process, or *negotiation,* continues until a deal is made or someone quits.

Understanding the fine art of negotiating can help you make a good offer to begin with and then handle any counteroffers. This chapter discusses negotiating techniques.

Understanding the Offer Process

When you decide you want to make an offer on a house, your agent will sit down with you and help you write it. The offer must be written; it cannot be verbal. (Chapter 8 explains the key items included in an offer.) After the offer is written, you sign it and attach your earnest money to show the sellers, "Look. I have some money, and I want your house."

Your agent then conveys the offer to the seller, usually in a face-to-face meeting with the seller's agent. In some cases, the offer may be made over the phone or faxed, then followed up with a face-to-face meeting. This is one area where your agent can help; she can present the offer favorably and start the negotiation process of making the deal.

When you write the offer, you should include a time limit for responding to the offer. During this time period, you'll be biting your nails and sitting by the phone, until finally your agent will give you the seller's response: yes, no, or maybe.

Buying a home is an emotional process. You may think that only one house will really fit you and your needs, and you may feel devastated if that deal doesn't go through. Keep in mind that there are many, many houses, and you will most likely find another house that you like.

The seller may choose to accept the offer, in which case you can skip to the section later in this chapter titled "Having an Offer Accepted." You've bought yourself a house.

Sometimes the seller chooses not to respond. In this case, no news is not good news. No news means *no*. If the seller rejects the offer and you really want the house, you may want to make another offer. Or, you can start looking at other houses of interest.

In many cases, the seller will return the offer with some changes. This is called a *counteroffer*. You can choose to accept the offer and go directly to the section titled "Having an Offer Accepted," or you can choose to counter with your next offer. In this case, see the section "Handling Counteroffers." The back and forth of countering will continue until one side quits or one side accepts the deal.

Offer Strategies

Did you ever notice that there's a fine line between too much and too little? Take, for example, salad dressing. First your salad has too little dressing. You add a tad more and *bam!*—it's too much. Finding that perfect spot between too much and too little is what you want to do when making an offer. Depending on your situation, you may want to use one of the following strategies:

The lowball offer. If you are looking for a house in a buyer's market and are not emotionally committed to having the house, you may want to make a lowball offer. A lowball offer is usually way below the asking price. Lowballs may succeed if the seller is desperate. Sometimes the seller will counter, but most times the seller will ignore this type of offer. You definitely don't want to make a lowball offer in a seller's market or if you really, really want the house.

An agent must pass along any offers you make. He may not want to take a lowball offer to a seller, but he has to.

The anxious offer. If you feel you must have the house, you may want to make your best offer first. This strategy leaves no room for negotiating, but might be necessary in a seller's market in which homes aren't on the market for long. Your agent will probably convey to the sellers that this is your best offer; the sellers may accept, counter, or reject the offer. If the market isn't red hot, you may not want to make your best offer first. Most sellers expect to receive an offer, counter, then receive another offer; that is, they expect to play tennis.

The bidding war offer. In a seller's market, you may find yourself bidding with other buyers for the same property. In this case, you lose all your negotiating strength. You have to see the bid, raise it, or fold your cards gracefully and move to the next game.

The negotiable offer. In most cases, the best offer is the one that leaves room for negotiating. You should plan on what you want to offer first and what you can go up to. If you are working with a buyer's agent, your agent can help you with this strategy. If you are working with a seller's agent or subagent, keep in mind that this agent is required to pass along all information. If you tell the seller's agent you can go higher, the seller's agent can pass that information along. The negotiable offer gives you a start in the point-counterpoint process, described next.

Handling Counteroffers

It's appropriate that *negotiate* includes the word *go,* because that's what you do—you go back and forth. If the sellers want to consider your offer, but make some changes, they will return a counteroffer. If you want to make some changes to this counter, you make another counteroffer. And so it goes. See the figure on the next page for an example of a counteroffer.

Receiving a Counteroffer

If a seller counters with another offer, that's usually a good sign—at least you know that the seller gave your offer some consideration. Your agent should return the counteroffer and explain the changes. Usually, there's a time limit for you to respond to the counteroffer.

Keep in mind that everything is negotiable. The seller may ask for more, may say no to what you asked for, or may ask for something else. For instance, the seller may ask for a higher price. Or the seller may say no to your request to pay closing costs. The seller may agree to the offer but ask for a different closing date or occupancy date. You should look over the counteroffer carefully and be sure you understand the changes.

Items that remain the same are not mentioned again after they have been found okay—only changes are noted on counters. If you're not sure which things are the same and which are different, ask. You may want to restate your understanding in the counter.

Don't accept or respond to any verbal counteroffers. If the sellers tell your agent that they want a higher price, have them convey that information in the form of a written offer.

In some cases, the counteroffer may be okay with you. You sign the counteroffer, and the deal is made. See the section "Having an Offer Accepted," later in this chapter.

In other cases, you may think the counteroffer is close, but you still want a few changes. In this case, you counter the counteroffer with another counteroffer!

COUNTER OFFER # _1_

_6_ (A.M.) (P.M.) _July 12_ , 19_94_

The undersigned hereby makes the following Counter Offer to a certain Purchase Agreement dated _July 12_ , 19_94_ , concerning real property commonly known as _3569 Correlation_ in _Clay_ Township, _Hamilton_ County, _Carmel_ , Indiana between: _Harry + Harriet Hamilton_ as Seller(s) and _Paul and Paula Pierce_ as Purchaser(s).

① _Purchase price to be 106,000._
② _Seller to pay purchasers closing costs not to exceed_
    _$1000._

All other terms and conditions of the Purchase Agreement and all previous Counter Offers shall remain in effect except as modified by this Counter Offer.

This Counter Offer # _1_ is void if not accepted in writing on or before _6_ (A.M.) (P.M.) (Noon) (Midnight) on _July 13_ , 19_94_

This Agreement may be executed simultaneously or in two or more counterparts, each of which shall be deemed an original, but all of which together shall constitute one and the same instrument. Delivery of this document may be accomplished by electronic facsimile reproduction (FAX); if FAX delivery is utilized, the original document shall be promptly executed and/or delivered, if requested.

Harry Hamilton _7/12/94_
(Seller) (Purchaser) Signature   Date

Harriet Hamilton _7/12/94_
(Seller) (Purchaser) Signature   Date

_306-75-1234_
Social Security # / Federal I.D. #

_317-18-1920_
Social Security # / Federal I.D. #

ACCEPTANCE OF COUNTER OFFER # _____

The above Counter Offer # _1_ is hereby accepted at _12_ (A.M.) (P.M.) (Noon) (Midnight) _7/13_ , 19_94_. Receipt of a signed copy of this Counter Offer is hereby acknowledged. This Agreement may be executed simultaneously or in two or more counterparts, each of which shall be deemed an original, but all of which together shall constitute one and the same instrument. Delivery of this document may be accomplished by electronic facsimile reproduction (FAX); if FAX delivery is utilized, the original document shall be promptly executed and/or delivered, if requested.

Paul Pierce _7/13/94_
(Seller) (Purchaser) Signature   Date

Paula Pierce _7/13/94_
(Seller) (Purchaser) Signature   Date

_108-03-4153_
Social Security # / Federal I.D. #

_116-32-6498_
Social Security # / Federal I.D. #

Approved by and restricted to use by members of the Metropolitan Indianapolis Board Of REALTORS®
This is a legally binding contract, if not understood seek legal advice.   ©MIBOR 1992   (Form No. 210-01/92)

An example of a counteroffer.

Responding to a Counteroffer

If the seller's counteroffer is close to what you want, but you want to make a few changes, you can offer another counteroffer. Again, your agent will help you draw up the offer. Usually the counteroffers are simply edited versions of the original offer, with changes written in and then initialed by all parties. In some cases, you may want to write a new offer.

If you are making lots of changes, you may want to use a new offer form. If the sellers see many items crossed off or written in, they may be more aware of the changes. The marked up form screams, "Here's where I'm trying to get you!" Instead, write up a new offer that looks cleaner. Be sure it says what you want it to say.

In responding to the counteroffer, you should consider what is important to you. Can you come up a little higher on price? Will you give on price in exchange for some help on closing?

When negotiating, be sure you stay within your financial limitations. Don't let the emotions of buying a house sway you into paying more than you can afford. It's easy to get into a nitpicking situation during countering. You may think that you want the last word. Keep in mind your goal: to buy the house. If you want to change something that is really important, by all means don't accept the counteroffer. If the reason you want to counter is trivial, consider just accepting the offer.

If you are close to a deal, the agent may recommend you "split the difference." For example, if you offer $105,000, and the seller counters with $108,000, you may want to split the difference and offer $106,500. In this case, both sides may feel as if they "won." Don't do this too soon.

The best type of negotiating is a win-win situation. The sellers should feel as if they got a good price, and the buyers should feel as if they got a good deal on the house they wanted.

When to Quit

If the counteroffering has become ridiculous—gone on for too long or fixated on small details—it's time to quit. Sometimes the buyer and seller focus more on the competitiveness of the situation and feel driven to win. The process can get ugly, and usually both the buyer and the seller end up with bad feelings.

Don't let the negotiation process drag you down. Your agent can help keep you focused on the goal (buying the house). Your agent may also be able to get the sellers to focus on their goal (selling the house). If not, you should consider walking away and trying to find another house suited to your needs.

You may also want to quit when it becomes apparent that you and the seller are too far off on terms and price ever to reach an acceptable agreement.

Having an Offer Accepted

The happy part of househunting occurs when the offer is accepted. This occurs when the seller signs and accepts your original offer or any counteroffers, or when you sign and accept the sellers' counteroffer. Once both parties have signed, the purchase offer becomes a legally binding document. You cannot back out now.

When your offer is accepted, you will probably feel two conflicting emotions: happy (you should be glad that you have purchased the house you wanted) and scared (you just made a big commitment, and the process isn't entirely over). You still have to get financing and close on the house. Wouldn't it be great if they made pills for buyer's remorse? Keep in mind that most people feel nervous after making such a big decision, and the feeling will probably pass.

When you have an offer accepted, make sure that you get a copy of the signed

An offer is accepted only when all parties have signed the same document. Don't be fooled if the seller or agent says, "The offer is accepted, with just a few changes." If the seller made any changes to an offer you presented, it is a rejected offer, and you are not bound to honor the agreement.

113

 If you are feeling anxious about the house, write a list of all the things you like about the house and all the benefits you will receive from owning the house. Start thinking about how you will decorate, who you will have over, and so on. Think about living in the house and enjoying it. Doing so may help ease your mind.

agreement. You may want to have an attorney look over the agreement before you sign it. If your attorney isn't available, you can write "Subject to the approval in form of my attorney." See the section "Do I Need a Real Estate Attorney?," later in this chapter.

You may be asked to increase the amount of money you put down on the home. This money will be held in escrow until you close on the house.

You will be required to get moving on any contingencies that you need to satisfy. For example, you may have a certain time period (specified in the contract) in which to arrange to have the home inspected. You may also have to apply for a loan within a certain time period. Your agent should remind you what you need to do next.

Withdrawing an Offer

Suppose that you change your mind and decide, "Oops—I don't really want to buy a house." Can you back out of a deal? In some cases, you can. In other cases, the seller is going to respond with, "Oops—you are getting a house whether you want it or not!"

When can you back out of a deal? You can withdraw from the deal with no legal repercussions in any of the following cases:

➤ You can withdraw an offer any time before the seller has signed and accepted the offer.

➤ You can walk away at any time during the offer–counteroffer process. If the seller gives you an offer you don't like, you do not have to respond. You can just quit.

➤ You can withdraw an offer if any of the contingencies included in the offer are not met. For example, if the offer is contingent on an inspection of the home, and the inspection turns up a major structural flaw, you may be able to withdraw from the offer. (Usually, though, the seller has the opportunity to make the repairs.)

If the offer has been signed by both parties, it is a binding contract. You cannot back out without forfeiting your deposit money. Also, the sellers may be able to sue you for damages if you don't fulfill the contract. On the other hand, the seller can't back out either. If the seller does, you can sue for damages or try to enforce the contract. You can't really force someone to buy or sell a house unless they want to, though.

Do I Need a Real Estate Attorney?

In addition to the services of an attorney, you may want to use a real estate attorney to look over the contract before you sign it. An attorney, for the most part, will not be involved in the price negotiation of the deal, but can help ensure that you don't get caught up in a bad deal. The attorney can look over the finer details of the agreement and make sure that you understand them and that they are acceptable.

An attorney can also help with the closing, ensuring that all the necessary steps are completed, and looking over any papers you are required to sign. (You will be signing a lot!)

She can help settle any difficulties that arise. For instance, suppose that the deal falls through because of one of the contingencies, but the sellers won't return the deposit. Your attorney can help handle this problem. In addition, the attorney may handle the escrow duties in some states. And, if nothing else, an attorney's presence can provide you with peace of mind.

If you decide to use an attorney, you will want to use one that specializes in real estate law. You can ask friends, relatives, your agent, or others for recommendations. Be sure to inquire about the attorney's fees. You may pay a flat fee or pay hourly. Also, be sure you explain exactly what you want the attorney to help with.

The Least You Need to Know

If you like to negotiate, you will enjoy the strategies of the home-buying process. If you hate negotiating, you can rely on your agent to keep your nerves calm and help you through the offer–counteroffer stages of the negotiation.

➤ When you make an offer on the house, the sellers can accept, decline, or counter with their own offer. If you receive a counter, you can then accept, decline, or counter with your next offer. This process continues until a deal is made or someone quits.

➤ When both parties agree to the offer and sign the offer, it becomes a legally binding contract. Once you have a binding contract, you cannot withdraw from the offer without legal consequences.

➤ You can withdraw from the offer before the seller signs it or any time during the offer–counteroffer process. If the contingencies you specified in your contract are not met, you may also be able to withdraw your offer.

➤ If you start to quibble about minor things and the process gets ugly, you may consider quitting and moving onto another house. You may also want to quit if it becomes apparent that you and the seller are too far away on terms and/or price.

Chapter 10

Buying a New Home

In This Chapter
➤ Finding a house
➤ Negotiating a contract
➤ Getting a home warranty
➤ Avoiding problems

Over one million new homes are sold each year. Perhaps you are one of the million that wants a brand-new home in a brand-new neighborhood with brand-new carpeting, brand-new appliances, brand-new everything. There's something thrilling about newness.

Buying a new home and buying an existing home are similar in some aspects. The process of finding a home, making an offer, getting financing, and closing are basically the same. There are some variations in finding a "good" home and in making a "good" offer, as covered in this chapter.

Chapter 5 discusses the pros and cons of buying a new home compared to buying an existing home.

Finding a House

Finding a newly built house is in some ways similar to finding an existing house. You want to first of all select a good location and a house plan that meets your needs. You want to select a good quality home. When you look at existing homes, you can see what you are getting. When you buy a new home—especially if it hasn't been built yet—you want to investigate the builder. This section explains all the items to consider in finding a new house.

Selecting a Subdivision

Finding a new home may be easier or harder than finding an existing home, depending on how you look at it. On the plus side, most new homes are built in new subdivisions. The developers and builders most likely advertise these new developments in the real estate section of the paper. You may also spot subdivisions as you drive around the city.

On the minus side, most new subdivisions are located outside the city, where there is room to expand. In this case, you may have to look a little harder to find a subdivision that is in an area acceptable to you. As you look at the subdivision, take into consideration the following questions:

Is the subdivision close to the place you work? Is the commute time acceptable? Do you have access to the interstate?

Is the area around the subdivision acceptable? If the subdivision is within an existing neighborhood, you can check out the neighborhood. If the subdivision is surrounded by land, you may want to investigate the plans for the area. For instance, you probably won't want to move into a subdivision if the rest of the surrounding area is planned for commercial growth.

What is the growth rate in that area of the city? No matter how wonderful the subdivision is in itself, you won't want to live in an area of town that is on the skids. Think about reselling the house. Will you be able to do so at a profit? Or are sales in the area flat? Are they on a down swing?

Is shopping convenient? Are there enough cultural and recreational facilities in the area to meet your needs? What is planned for the community?

What are the local schools like? Even if you don't have children, you will want to consider the school system. Living in a "good" district can improve the resale value of your home.

What police and fire services will be provided in the new subdivision?

What will the taxes be? Will you have to pay for any special assessments—for instance, pay to install the sewer lines or sidewalks? Is there any difference in taxation between a new home and a resale? What is the likelihood that the subdivision will be completed with like-quality homes? How many homes are sold in the subdivision?

Selecting a Good Builder

When you think about selecting a house, think about the three little pigs. You don't want to purchase a house that a huff and puff will blow over. The quality of the homes depends a lot on the builder.

Many subdivisions will include houses built by several different builders, so you can select a builder you like. You may want to tour several homes in the subdivision to see which homes you like. Try to focus on the quality of the home—not the "Wow!" factor or the price.

Investigate the sales of homes in the subdivision. Which are the best-selling homes? Why? Are they better quality? Better price?

If you have a friend who works in home construction or home maintenance, ask that person for recommendation. He or she may be able to tell you that houses by SlapEmUp Homes are a nightmare, and tell you which builders have the worst and best reputations.

Ask the builder reps why one house is better than another. Of course, they are going to give you a sales pitch, but look for concrete details. Do they use better roofing materials? Do they include other extras as part of the deal (for instance, landscaping)?

Determine what the basics and extras are for a given home. Find out the costs for upgrading. For example, if one builder offers more extras in a home or charges less for upgrades, you may want to consider that builder.

Visit homes built by the builder and talk to homeowners. You can visit recently built homes. These owners may be able to tell you about

119

any problems they've had. You may also want to visit a more established subdivision in which the builder has built homes. These homeowners can tell you how the houses have stood up in the long term. Ask the homeowners what they like and what they dislike. Which builders have good resale track records? Do the homes appreciate, do they sell quickly once placed on the market, or is there something that keeps buyers away?

Check out the reputation of the builder. How long has the builder been constructing new homes? Is the builder solidly financed? Check with the Better Business Bureau and other consumer groups to see whether any complaints have been made against the builder.

Selecting a Plan

After you decide on a particular builder, you can focus on the fun part—selecting the home you want. Many builders have several styles of homes that you can choose from. Do you want the Cape Cod style? Or are you more of a Colonial person? The houses may vary in style, size, amenities, and other aspects. You should tour the various styles of homes and see which one you prefer.

Keep in mind that the model home has the top-quality carpet, cabinets, tiles, appliances, and so on. Your home may not include the same features. If you are touring the model home, be sure to ask whether you will get the exact carpet, exact tile, and so on. If not, check out the quality of the materials that will be used. If you want to upgrade, inquire about the costs of upgrading.

If possible, it's a good idea to buy a home that is already built—you know exactly what you are getting and you know the house is ready. If you have the house built, you may be able to select some aspects of the home, but you won't be sure it will turn out exactly how you envision it, and you will probably encounter delays.

When you look at the house plans, think about you and your family's needs now and five years from now. Consider the following questions:

➤ How many bedrooms do you need? How many bathrooms? How large are the rooms?

➤ What "living" rooms are included—great room, living room, den, dining room, and so on? Do you like the placement of the rooms in the house, that is, the traffic pattern?

➤ What type of kitchen does the plan include? An eat-in kitchen? A country kitchen? What items in the kitchen can you select—the appliances? Tile? Cabinets? What do you have to pay extra for?

➤ How big is the yard? Is landscaping included?

➤ Is a garage standard? Is it finished or unfinished?

➤ Does it have a basement? How much will it cost you to have a full basement? Half basement? Finished? Unfinished?

➤ How is the house heated? Does it use the most energy-efficient heating source? What about central air? Insulation?

➤ Which decorating options do you get to select? Can you pick the floor coverings? Wall coverings? Window treatments? If so, compare the quality and selection of each of these options. Do you have to pay more to upgrade the carpet or other decorating features?

➤ What's included in the sale and what's extra? For instance, is a fence included or do you have to pay extra for it? Is the patio or deck included? How big is the standard patio and deck? Can you get a bigger one? For what price?

Selecting a Good Lot

You've got your house and neighborhood. Now you have to plunk it down somewhere in that neighborhood. Where? You may be able to select any location in the subdivision you want. The best lot isn't the largest lot; it's the one with a view. Keep in mind that you may have to pay more for the house, depending on the lot you select. In some cases, you may not have a wide selection for the placement of the home. The builder may have only a few lots left.

Just because your house backs up against a beautiful row of trees when you move in, doesn't mean those trees won't be ripped out to ready another lot. If the trees aren't actually on your own lot, you should ask the builder if they're there to stay.

When you select a lot, be sure to consider the traffic pattern in the neighborhood. Does everyone in that neighborhood have to drive by your house to get to their home? Will the street be busy? Does the house back up to a main road? Consider your view. Does the house back up to trees? Is your lot next to a schoolyard or church?

Negotiating a Sales Contract

When you talk to a builder, you may get the impression that nothing is negotiable; the price is fixed. In some cases, the builder will hold firm to the price. That's because the builder has fixed costs that can't be avoided. The lumber is going to cost so much, the electrical work is going to cost so much, and so on. Most builders operate on a slim margin, so they don't usually give you too much of a break on the price. But there is still some room for negotiation. See the figure at the end of this chapter for an example of a "Home Purchase Agreement" on a new home.

Negotiating for Upgrades

Remember: What you see in the model home and what you get are different. The carpeting, wall covering, cabinets, tile, fixtures, etc., used in your home may vary, but for a price, you can upgrade to the better stuff. Here's where you can negotiate. Consider asking for any of the following improvements:

Better quality outside materials (roofing and exterior walls).

Landscaping. In some cases, the covenants, conditions, and restrictions of the area may require a certain type of front yard, and in this case, the landscaping may be included as part of the price. If it's not, you may want to ask for landscaping.

Better quality floor and wall coverings (carpet, tile, wallpaper, and so on).

Better quality appliances. First find out what appliances are included as part of the deal. The model home may include a dishwasher, but do all the homes? You may ask the builder to throw in some freebies.

 Usually a builder will clear an entire area of trees before he starts building. If you find a lot that still has mature trees on it, though, you should ask the builder if he will leave them. If the builder says no, and it's important to you, try negotiating. Offer to give up another perk in exchange for the trees.

More or better amenities. Is the fireplace extra? How about a free one? Is the deck included? How about a free hot tub?

You may not get all that you ask for, but you can still ask.

Negotiating Contract Terms

Another area for negotiation includes the terms of the contract (flip to the end of the chapter to see a sample "Home Purchase Agreement" for a new home). For example, perhaps you will want to ask the builder to *buy down* the mortgage. (See Chapter 15 for information on this type of financing.) Or you can ask for the builder to provide help with the closing costs. You may ask to do some of the work yourself in exchange for a break on price or features. Your agent can help you negotiate a favorable contract—which brings up a good question: Should you use an agent?

Using an Agent

As you look through a new house, the builder's rep may try to convince you that you don't need an agent. He may tell you, "You can buy directly from me and avoid the middle-man!"

Be careful! Sometimes you need the middleman. For instance, if you have to negotiate face to face with the builder, you may lose your negotiating power. An experienced agent knows where you can push for a deal. Plus, the agent is an impartial negotiator. If you go to the builder with that "please-please-please-I-want-this-house" look on your face, you lose. It's difficult to not be emotional.

The builder may sell you on one-stop shopping—buy the house and arrange for the financing. That's okay as long as you are getting a competitive loan package. Shop around.

Also, the builder's rep may get the commission on the house himself. That's like the wolf being the three little pigs' insurance salesperson.

The builder should accept working with your agent and should pay for the agent's commission. You pay the same price regardless of whether you use an agent. In many cases, the builder is happy to get buyers with agents because they know they are serious and qualified buyers.

If you don't work with an agent, be sure to have an attorney look over all the contracts. Also, be sure you are getting something in return. Into whose pocket does the saved commission go?

Getting a Deal

Keep in mind that builders are motivated to sell. They don't hold any emotional ties to the home. The builder's motivation determines the flexibility in sales terms. In some instances, you may be able to negotiate a better deal. Here are some examples:

You may want to buy early in the development process. When a subdivision has homes that have been sold and are lived in, it makes the area more appealing to new buyers. The builders want to be able to say that *x* number of homes have sold. They want to give other buyers the illusion that they better buy now or be locked out of the swanky neighborhood forever. For these reasons, the builders may be more willing to deal. The builder will tell you about a price increase on a certain date to convince you to buy early.

You may want to negotiate to buy the model. The model will include top quality furnishings, plus you can see exactly what you are getting. You may arrange for the builder to sell you the model and then let them rent the home from you until the development is complete.

If you move into your new home while the rest of the subdivision is still under construction, you should be prepared for a lot of construction noise.

If you can, buy in a down market. If new home sales are slow, the builder may want to unload the excess units. If he doesn't, he has to pay the costs to maintain and promote these empty units. Also, he has sunk a great deal of money into supplies and labor (he has to pay the subcontractors whether the house sells or not), so a builder in a bind may be willing to sell a house for what he has invested in it, just so he can pay off his bills.

Buy the last unit. As more and more homes in the subdivision sell, the builder gets more and more profit. He may be less worried about meeting expenses and may be flexible on price. Plus the builder is likely to want to move on to the next development and may be motivated to sell the last one.

Home Warranties

What's a new home warranty? Do you need one? What types are there? What should the warranty include? Read on for the answers to these and other warranty questions.

What's a Warranty?

A warranty is a guarantee that a product will function for a certain period of time. For example, your toaster may come with a 30-day warranty. If the toaster doesn't toast, you can get a new toaster or have it repaired. Home warranties work the same way.

Types of Warranties

On a new home, there are different types of warranties. All homes come with an *implied warranty* from the builder. This means that the builder should replace or repair anything that threatens the home— that is the structure, soundness, and function of the home and its components. In addition, some homes come with an expressed *builder's warranty*. This warranty explicitly lists which features are covered and for how long.

Some builder's warranties are backed by insurance. If the builder defaults, the insurance company will guarantee the claim. For example, a Home Owners Warranty, or HOW, includes the following coverage:

Year 1	Covers defects in workmanship and materials; structural defects; flaws in electrical, plumbing, heating, cooling, ventilating, and mechanical systems. Does not cover appliances, fixtures, and equipment.
Year 2	Covers major structural defects, certain major electrical, plumbing, heating, cooling, ventilating, and mechanical systems. No longer covers defects in materials and workmanship.
Years 3–10	Covers certain major structural defects.

What Should Be Included in the Warranty?

A good warranty should include the following information:

➤ The name of the person who is warranted and a statement telling whether the warranty can be transferred.

➤ The length of warranty.

➤ An exact explanation of what is covered and what is not. The appliances? The roof? The plumbing?

➤ A description of what will happen if a problem occurs. Will the problem be fixed? By whom? In what time frame? How do you file a claim? Do you have to pay a deductible? If so, how much?

➤ Any limitations on damages. If the ceiling leaks and ruins your mink fur collection, is the collection covered?

Avoiding Problems

Buying a new home probably doesn't have any more or any less hassles than buying an existing home. But you will encounter a different set of problems. You may want to include the following information in your sales contract.

You should insist on a final walk-through inspection. Insist that any incomplete, missing, or broken items be fixed. If possible, don't close until the changes are made.

If you close before any final repairs are made, make sure that no money exchanges hands until the repairs are done. If the builder is paid, he may not be motivated to fix the dripping sink. If the money is still held in escrow until that drip is fixed, you then have some leverage to ensure that the repairs are made.

Make sure that your home is built to the standards of the model you visited. In some cases, the builder may make changes—for instance, if the housing market changes.

Ask for ongoing inspections. If you know someone with home-building experience, have him check out the house during its building phases. It's easier to spot shoddy electrical work—and have it fixed—when the work is being done.

Prepare for delays. The builder may take longer to build the house than planned. This can cause problems if you don't have anywhere to live or if you have locked in the interest rate. First, make sure you have someplace to stay if the house isn't built on time. Second, consider locking in the rate until the closing date. You may ask for this if you are using the builder or mortgage company for financing. Third, check up on the progress. If four months have gone by since you made an offer and they haven't started the basement yet, you're in trouble.

The Least You Need to Know

Buying a new house can be exciting because you can choose many of the details of the home—the floor plan, the carpet, the cabinets, and so on. When you purchase a new home, you don't want to get carried away in this excitement. You want to negotiate a good deal.

➤ The key items to consider when purchasing a new home are the area, builder, plot, and plan.

➤ Check out the builder's reputation. Talk to homeowners already living in houses built by the same builder. Check with the Better Business Bureau. Ask those acquainted with home builders for their opinions.

➤ New builders may not be too flexible on price, but you can negotiate for upgrades to the carpeting, roof, yard, etc. You can also negotiate on the terms of the contract.

➤ If you are having the home built (rather than buying a newly built home), expect delays.

➤ There are three types of new home warranties: an implied warranty, a builder's warranty, and an insurance-backed warranty. You should get all three.

Davis
HOMES, LP

HOME PURCHASE AGREEMENT

Davis Homes, LP, an Indiana corporation having its principal office at 3755 East 82nd Street, Suite 120, Indianapolis, Indiana 46240 ("Builder"), and _____ ("Purchaser") hereby convenant and agree as follows:

1. **Description of Home.** Builder agrees to build and Purchaser agrees to purchase from Builder a custom built home, model _____, elevation _____, to be constructed on lot number _____, in the _____ Subdivision, _____ County, Indiana. The custom built home will include the lot referred to above and will be constructed in substantial compliance with the General Specifications described on **Exhibit A**, which is attached hereto and incorporated herein by this reference.

2. **Purchase Price.** For the real property and improvements described above, Purchaser agrees to pay Builder the sum of $_____ payable as follows:

Earnest money due at signing	$_____
Down payment due at mortgage approval or authorization to begin construction	$_____
Mortgage Amount	$_____
Cash payment due at Closing	$_____

3. **Mortgage Application.** Within five (5) days after the date of this Agreement, Purchaser shall make formal application to a mortgage lender for a commitment for a mortgage loan of at least $_____. Purchaser agrees to use his best efforts to obtain the mortgage loan commitment and to provide all supplementary information requested by the mortgage lender in connection with such application. Purchaser agrees not to increase his present indebtedness such that it impairs Purchaser's current ability to secure financing of the above amounts. Purchaser understands and agrees any increase in indebtedness which impairs his ability to obtain financing shall constitute a violation of Purchaser's promise to use his best efforts to obtain a mortgage loan commitment. Purchaser agrees any failure by Purchaser to respond to a request for information or assistance from a potential mortgage loan lender within five (5) days of the request shall constitute a violation of Purchaser's promise to use his best efforts to obtain a mortgage loan commitment. Purchaser acknowledges that interest rates, terms and closing cost payable by Purchaser in connection with a mortgage loan are set by the mortgage lender and that Builder is not responsible for fluctuations in interest rates, terms or fees. In the event that Purchaser is unable to obtain a mortgage loan commitment in the amount stated above (or such lesser amount as Purchaser deems sufficient to proceed) within sixty (60) days after the date of this Agreement, Purchaser shall give Builder written notice of Purchaser's inability to obtain financing and send a written request to the mortgage lender requesting the mortgage lender verify the failure to obtain financing, and reasons therefor, to Builder. Upon Purchaser's written notice to Builder that despite Purchaser's best efforts he has failed to obtain such a commitment, Builder shall have the option to either cancel the Agreement and refund all earnest monies to Purchaser or to attempt to procure a mortgage commitment for and on behalf of Purchaser. However, if Purchaser's failure to obtain a financing commitment has been caused in whole or part by Purchaser's failure to use his best efforts to obtain a mortgage loan commitment, Purchaser understands and agrees Builder will retain all earnest money deposited and may also pursue all other legal remedies or relief. In the event Builder does not obtain a mortgage commitment for Purchaser within sixty (60) days after Builder's receipt of such notice, Builder or Purchaser may cancel the Agreement by delivering a written notice of cancellation to the other party, and Builder shall return Purchaser's earnest money deposit. Until one of the parties cancels the Agreement, both may continue to attempt to obtain a financing commitment, and upon receipt of such a commitment, the Agreement shall become non-cancellable. Prior to any cancellation, Purchaser agrees to cooperate with Builder and execute any and all necessary applications and provide all information required to obtain such loan. Purchaser understands and agrees that any job transfer, or other change in employment status, will not release Purchaser from his duties and obligations as contained in this Agreement. In the event any such change in employment status occurs which prevents Purchaser from obtaining the required financing to complete this Agreement, Purchaser understands and agrees that Builder will retain all funds received and may also pursue all other remedies and relief.

4. **Color Selections.** Within ten (10) days after the date of this Agreement, Purchaser shall deliver to Builder a completed Color Selection sheet which shall become a part of this Agreement. If prior to the start of construction, Builder determines that any item or color requested is or will be unavailable, then Purchaser shall select a substitute item or color within seven (7) days after receipt of written notice from Builder of such unavailability. If Purchaser fails to make any choice within the above time limit, Builder shall make such choice for Purchaser.

5. **Mortgage Commitment.** Within sixty (60) days after the date of this Agreement Purchaser shall deliver to Builder (a) a written commitment letter from a mortgage lender, or other evidence of sufficient cash to complete this transaction in a form acceptable to Builder and (b) all sums due as a down payment prior to start of construction under Paragraph 3. If Builder does not receive the above documents and sums, he will have no obligation to proceed and may, at his option, cancel this Agreement and refund all earnest monies to the Purchaser less any actual out-of-pocket expenses incurred by Builder on account of Purchaser.

6. **Change Orders.** Any changes or alterations requested by Purchaser in the General Specifications or Color Selections must be approved in writing by Builder and, in the case of General Specification, by F.H.A., V.A., or other mortgage lender. Such changes or alterations shall not be valid unless Purchaser provides the above mentioned parties with a written change order on a form provided by Builder setting forth the description and additional cost of the change. Purchaser shall pay such additional costs at the time such change order is signed by the appropriate parties, plus any applicable processing fees pursuant to Builder's change order policy. No change orders will be accepted after Builder has received Purchaser's mortgage commitment or other authorization to begin construction.

7. **Construction, Schedule, Delays.** Builder estimates that all work to be performed by it under this Agreement will be completed within _____ (_____) days after the start of construction, but, Builder does not guarantee a firm completion date. The start of framing on the house will constitute the start of construction. Builder will make reasonable and diligent efforts to meet the estimated construction schedule, but Builder will not be obligated to provide or compensate for any accomodations to Purchaser as a result of unavoidable construction delays, including, but not limited to, Builder's inability to convey clear title; the act, neglect or default of Purchaser; damage by fire, earthquake, weather or other casualty; and delay caused by strike, walkout, or any other act by employees or suppliers of labor or materials. Such delays shall not serve to cancel, amend, or diminish any of the Purchaser's obligations under this Agreement. If such delay occurs, the time fixed for completion of the construction shall be extended for a period equal to the time lost by reason of such delay. In the event of late completion not caused by the aforementioned delays, Builder will pay to Purchaser at closing a sum equal to Ten Dollars ($10) for each day Builder's work is incomplete after expiration of completion date, which shall constitute liquidated damages to Purchaser, and shall be the only recovery for delay to which Purchaser shall be entitled. If after the start of construction Builder is unable to obtain the materials specified on the General Specifications or the Color Selections, Builder shall have the right to substitute materials of similar pattern, design and quality.

8. **Permits, Insurance and Assessments.** Builder shall secure building permits as required; and shall maintain workmen's compensation and liability insurance during the construction period; and shall pay any special assessments or improvement bonds, including those payable in the future, for the work covered by this Agreement.

9. **Construction Liens.** Builder agrees to indemnify and hold Purchaser harmless from any and all liens which may be filed in connection with Builder's construction under this Agreement. Purchaser agrees as a condition precedent to Builder's obligation under this Paragraph, to notify Builder in writing of the existence of any such lien within ten (10) days from the date on which Purchaser receives notice of the intention to hold such lien.

10. **Disputes.** Should any dispute arise between Purchaser and Builder with respect to the meaning of the General Specifications or the quality of materials or work required by this Agreement, the dispute shall be reviewed by two qualified persons chosen by Purchaser and Builder, respectively, and if these two persons are unable to agree on the disputed matters, they shall name a third person as umpire, and the decision of the majority of the three persons shall be binding on both Purchaser and Builder. If such persons determine that the work or materials were not finished in good workmanlike manner, they shall specify the additional work or materials to be furnished by Builder and Builder shall complete the work to their specifications within a reasonable time. If, in the sole opinion of Builder, a dispute is unlikely to be resolved pursuant to this Paragraph, Builder may, at its election, cancel this Agreement by written notice to Purchaser accompanied by Builder's check refunding all monies previously paid to Builder by Purchaser, plus interest at the rate of six percent (6%) per annum; whereupon, this Agreement shall terminate, and neither party shall have any further liability to the other party hereunder whatsoever.

11. **Builder's Control of Premises.** The real property described in Paragraph 1 shall be under the Builder's control and possession from the commencement of the work thereon until the Builder receives payment in full pursuant to Paragraph 2 including any amounts due for changes or alterations. Purchaser further convenants and agrees that he will not occupy or take possession of such real property until he has fully inspected and accepted it, all sums due Builder under this Agreement have been paid in full, and title has been conveyed to him.

12. **Closing.** Purchaser and Builder agree that an acceptable final inspection by V.A., F.H.A., or other lender shall constitute evidence of completion of Builder's obligation under this Agreement. Purchaser agrees to close within five (5) days after such inspection. In the event that Purchaser fails to close within five (5) days after final inspection, the Purchaser will be deemed to be in default of this Agreement. In such case, Builder may/at his option, extend the time for closing for successive periods of thirty (30) days, provided that Purchaser pays to Builder a fee of 1½% of the sales price in advance for each extension period; or Builder may, at his option, elect not to offer any such extension, retain all sums paid by Purchaser as liquidated damages and seek to enforce any of his legal remedies under this Agreement.

P _____

Initials B _____

A sample new home contract, page one.

13. **Deed and Title Insurance.** Builder will convey fee simple title to Purchaser by Corporate Warranty Deed at closing and shall deliver an Owner's Policy of Title Insurance in an amount equal to the total price as specified in Paragraph 2. Purchaser will assume and agree to pay the first installment of real estate taxes which will become due and payable after closing.

_____ (Initial if applicable)   14.   **F.H.A. Amendatory Clause.**   The following clause is applicable only if this Agreement is contingent upon Purchaser's securing an F.H.A. insured loan: "It is expressly agreed that, notwithstanding any other provision of this Agreement, the Purchaser shall not be obligated to complete the purchase of the property described herein or to incur any penalty by forfeiture of earnest money deposits or otherwise unless Builder has delivered to the Purchaser a written statement issued by the Federal Housing Commissioner setting forth the appraised value of the property for mortgage insurance purposes of not less than _____ ($_____). Builder hereby agrees to deliver the above statement to the Purchaser promptly after such appraised value statement is received by Builder. The Purchaser shall, however, have the privilege and option of proceeding with the consummation of this Agreement without regard to the amount of the appraised valuation made by the Federal Housing Commissioner."

_____ (Initial if applicable)   15.   **V.A. Amendatory Clause.**   The following clause is applicable only if this Agreement is contingent upon Purchaser's securing a V.A. guaranteed loan: "It is expressly agreed that, notwithstanding any other provision of this Agreement, the Purchaser shall not incur any penalty by forfeiture of earnest money or otherwise be obligated to complete the purchase of property described herein, if the Agreement price exceeds the reasonable value of the property established by the Veterans Administration. The Purchaser shall, however, have the privilege and option of proceeding with consummation of this Agreement without regard to the amount of the reasonable value established by the Veterans Administration."

16.   **Warranty.**   Upon full payment by Purchaser to Builder of the price as specified in Paragraph 2, including any charges or alterations requested by Purchaser, Builder will enroll Purchaser in the "2-10 Home Buyers Warranty" program, providing Purchaser with up to two (2) years of warranty protection on certain components of the custom built home. THE 2-10 HOME BUYERS WARRANTY IS THE SOLE WARRANTY MADE BY BUILDER AND IS SUBJECT TO PURCHASER PROPERLY MAINTAINING ALL ITEMS CONNECTED WITH HOME AND PROPERTY OWNERSHIP. THIS IS A LIMITED WARRANTY AND DOES NOT COVER ANY CONSEQUENTIAL DAMAGES. BUILDER MAKES NO OTHER WARRANTIES, EXPRESSED OR IMPLIED, INCLUDING NO IMPLIED WARRANTY OF HABITABILITY, MERCHANTABILITY OR FITNESS FOR PARTICULAR PURPOSE. IF ANY WARRANTY IS IMPLIED FROM THIS AGREEMENT, IT SHALL NOT HAVE A DURATION LONGER THAN THE EXPRESSED WARRANTY IN THE 2-10 HOME BUYERS WARRANTY AGREEMENT. Purchaser shall give Builder a written notice of any claim under the 2-10 Home Buyers Warranty agreement. Builder shall have sixty (60) days after receipt of such notice to inspect the custom built home and, if such inspection shows defects covered by the home warranty agreement, Builder shall make necessary repairs or adjustments without cost to the Purchasers within ninety (90) days (weather, labor, and supply conditions permitting). Purchaser agrees to allow a "break-in" period of six (6) months after occupancy before requesting repairs of or adjustments except of emergency matters.

17.   **Mortgage and Closing Costs.**   Mortgage application fees, legal closing costs and pre-paid interest, taxes and insurance required in connection with this transaction shall be allocated between Builder and Purchaser as shown on the attached Closing Costs Addendum to Home Purchase Agreement.

18.   **Utilities.**   Purchaser agrees that all utilities to be billed to the custom built home will be changed from Builder's name no later than three (3) days after closing. Other connections of utilities shall be in Purchaser's name and will be at the expense of Purchaser.

19.   **Purchaser's Acknowledgement.**   Purchaser acknowledges receipt of a true copy of this Agreement and acknowledges that he has read and understands the contents thereof.

20.   **Miscellaneous.**   This Agreement shall be binding upon the heirs, administrators, executors, and the assigns of the respective parties hereto. If any provision of this Agreement is held to be invalid by any court of competent jurisdiction, the invalidity of such provision shall not affect any other provision of this Agreement. The headings of this Agreement are intended solely for convenience of reference and shall be given no effect in the construction or interpretation of this Agreement. This Agreement constitutes the entire understanding and agreement between the parties concerning the subject matter of this Agreement and may not be amended, supplemented or modified except by a written document signed by all parties. Any and all previous agreements, whether written or oral, between the parties concerning the subject matter of this Agreement are hereby cancelled and superseded by this Agreement. The failure of any party to insist upon performance of any of the provisions of this Agreement shall not be construed as a waiver of such provisions. This Agreement shall in all respects be interpreted and construed in accordance with and governed by the laws of the State of Indiana. This Agreement or any notice thereof is not recordable in any public record.

21.   Purchaser understands and agrees that all desired features and specifications must be included on the final signed blueprints which will determine the course of construction of the home. Purchaser understands and agrees that any feature, specification, or other construction detail not clearly specified in the final signed blueprints will be determined by Builder.

22.   Builder's obligation hereunder is conditioned on its ability to obtain all necessary permits and licenses including, but not limited to, a building permit to allow for construction of the home. This includes plotting of the subdivision and improvements to be made thereon. If Builder is unable to obtain all such permits within ninety (90) days from date, Builder shall have the right in its sole discretion to cancel this contract by written notice to Purchaser, accompanied by a refund of all amounts paid Builder by Purchaser together with interest at six (6%) percent per annum; whereupon, this agreement shall terminate without further liability or rights hereunder.

23.   **Further Specifications, Conditions and Options.**

_____

_____

_____

_____

IN WITNESS WHEREOF, the parties hereto subscribe their names, this_____ day of _____ , 19___ .

PURCHASER(S) _____   _____

   ADDRESS _____
   CITY/STATE/ZIP _____
   HOME PHONE_____
   BUSINESS PHONE: HIS _____
                              HERS _____

BUILDER ACCEPTANCE   DAVIS HOMES, LP

Date_____   By _____
                                                              Title

* *

MORTGAGE LENDER _____ TYPE FINANCING _____
CO-OP REALTOR _____ REALTY COMPANY_____
ADDRESS_____
CITY/STATE/ZIP _____
PHONE _____

A sample new home contract, page two.

My precept to all who build is,
that the owner should be an ornament
to the house, and not the house
to the owner.

—Cicero

Buying a Condominium or Co-Op

Hate to do lawn work? Want to live someplace where someone else cuts the grass, takes care of maintenance, but still have your "own" place? If so, you may want to buy a different kind of home—a condominium, co-operative, or townhouse. This chapter explains each of these types of residences as well as how to make a smart purchase decision if you decide this style of living is for you.

Buying a Condominium or Townhouse

Take this little quiz:

True or false?	The term *condominium* refers to an apartment-style building where the tenants own the "apartment."
False	*Condominium* actually refers not to the style of the house, but to the form of ownership. Also,

condominiums come in many shapes and sizes. A condominium may be an apartment-style building, a duplex, a townhouse, or a freestanding home. A condominium may be part of a PUD, or planned unit development.

True or false? When you own a condominium, you don't actually own anything physical. You own airspace.

Basically, true When you purchase a condominium, you own the airspace inside the walls and a portion of the shared or common elements—for instance, sidewalks, pool, elevator, and so on. You do not own the walls or the ceilings of your residence. You own what's inside the walls and ceilings.

What are the benefits, then, of purchasing this type of residence? What are the drawbacks? The next section should help you decide whether condo living is right for you.

Advantages and Disadvantages of Condominium Living

There are a variety of reasons why you should consider buying a condominium: You receive all the **tax breaks** and benefits of homeownership. You can deduct your property taxes and interest paid on the condo. Unlike an apartment that you pay rent for, when you own a condominium, you **build equity** during the time you live in the condo, and you can resell the condo. It is yours.

You have **less maintenance** to worry about, because exterior repair and maintenance work is taken care of by the condominium association. (Interior maintenance is still up to you.) Your condominium may include **recreational facilities**: a swimming pool, tennis courts, recreation room, and more.

If you want to live in a certain area, a condominium may be your only option. For instance, in large cities such as Chicago you may find a better selection of condos than single-family homes in certain areas. In some cases, you may pay less for a condo than for a single-family home.

What are the drawbacks? In a slow market, condo prices are usually the first to suffer and the last to rebound. That means if you have to sell during a downtime, you may not get the price you want, and it may take longer to sell the condo. Also, you are living in a community, and as such, you must abide by the rules set up in that community—the board, for instance, decides which improvements you can make.

Be sure to include the monthly fees for a condominium in figuring the monthly payments. In addition to PITI (Payment, Interest, Taxes, Insurance), you will pay a monthly maintenance fee.

You may have less space and less privacy in a condo than in a single-family dwelling. Remember that your neighbors are just a wall away. Neighbors can affect resale value of a condo even more than they can a house. People are going to be choosier about who they share a wall with than about who lives a yard away.

The Board Rules!

When a condominium community is established, a condo association is formed. This association then elects the board. As a member of the condominium community, you can vote for board members and other issues. The number of votes you have may vary depending on certain factors, such as the size, location, view, or floor plan of your condominium. The better-placed condos may have more votes, for example. Or the votes may be assigned one vote per unit.

Become a board member of the condo association. Doing so enables you to keep up on what's going on in your community, plus you have a say in the decision-making process.

Once the board is created, it establishes a budget and assumes the responsibility of collecting fees, enforcing rules, deciding on which repairs and improvements to make, and overseeing repairs and improvements. The board will most likely hire a management company to run the condo community, but the board will oversee this management.

133

The board is, in effect, a mini-government. They may create guidelines for changes you can make to your condominium. If you don't make your payments on time, the board can put a lien against your property. What does this mean to you? A couple of things: Before you buy a condo, be sure you understand the authority of the board and that you are comfortable with this structure. If it bothers you that you have to get permission to redo your bathroom, you may be frustrated with condominium living.

If you decide to purchase a condominium, it's a good idea to get to know the board members. The board members reflect the values and opinions of the other residents. Keep in mind that you will be living in a close community with these residents. Are you comfortable with the philosophy? Do you fit in?

Be sure that you understand all the financial obligations that come with owning a condominium. The section "Making an Offer," later in this chapter, discusses this topic in more detail. For instance, you might want to find out about plans for improvements or major repairs. In some cases, the board can make the residents pay a special assessment for repairs and improvements.

Selecting a Community

If you are considering a condo, the first aspect you should check out is the community. Here are some points to consider:

Is the condo association financially sound? You don't want to purchase a condo in a community where the treasurer has just absconded with all the condo fees. The association should keep a reserve of funds for repairs and improvements. If that reserve is empty, you as a condo owner can be charged a "special assessment" for any repairs that have to be made. Ask how many special assessments have been made in the past few years. Ask about any planned improvements or repairs and how they will be financed.

Is the condo well-managed? Remember that one of the benefits of living in a condo is leaving the maintenance up to the condo association. If that association isn't responsive and your grass grows up to your waist, what's the benefit?

How many condos are sold? Vacant? Rented? If many of the condos are sold, it may indicate a solid community. If many are vacant, you should wonder why. Also, if a lot are vacant, that means there is less money in the maintenance kitty. Finally, the percentage of rentals may control the type of financing that is available.

Which facilities are part of the community? Is there a gym, swimming pool, meeting rooms? Are you part-owner of the facilities, or do you have to pay a fee to use them? Make sure the facilities are adequate for the community. That pool may look nice now, but when all 200 kids from the community pile in, the pool isn't going to look so fun.

What are the by-laws and restrictions that you must abide by? Can you have a dog? Can you paint your garage a different color? You should look closely at the master deed, which should list the conditions, covenants, and restrictions. Read the by-laws to see who's responsible for what. What authority does the board have?

> **Some rules are good!** You may want your freedom, but you'll quickly find that a few rules are necessary when a family with 17 children, two aunts, one uncle, two grandpas, four dogs, and one cat moves in next door, and they all think that fireworks every night are a great way to keep the kids entertained. Rules will help keep peace in the community.

What are the monthly charges for the condo association fees? What percent of this payment is deductible?

Checking Out the Condominium

In addition to looking at the community, you should carefully check out the unit itself. Is it well maintained? What is the square footage? What amenities are included? Do you like the floor plan?

Making an Offer

Before you make an offer, you should review the master deed, by-laws, and house rules carefully with your agent and/or attorney. If you do not review these documents before making the offer, you should make the review and acceptance of these documents a contingency in the contract.

 You cannot be turned down for housing based on race, gender, or national origin. If you think you have encountered discrimination, you can contact U.S. Department of Housing and Urban Development to report the discrimination. See Appendix B.

The sales contract is similar to a single-family home contract. The contract includes the offer price, the terms, and any contingencies. (Information on drawing up and negotiating a contract can be found in Chapters 8 and 9.)

Getting financing on a condominium is similar to getting financing on a house. One difference is that the lender will include your monthly condo association fee as part of your PITI (principal, interest, taxes, and insurance). Also, you may be required to make a larger down payment. Finally, some lenders may make loans only for "approved" condos (those that qualify for FHA financing).

Buying a Co-Op

In some ways, a co-operative (or co-op) is similar to a condominium. The key difference is in the structure of ownership. Rather than owning real estate, you buy shares in a corporation that owns the building. When you purchase a certain amount of shares, you then have the right to live in a particular unit. This is called a proprietary lease. Unlike a condominium, where you can buy a home if you have the money, you must be "approved" by the board before you can purchase a co-op. The board members must vote you in before your purchase is approved. Sound snobby? It can be.

Most co-ops are found in New York City, but you may find this type of living arrangement in other large cities, such as Boston or San Francisco.

Financing Your Co-Op

Before 1984, if you wanted to buy a co-op, you had to pay cash or take out a personal loan. Then in 1984, Fannie Mae agreed to buy co-op loans. (For more information about Fannie Mae, see Chapter 16.) Once Fannie Mae started buying the loans, lenders starting making the loans. One of the largest co-op lenders is the National Cooperative Bank (NCB).

How is the financial situation different? Because you do not own "real" estate, you do not get the same tax deductions as a condo or home owner. That doesn't mean you don't get any tax breaks; you just have a different tax situation. If you are thinking about buying a co-op, you may want to talk to your accountant about the type and amount of tax deductions you will be allowed to take.

To get approval on most co-op loans, the lender requires that the participating co-op meet certain standards: structural soundness, restricted commercial use, fiscally responsible budget, and good management. You can expect to pay a higher interest rate on a co-op, but the closing costs may be less. You may also be required to make a higher down payment.

Your monthly payment includes your monthly maintenance fee. A lender will probably include this fee in your total monthly payment when qualifying you for a loan.

In addition to satisfying the lender's criteria, you will also have to pass inspection from the board members. You may need to submit personal references and financial statements. The board may also interview you.

Selecting a Co-Op

Selecting a co-op is similar to selecting a condominium. You should investigate the building and management carefully. You should review the proprietary lease, by-laws, and financial statements of the corporation. Here are some items to consider:

Is the co-op financially sound? Do they meet all the expenses for running the co-op? Do they have reserves to cover renovations and repairs?

What is the age and condition of the building? Does it need repairs? New roof? New elevators? You may want to have the co-op professionally inspected.

What are the covenants, conditions, and regulations you have to observe? You should know the rules you must follow. You should also investigate whether you can sublet the unit.

The Least You Need to Know

Many first-time buyers or retiring couples decide to purchase a condominium rather than a single-family home. In big cities such as New York, you may find buyers who own a co-op, which is a different form of home ownership.

➤ The term *condominium* refers not to the style of home, but to the form of ownership. When you own a condo, you don't own the walls, floors, or ceilings of your unit. Instead, you own the airspace within those walls. You may also own a part of the common facilities.

➤ If you live in a condominium, you don't have to worry about maintenance. Instead, you pay a monthly fee, and the maintenance of the property is taken care of for you. This monthly fee will vary depending on the community.

➤ When you purchase a co-op, you don't own property. Instead, you own shares in the corporation that owns the co-op. In return for the shares, the corporation grants you a proprietary lease which gives you the right to live in a certain unit.

➤ Be sure to check out the condominium or co-op by-laws, rules, restrictions, and other management and financial information. You should select a community that is financially sound and well-managed.

Part III
Get Financing

After looking at house after house until all the rooms merge into one never-ending maze of homes, you find the house you want and have an offer accepted. Now you can relax, right?

Wrong! The next maze is the financial maze—finding the right type of financing for you. Put on your blue suit and get ready to play banker, because this part explains all the financial options available for purchasing a home.

Chapter 12

Getting Financing

> ## In This Chapter
>
> ➤ Understanding how lending works
>
> ➤ Understanding how mortgage lending works
>
> ➤ Understanding the different types of financing
>
> ➤ Deciding which type of financing is most appropriate for you

Once you have an offer accepted, you have a piece of paper saying you are buying that house. Now you have to put the money behind that paper and secure financing.

When you think about securing financing, think about a high-school dance. The lenders are on one side of the room, and the buyers are on the other. Getting together requires agreement by both sides. For example, which lender do you want to dance with? And will that lender dance with you?

This chapter helps you decide which dance partner is right for you.

How Lending Works

Bankers aren't in the business because they like to handle money; they like to make money. Banking is a business, just like any other business. What bankers "sell" is money.

Here's how it works: Your Aunt Betty deposits $500 in her savings account, and the bank agrees to pay her five percent interest on that money. The bankers then take Aunt Betty's $500 and loan it to you. In exchange for letting you use "their" money, the bank charges you nine percent interest.

The nine percent interest rate you pay covers the five percent the bank has to pay Aunt Betty, any costs for moving the money around, and of course, a profit for the bank. The difference between the savings interest and lending interest is called the *spread*.

When money is tight, more people want money. Lenders can be picky about who gets the money and can charge a higher rate to borrow the money. When money isn't tight, there is more money than there are borrowers. Lenders want to make the loans attractive, so rates go down.

Interest Rates, or What's the Charge?

If all the banks offered money to all buyers at the same rates, selecting a lender would be easy. Remember that lending is a business, and as such, the lender will compete for your business. This competition means the terms of the loan—how much you will pay and how often you pay—can vary.

Lenders differ in how much they charge you to use their money. This charge is called the *interest rate* and will vary depending on the lender, the economy, the type of loan, and other factors. Interest rates can range from 4% to 15% or higher. The interest rate has a huge effect on how much you pay for an item. Consider the following example:

If you borrow $100,000 at 8% for 30 years, your monthly payment will be $733. If you borrow the same amount of money for the same amount of time but at a higher interest rate, your payment increases significantly. Table 12.1 compares a loan at 8% to a loan at 13%. The monthly payment amount difference is $372!

Table 12.1 How Interest Rate Affects Payments

Example 1		Example 2	
Loan Amount	$100,000	Loan Amount	$100,000
Interest Rate	8%	Interest Rate	13%
Term	30	Term	30
Monthly Payment	$733.76	Monthly Payment	$1,106.20
	Difference $372		

APR or the Real Rate

When a lending institute makes a loan, it amortizes the loan—that is, it calculates the loan amount plus interest and then divides that total by the number of months you are paying on the loan (the term). The interest is front-loaded so that on the first few years of payments you are paying mostly interest. (The bank gets its money first.)

The interest rate quoted and the interest rate you actually pay will be different because the real interest rate will include points, application fees, and other fees you pay for the loan. The real interest rate is called the APR or annual percentage rate. When you apply for a loan, the lender will tell you the true APR.

Points

In addition to the interest rate, you may also be required to pay points. One point is equal to 1% of the loan. A lender uses points to trick you into thinking you are getting a lower rate than you really are. The points are sometimes called *discount points*. Usually the lower the rate, the more points you have to pay. For example, a lender may offer a loan for 8.5% with zero points. Or you can get a lower rate (8%) by paying 2 points up front.

The number of points will vary depending on the lender and on the mortgage package. You pay points at the closing.

Term

Loans vary depending on how long you make payments. You can get a 30-year loan, a 15-year loan, or a loan on which you make 26 payments a year (every other week). The length of time you pay is called the *term*.

Most lenders today allow you to prepay on the loan amount. Prepaying on a loan will pay off the loan earlier and can save you a lot of money on interest.

Types of Financing

My mom and dad live in the same house that I grew up in. They have been paying on the house for almost 30 years. They pay the same monthly payment now that they did in 1965 when they bought the house. (Their house payment is less than my car payment!) Back when they purchased their home, most people selected this type of financing, which is called fixed-rate financing. Most people expected to stay in their homes for 30 years and wanted the stability of fixed payments.

Times have changed! First, people don't stay in the same spot as long, and second, lenders have gotten more creative with the financing that is offered. Now you can shop around for different types of loans.

As mentioned earlier, loans differ in the interest rate and points charged. Loans also can vary depending on who offers the loans and how they are backed. The two most common types of loans are conventional and government-backed. You can get your loan from Bill Banker or from Bill Banker with Uncle Sam backing you. Loans vary depending on how the payments are structured. The two most common structures are fixed-rate mortgages and adjustable-rate mortgages. Remember, the term *mortgage* doesn't refer to the payments you make on your home. A mortgage is the lien or claim against your property.

Death Grip

The word **mortgage** dates from the 13th century and comes from the Old French *mort* (death), and *gage* (promise or pledge). Mortgage, therefore, translates to "death pledge." And you thought loan officers today were tough!

Conventional Loans

I'm not sure where the term "conventional" originated. Perhaps this term got tagged on this type of loan because most conventional loans are made by bankers, and bankers are known to be conservative, traditional, yes, even conventional. Think blue suits, white shirts, boring ties.

Conventional loans are secured from a lender, usually a bank or savings and loan institute. (Chapter 16 discusses sources of conventional loans.) Conventional loans usually require at least a 20% down payment. You can put down less than 20%, but most lenders will require that you purchase private mortgage insurance (PMI). This insurance increases the costs to you with no benefit to you; it merely protects the lender in case you default on the loan.

Government-Backed Loans

To make homeownership more affordable, the government got involved in the loan business and decided it would back home loans. The lender still makes the loan, but the government backs, or insures, the loan.

The two most common types of government loans are FHA (Federal Housing Authority), which are insured by the Federal government, and VA (Veteran's Administration) which are guaranteed. VA loans are covered in Chapter 15.

FHA loans offer many benefits to first-time buyers. Because FHA insures the loan, the lender will accept a smaller down payment. On an FHA loan, for instance, you may be able to put just three to five percent down. A lower down payment helps new buyers who don't have a lot of up-front cash afford a home.

You can finance some of your closing costs. Again, this feature helps first-time buyers who don't have a lot of up-front money. The monthly payments on the loan will be more (because the amount financed is more), but you don't have to come up with the money when you purchase.

FHA loans are attractive because they are *assumable* (someone else can take over the payments). Assumable loans may be an added attraction when you sell your home. (Assumptions are covered in

Chapter 15.) In the past, some FHA loans were freely assumable, meaning the buyers did not have to qualify. Newer FHA loans are qualified assumptions, meaning that the buyers must qualify to take over the loan. This has really diminished the attractiveness of the FHA.

There are no penalties for prepaying your loan.

Many buyers think that they can qualify for an FHA loan on only their first home. That's not true. You don't have to be a first-time buyer to get an FHA loan. Your loan amount must be within a certain range to qualify, and you may not have another FHA loan outstanding.

Flip the coin, and there are drawbacks to an FHA loan. You are required to put less down on the house, so you have less up-front money invested. To balance this, you are required to pay mortgage insurance premium (MIP) up front. This fee can be pretty high. You can finance the insurance, but keep in mind that your monthly payment will be higher.

The house must be appraised by FHA appraisers. Sometimes FHA will require certain repairs before approving the loan. FHA loans will finance homes that cost up to a certain amount. The amount varies depending on the area. A rough figure is $100,000, but that figure may be higher if you live in areas where the cost of living is higher. Also, an increase in the limit is planned.

Finally, FHA loans must be paid to the end of the month rather than to the date of payoff when you sell your home.

Fixed-Rate Loans

Until 1970 or so, almost all loans made for homes were fixed-rate mortgages. On a fixed-rate mortgage, your monthly payment never varies. You pay the same amount for the first payment as you do for the last. If interest rates go up, it doesn't matter; your payment stays the same. Likewise, if interest rates go down, your payment still stays the same. Fixed-rate loans are covered in Chapter 13.

Adjustable-Rate Mortgage Loans

Before 1972, interest rates were low (around 7%), and lenders were doing okay. Then the U.S. economy hit a rough spot. From 1972 to 1980, interest rates skyrocketed, at one point reaching 20%. Lenders lost money because they had to pay a high interest rate on savings accounts, but borrowers with fixed-rate mortgages were still paying them the low rate that they had secured before the spike in rates. The lenders, of course, didn't like this, so they decided to have borrowers share in the risk in future loans made. Hence, the adjustable-rate mortgage, or ARM.

When you get an ARM loan, you usually pay a lower rate initially than a fixed-rate mortgage. The interest rate on the ARM loan is tied to an index that reflects the current money market. If the interest rates go up on your renewal date, your payments go up. If the interest rates go down, your payments go down. Chapter 14 covers ARM loans in detail.

If you have a fixed-rate loan, you may not be stuck with that loan for the rest of your life. You can refinance the loan to get a better interest rate. Generally, it's a good idea to refinance if interest rates drop by two percent or more. Calculate the costs to see how long you must have the new loan for you to break even on the closing costs you will have to pay.

Other Loan Types

The conventional and government-backed loans and fixed-rate and adjustable-rate are the most common loan types. There are other ways to finance the purchase of a home, though. For instance, you can assume someone else's mortgage. You can ask the seller for financing. Other loan arrangements are the topic of Chapter 15.

How to Decide on the Type of Financing

You've now surveyed the market; you know what your options are when shopping for a loan. How do you pick one? Unfortunately, there's no one right answer. Which loan is right for you will depend on your current financial situation, your future plans, and other factors. This section helps you narrow down your choices.

Your agent can help you decide which type of financing is best for you.

Deciding which type of loan you take will depend on several factors. This section includes some simple summary tables. Keep in mind that these tables summarize general circumstances. Your own situation will depend on all the factors—not just one.

How Much Can You Afford for a Down Payment?

Money, as usual, is the first consideration. If you have piles and piles of money sitting in your closet, you can pick and choose among the different lending options. If you are like most people, though, you probably lack those piles of money. You may have just one pile, and that pile will affect which type of loan you can get.

For example, conventional loans require a 10 to 20 percent down payment. If you can't come up with that amount, you have to consider a different loan type—perhaps an FHA loan.

Down Payment	Loan Type
20% or more	Conventional
5–19%	Insured conventional
Less than 5%	FHA or VA

How Much Can You Afford for a Monthly Payment?

In addition to the down payment, you should take into consideration how much you can afford—and how much the lender thinks you can afford. Deciding how much you can afford is covered in Chapter 3. This chapter explains the ratios that the lender uses to qualify you for a loan amount.

Remember that lenders calculate your monthly house payment as a percentage of your income. Also, keep in mind that your monthly house payment will depend on the interest rate. You may want to select a loan type with the lowest initial interest rate in order to qualify for the house.

For example, suppose that you can afford $700 for monthly payments. This payment amount includes principal, interest, taxes, and insurance. If the fixed-rate loan charges 8%, the payment on the principal and interest alone is $733. You won't qualify for this type of loan.

On the other hand, if the initial rate for an ARM loan is 6%, the monthly payment for principal and interest is $600. You could qualify for this type of loan.

How Long Will You Live in the House?

Another item to consider when selecting a loan type is how long you plan to live in the house. A recent survey shows that most people stay in a home an average of five to seven years.

If you plan to stay in the house five years or so, you may want to consider an adjustable-rate mortgage. The first few years of the loan will be at the lowest rate, or teaser rate. The following years will be adjusted according to the market. The payments could go up or down, but even if they go up, most can jump up only a certain amount each year. If you have one year at the teaser rate and then two years with a rate cap, you may find the interest rate has only risen 4%. This type of financing might be much more advantageous than a fixed-rate.

Consider this example:

Fixed-rate		ARM	
Year 1	9%	Year 1 (initial rate)	5%
Year 2	9%	Year 2 (+2%)	7%
Year 3	9%	Year 3 (+2%)	9%

If this was your situation, you would have had two years below the fixed rate and one year at the same rate. In this case, the ARM would definitely be a better choice.

Keep in mind that ARMs differ in the way they are structured. Not all include rate caps, or the rate cap may work differently. Chapter 14 discusses what to look for in an adjustable-rate mortgage.

On the other hand, if you plan to live in your home for the next 10 or 20 years, you may want to lock into a fixed-rate mortgage. Doing so ensures your payments will remain the same. In the long run, you may benefit from the fixed rate. As a rule of thumb, if you plan to stay in a house five years or less, consider an ARM. If you plan to stay five years or more, consider a fixed-rate mortgage.

What Are the Current Interest Rates?

The current interest rates will also be a factor to consider in deciding on a loan type. If the rates are high, you may only qualify for an ARM loan. If rates are low, you may want to lock into the low rate over the life of the loan.

The following two charts illustrate how interest rates have fluctuated over the past 22 years.

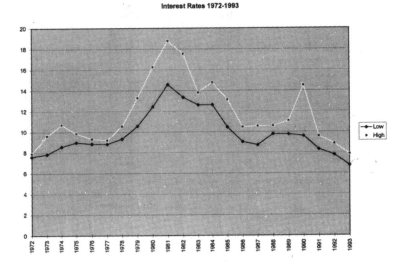

Charting interest rates for the past 22 years.

A Glance At the Past

Year	Low	High
1972	7.61	7.9
1973	7.84	9.61
1974	8.56	10.69
1975	8.98	9.84
1976	8.84	9.31
1977	8.82	9.19
1978	9.32	10.56
1979	10.57	13.27
1980	12.43	16.25
1981	14.58	18.77
1982	13.34	17.54
1983	12.61	13.78
1984	12.62	14.75
1985	10.46	13.1
1986	9.03	10.48
1987	8.73	10.55
1988	9.79	10.59
1989	9.76	11.06
1990	9.6	14.47
1991	8.3	9.59
1992	7.76	8.85
1993	6.75	7.85

What's Your Risk Level?

Finally, you will want to consider your own personality. If you enjoy taking risks, having a mortgage that could get more and more expensive may not cause you to lose any sleep. If you are a worrier, you may not want to get an adjustable-rate mortgage, even if it is a better deal. The added worry of rising payments may not be worth the added savings in money.

The Least You Need to Know

When shopping for a loan, you have to take into consideration your particular situation. Then shop for a lender that offers a loan package suited to your needs.

➤ Loans vary on the amount the lender charges. You can expect two types of charges: an interest rate that you pay over the life of the loan and points that you pay up front.

➤ One point is equal to 1% of the loan amount. Therefore, if you have to pay two points on a $100,000 loan, your points will total $2,000. Interest rates and points are usually tied together. The lower the interest rate, the higher the points.

➤ You can secure a conventional loan or you can get a government-backed loan, such as an FHA or VA loan.

➤ FHA loans usually allow for a lower down payment, but you have to pay mortgage insurance. FHA loans aren't available solely to first-time buyers.

➤ When you get a fixed-rate loan, your first payment and last payment are the same—that is, the payment never varies. Fixed-rate loans are a good idea when the interest rates are low, when you plan to stay in your house for a while, or if you do not like taking risks.

➤ With an adjustable-rate mortgage (ARM), the payment varies over the life of the loan. Usually the first couple of years are at a low or teaser rate, then the payments are adjusted according to an index.

Chapter 13

Getting a Fixed-Rate Mortgage

> **In This Chapter**
>
> ➤ Understanding the advantages and disadvantages of a fixed-rate mortgage
>
> ➤ Checking interest rates and points
>
> ➤ Choosing a loan term
>
> ➤ Prepaying a mortgage

Not a risk taker? Then you'll probably be most comfortable with a fixed-rate mortgage. Fixed rates are a good idea in many circumstances. Which ones? Read this chapter to find out.

Weighing the Pluses and Minuses

You've probably picked up on the theme of this book: good and bad, advantages and disadvantages, benefits and drawbacks, pluses and minuses. That's because there's no easy answer. For every situation, there's something beneficial about it and something not so beneficial. You have to weigh the pros and cons to decide which decision is right for you.

Here the decision being weighed is whether a fixed-rate mortgage is best for you.

Pluses

A fixed-rate mortgage was about the only type of mortgage before the 1970s. If you had a mortgage then, you most likely had a fixed-rate mortgage. That's probably the kind of mortgage your parents have if they have lived in their home for some time. What that means is that your parents are likely to say "fixed-rate" all the way.

In some cases, your parents are right.

A fixed-rate mortgage gives you the benefit of knowing your exact payment for the life of the loan. What you pay in 1994 will be the same amount you pay in 2024. To some buyers, the financial security of having a set payment greatly outweighs any cost savings they might gain from getting another type of mortgage.

Fixed-rate mortgages are especially sensible when interest rates are low. Why take the chance of playing "spin the interest rate" when you can lock into a favorable rate now?

If you plan to stay in your home for a long time, a fixed rate becomes even more desirable. You gain most of the benefits of an adjustable-rate mortgage during the first few years of the loan. After that, you may end up paying a higher rate than the going fixed rate. As stated before, if you know you will be moving on to a different city, job, or house in a few years, the ARM makes sense, but if you are moving to your dream house to stay, a fixed-rate mortgage is the mortgage for you.

Finally, you'll want to keep in mind that if your income is likely to rise, the burden of making payments will not be as great. When you are making twice the money, your house payments will still be at the original payment amount. That's a plus. And if your income is likely to decrease or remain steady—for instance, if you are retiring—a fixed-rate mortgage might also be the best bet. Your payments will be the same, so you can plan accordingly.

Minuses

When interest rates are high, the picture changes. In this case, the rates for a fixed-rate mortgage may be so high that you cannot qualify for a fixed-rate loan. Also, why lock into a high rate for the life of the loan? Instead, consider an adjustable-rate mortgage which is usually offered at a lower "teaser" rate with a cap that will ensure your rate stays low for the first few years. After that, if you find that the economy has shifted, and interest rates are low again, you have the option of refinancing at a lower, fixed rate.

Checking Interest and Points

When shopping around for a fixed-rate mortgage, you'll want to look at the interest rates that are offered and the points you have to pay. Keep in mind that the lender may offer a lower interest rate, but jack up the points. You'll want to carefully compare the different loans offered.

Suppose that you are purchasing a home for $100,000. The lender offers two rates: 8.5% with no points, and 8% with two points (see Table 13.1). Which is better? The answer depends on your situation.

Table 13.1 Price of Paying Points

Description	Amount
Price of Home	$100,000
Price of 2 Points	2,000
Monthly Payment at 8.5%	769
Monthly Payment at 8%	734
Savings	35
Months to Recoup Points Cost	57

If you can't come up with the additional $2,000 for the points, you'll want the option with zero points.

If you are going to live in the house longer than five years, you'll probably benefit from paying down the rate. Here's why. The difference between your monthly payments for the 8.5 percent rate and the 8 percent rate is $35 a month. If you divide the up-front costs of the points ($2,000), you can see that it will take you around 57 months (almost five years) to recoup that expense. After that, the $35 is money you are saving.

155

The shorter time you are in the house, the less willing you should be to pay points. Points are interest in advance. Lenders like for you to pay the points and then pay off the loan early.

If you are going to live in the house for less than five years, you won't recoup the expense of the up-front points. You end up paying more, even though you have a lower interest rate and lower monthly payments.

Ideally, you want the lowest rate with the lowest points. When you have to decide (higher rate, fewer points or lower rate, more points), first decide whether you can afford the extra expense of points. If you can, be sure you'll live in the house long enough to gain the cost savings from the lower interest rate.

How Long to Pay?

Fixed rates come in various sizes, or *terms*. The term is the length of time you make payments. Which term is right for you? Read this section to decide.

30-Year Versus 15-Year Versus Biweekly

The most common term is the 30-year fixed rate. Your payments are amortized over 360 months, or 30 years.

You can also get a shorter term, for instance, a 15-year mortgage. In this type of mortgage, your monthly payment is more (around 20 to 30 percent higher), but you pay off the interest and principal faster. You end up paying less. You can also get a 10-year or 20-year mortgage.

An additional option is a biweekly payment, available on a 30-year mortgage. With this type of mortgage, you make a payment every other week. You make 26 payments a year, basically one extra month's payment a year. Again, because you are paying off the mortgage faster, you end up paying less. With this type of mortgage, you'll pay off the loan in less than 20 years.

Table 13.2 compares the total payments for a 30-year, 15-year, and biweekly mortgage for the same amount ($100,000) and same interest (8%).

Table 13.2   Comparing Mortgages

	30-Year	15-Year	30-Year Biweekly
Interest Rate	8%	8%	8%
Monthly Payment	$844	$1,099	$422
Principal Paid	115,000	115,000	115,000
Interest Paid	188,779	82,820	135,195
Total Amount Paid	303,779	197,820	250,195

Notice that you can save a significant amount of money when you choose the 15-year mortgage—over $100,000 in interest savings. And in 15 years, you'll own your house free and clear.

Is the Shorter Term Better?

Some real estate professionals advise that the 15-year mortgage is a smart investment. You end up saving a considerable sum if you stay in the home for a long period of time. Also, the interest rate on a 15-year mortgage may be slightly lower than for a 30-year mortgage.

Other experts disagree. These experts say that you may not want to tie up your money for housing expenses. You can always make double payments on the 30-year loan, but then if you find yourself in a financial bind, you're not locked in to these higher payments. (See "Prepaying Your Mortgage," below). Or you can put the extra money in a savings account or mutual fund that earns more money than your mortgage rate. This leaves the money readily available in case of an emergency.

Whether or not to go with a shorter-term loan is primarily up to you. If you cannot afford or qualify for the higher payments of a 15-year loan, you could consider a 20- or 25-year loan. If you still do not qualify, though, you're limited to the traditional 30-year loan. You'll still get to decide, though, how often you'd like to make those payments. (Up to a point anyway—every six months isn't really an option.)

Biweekly payments can save you a lot of money, as you can see in Table 13.2, but they may also be more of a headache. You have to make twice as many payments, and some lenders charge a handling fee for this type of mortgage. You'll want to consider this fee against any cost savings.

Prepaying Your Mortgage

When you are shopping around for a mortgage, you'll want to inquire whether you can prepay on the mortgage without penalty. Why prepay?

Remember that the lenders want their money first, so most of your money in the first few years of the loan goes toward interest. Take a look at Table 13.3 to see the amortization schedule of the first 12 months of a 30-year loan for $115,000 at 8% interest.

In the first year, you pay around $10,000 in monthly payments, but less than $1,000 of that goes toward the principal. After one year, you still owe $114,000.

 Keep in mind that prepaying does not reduce your monthly payment obligations. You can't tell the lender that you paid an extra $1,000 last year, so this year you are going to skip the first few payments. You *must* still make the regular payments.

Here's where prepaying can be beneficial. When you prepay, the money goes directly to the principal. If you have an extra $1,000 after paying your monthly bills, (yeah, right) you can pay that $1,000 toward the mortgage. That money goes directly toward reducing the principal.

Again, financial experts disagree on whether prepaying the mortgage is beneficial or not. It does reduce the amount of money you pay for the home. You'll pay off the home more quickly if you prepay. Even if you make one extra payment a year, you can pay off your loan more quickly and save money.

Advocates against prepaying argue that you can put your extra money to better use. For example, if you prepay that $1,000 you get no tax benefit. If you put that money into a retirement account, you'll get a tax break. If you put the money into a savings account, you'll have access to it if you need it. If your mortgage rate is 7%, and you invest in a mutual fund paying 10%, you can make 3% on your money rather than paying off your mortgage.

Table 13.3 Amortization Table for First 12 Months of a Loan

Loan Amount	Interest	Term	Payment
$115,000	8%	30	$843

#	Payment	Principal	Interest	Balance
1	$ 843	$ 77	$ 766	$ 114,923
2	843	77	766	114,846
3	843	78	765	114,768
4	843	78	765	114,690
5	843	79	765	114,611
6	843	79	764	114,532
7	843	80	763	114,452
8	843	80	763	114,372
9	843	81	762	114,291
10	843	81	762	114,210
11	843	83	761	114,128
12	843	83	760	114,045
		Total Paid	**$10,116**	
		Total Principal Paid	**$955**	

The Least You Need to Know

Fixed-rate mortgages are appropriate in several situations. If you want a fixed-rate mortgage, be sure to shop around for the best combination of interest rate and points.

➤ Fixed-rate mortgages offer you the financial security of having a fixed payment over the life of the loan. If interest rates are low, you may want to lock into the low rate. On the other hand if interest rates are high, you may want to consider a different type of mortgage.

➤ Many lenders will offer a lower interest rate in exchange for paying points up front. Whether this is a good decision depends on how long you plan to stay in the house. Figure out how much you'll save a month with the lower interest rate, then figure out how many months it will take you to recoup the points.

➤ You can select a 30-year, 15-year, or biweekly fixed-rate mortgage. Your lender may also offer 10- or 20-year mortgages. The shorter the term, the less you pay in interest over the life of the loan, but the larger the monthly payment.

➤ When shopping for a fixed-rate mortgage, be sure to ask whether you can prepay on the loan without penalty. Prepaying reduces the principal (the amount you owe) more quickly than just making regular payments.

Chapter 14

Getting an Adjustable-Rate Mortgage

In This Chapter
➤ Weighing the pros and cons of an adjustable-rate mortgage
➤ Understanding how an adjustable-rate mortgage works
➤ Shopping for an adjustable-rate mortgage
➤ Considering a two-step mortgage

Are you a gambler? Fancy yourself a risk taker? If so, you may want to finance your home with an adjustable-rate mortgage (ARM). With an ARM, you're gambling that the interest rates will go down, hence, your payments will go down; the interest rates will go up, but you'll sell before your adjustable-rate catches up with the current fixed rate; or you'll switch to a fixed-rate mortgage before your rate catches up.

Shopping for an adjustable rate is trickier than shopping for a fixed-rate. You have to study the details of the loan, sort of like studying the tip sheets for racing horses. This chapter explains how an ARM works and how to select a good one.

Weighing the Pros and Cons of an Adjustable-Rate Mortgage

What do you gain by getting an ARM? What can you lose? This section helps you tally up the wins/losses for ARMs.

Pros

You may have an easier time qualifying for the loan. Remember that a lender will qualify you for a loan by comparing your monthly gross income to your monthly house payment (principal, interest, taxes, and insurance). If your payments are initially low, you can more easily make the grade.

Different lenders will look at different factors when qualifying you for a loan. FNMA (Fannie Mae Guidelines) requires you to qualify at the start rate plus 2.0% (second year rate). Some lenders may use a different qualifying test.

If you're just starting out, you're gambling that your income will rise. Even if your payments do increase, you may be in a better situation to afford the increased payments. For example, your spouse may go back to work, or your children may finish college.

If you plan to stay in the home only a few years, you'll gain the most benefit from the ARM. During the first few years is when you get the breaks on payment. You can sell before your rate rises and catches up with the current fixed rate.

If the current fixed rates are extremely high, an ARM may be the only type of loan for which you qualify. Also, if interest rates are high, you may gamble that they will go down sometime in the future. Finally, the principal and interest are recalculated at each term. If you prepay, you have more control.

Cons

If there's not much difference between the fixed rate and ARM or if the fixed rates are low, you may want to lock into the low rate rather than have your payments bob up and down.

If you aren't a risk taker, you may worry too much about your house payments going up. You may want to get a fixed-rate mortgage for the peace of mind of knowing you have one payment and it will not vary.

If you plan to stay in the house for a long time, you may want to lock into a fixed-rate mortgage (unless that rate is incredibly high).

Understanding How an Adjustable-Rate Mortgage Works

Think about two football teams. The Bears have won all ten of their games this season. The Colts haven't won any. Which team would you bet on? Probably the Bears—if all things are equal.

Now consider a different situation. To make the gambling more competitive, the bookie makes the Colts more attractive by giving you points. Instead of making the bet contingent on winning or losing, the bookie makes the bet also contingent on the number of points the winning team wins by. If the Bears win by 14 or more, they are the winners. But if the Bears lose or win by 14 or less, the Colts are the winners. Now it's not so clear cut which is the best bet.

ARMs work in the same way. First, lenders make this type of loan more attractive by making its rates more competitive. Second, lenders use different methods for figuring out the *spread*—the difference in the rates charged. This section explains how an ARM works.

Initial or "Teaser" Rate

To get you interested in an ARM, lenders usually offer a really low initial rate. This rate, often called the *teaser rate,* is usually good for a limited period of time—sometimes six months, sometimes one or two years.

If you're looking through the advertised rates, you may see one loan for four percent and another for eight percent. The four percent is most likely an ARM, while the higher rate is most likely for a fixed-rate mortgage. You may wonder with a difference like that, what the risk is on an ARM.

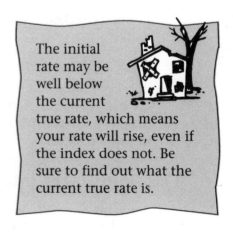

The initial rate may be well below the current true rate, which means your rate will rise, even if the index does not. Be sure to find out what the current true rate is.

The risk is that the initial or low rate is only available for a short period of time. Then the rate will adjust. How it adjusts depends on the index.

The Index

All ARMs are tied to a certain economic index, some national indicator of current rates that is not controlled by the lenders. Different lenders tie the ARM to different indexes. Some common ones used include:

➤ The rate of sales on treasury notes and bills (six-month, one-year, three-year, or five-year T-bills)

➤ The average rate for loans closed, called the Federal Housing Finance Board's National Average Contract Mortgage Rate

➤ The average rate paid on jumbo CDs

➤ The cost of funds for the lender

These indexes are usually printed in the newspaper so that you can see what the current rate is. When you are investigating ARMs, find out the index used and where the current rate is published.

The Margin

The index isn't the rate used to determine your interest rate. It is the first part in the calculation. The lender adds something on top of the current index rate. This is called the *margin* and can run from one to five percent. To get the rate you'll pay, the lender then uses this formula:

index rate + margin = your rate

For example, if the index used for your ARM is seven percent and the margin is two percent, your interest rate will be nine percent. The margin is usually fixed for the life of the loan and should be included in the contract.

The Adjustment Interval

If you get an ARM, you understand your payment will then be adjusted according to the index used. How often it is adjusted varies.

For example, if you get a one-year ARM, your payments will be adjusted every year. At the end of a year (usually the anniversary date of your loan or the date stated in your contract), the lender will calculate the new interest rate, and you'll make payments accordingly until the next adjustment period, a year later.

Lenders can make mistakes. Know how to check their calculations so that you can be sure the payment amount is adjusted correctly.

You can also get a three-year ARM or five-year ARM. The adjustment interval will vary depending on the lender and should be included in the contract.

ARMs are recalculated at each adjustment period and payments are based on the outstanding balance of the loan.

Caps

Your interest rate (and hence your payments) are like a tethered balloon. They can go up; they can go down, but only so far. Many lenders put a limit, or cap, on the increases and decreases. There are two types of caps: *rate caps* and *payment caps*.

A rate cap limits how much the interest rate can increase or decrease during the adjustment period (called a *periodic cap*) and during the life of the loan (called a *lifetime cap*). For example, an ARM may have a 2% periodic cap with a 6% lifetime cap. If your rate started at 5%, your interest rate could only raise 2% each period and would max out at 11%.

A payment cap limits how much your payment can increase during the adjustment period. Payment caps may sound reassuring because your payments will be within a certain limit, but this type of cap can cause problems—in particular, negative amortization.

Negative Amortization Is a No-No

If you want your loan balance to go down (which you do), you must make a certain minimum payment to cover the interest with enough left over to pay off some of the principal, or balance. If your payment doesn't cover the interest (which can happen if you have a payment cap), the unpaid interest is added to the principle. You can make payment after payment and end up owing more than you initially borrowed. This is called *negative amortization.*

To get out from negative amortization, you may be able to negotiate a new mortgage or prepay enough to cover the cost of interest and principal. Or, better yet, avoid situations that enable this to occur.

Selecting an ARM

When you're shopping for a fixed-rate mortgage, you need to look at one rate—the current interest rate, plus any points paid.

When you're shopping for an ARM, you need to look at several factors and consider the payments at various rates. You need to check out the initial rate, true rate, adjustment interval, caps, index, and margin.

Most lenders publish this information in the following format:

1 yr ARM   5.25   0   10%   30 day 2/6

The first figure tells you the adjustment interval (1 year). The next figures are, in order, the interest rate, the points paid, the down payment required, the lock-in period, and the period cap/lifetime cap.

What to Look For in Interest Rates

When you're comparing the rates of ARMs, don't get wooed by the teaser or come-on rate. This rate is temporary and at the first adjustment period, your interest rate will go up. Instead, ask what the true rate is—what would the rate be today by adding index and margin.

You'll also want to find out if there is a minimum rate. Some lenders will charge a minimum rate even if the index goes below that rate.

What to Look For in an Index

Unless you can look into your crystal ball and predict what will happen in the economy, you probably aren't going to have much luck in picking the "best" index. You can try guessing which index will do what, but it's usually better to look at past performance.

Ask for a chart that shows the changes in the particular index used for your loan. Look at a few year's worth of change so that you can see how stable or volatile the index was. (You may want to ask to see the years 1979 through 1981 because this was an extremely rough economic period.)

What to Look For in Margins

To compare ARMs with the same index, look for one with the lowest margin. Some lenders offer a lower initial rate, but a higher margin. This structure enables them to increase the rate more quickly.

What to Look For in Adjustment Intervals

As for adjustment intervals, keep in mind that the more frequent the adjustment, the more volatile your monthly payments. A longer interval is usually better because your payments don't change as much. For example, suppose that you know you'll be moving within five years. In this case, you may want to get a five-year ARM because you'll be moving sometime before the adjustment interval.

What to Look For in Caps

A lifetime cap offers the most protection. If you have a lifetime cap of five percent, you know that your payments will never go more than five percent higher than the existing rate—no matter how high the rates go. Sometimes this cap also applies to how low the rate can go—that is, the rate cannot decrease more than five percent. Be sure to ask the lender.

Be sure to find out what the cap applies to—the initial rate, or the true rate. If you get a low initial interest rate, you may calculate your highest rate at a certain percentage. For example, if the rate starts at four percent with a lifetime cap of five percent, you may think nine percent is the tops. But if the cap is actually tied to the true rate, you have a totally different situation.

You should also get an ARM with a periodic cap so that even if the rates do go to 12 percent, they can do so only at a certain percentage at a time. FHA ARMs are capped at one percent an adjustment period. Conventional ARMs are generally capped at two percent. If you have a periodic cap and the rate jumps more than that cap, be sure to ask

167

what happens. Is this extra percent added onto the next adjustment cycle, even if the rate hasn't gone up?

Payment caps, for the most part, are not a good feature because they can allow negative amortization.

What Other Features to Look For

You should ask in what situations negative amortization could occur with your loan terms. Ask whether the lender will alert you when this is a problem and ask how the lender handles negative amortization.

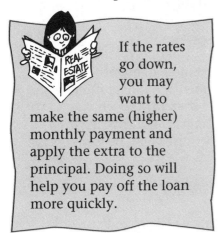

If the rates go down, you may want to make the same (higher) monthly payment and apply the extra to the principal. Doing so will help you pay off the loan more quickly.

Check to see whether you can convert the adjustable-rate mortgage to a fixed-rate mortgage. If the fixed rates are low, you may want to lock in at that rate. Be sure you know exactly what is involved in converting. Just finding out whether a loan is convertible isn't enough. The lender may charge a fee for the conversion and may also only allow you to lock into the current fixed rate, plus a margin. Also, you may be able to convert only at a certain date.

Also, find out whether the mortgage is assumable. If you sell the house, can the buyer assume the mortgage? Most are not assumable without lender approval.

Finally, inquire about whether you can prepay on the mortgage and if so, if there are any penalties.

Look at the Worst-Case Scenario

To understand how much your payments can rise, have the lender show you the worst-case scenario. Remember that lenders are trying to sell you something—the use of their money. They may stress the low initial payments.

Don't get caught up by the initial payments. Your payments are most likely going to go up. How much they go up and how much that means in monthly payments is something you should look at.

Table 14.1 shows the worst-case scenario for a one-year ARM for $115,000 at a teaser rate of 4%, a true rate of 8%, a periodic cap of 2%, and a lifetime cap of 6%.

Table 14.1 A Worst Case Scenario for an ARM

Evaluating an ARM

		Loan Amount	$115,000	
		Initial Rate	4%	
		Periodic cap	2%	
		Lifetime cap	6%	

Year	Rate	Explanation	Monthly Payment
Year 1	4.0%	Initial Rate	$549.03
Year 2	6.0%	Increase to periodic cap	689.48
Year 3	8.0%	Increase to periodic cap	843.83
Year 4	10.0%	Increase to lifetime cap	1,009.21
Year 5	10.0%	Increase to lifetime cap	1,009.21

Two-Step Mortgages

The two-step mortgage is a combination adjustable-rate mortgage and fixed-rate mortgage. During the first step, you pay one interest rate for that loan period. During the second step, you pay another interest rate for the life of the loan.

Types of Two-Steps

Two-step mortgages currently come in two variations:

➤ *5/25*. With a 5/25 two-step mortgage, you pay one rate for the first five years. Then in the sixth year, the rate is reset for the remaining 25 years of the loan.

➤ *7/23*. A 7/23 mortgage works the same way, only the time frame is different. You pay one rate for the first seven years, and in the eighth year the rate is recalculated for the remaining 23 years.

You may also find other variations of this two-step mortgage, but they all basically work the same way.

169

How to Do the Two-Step

A two-step works like this. During the first term of the loan you pay a low initial rate. This rate is fixed; that is, your payments do not vary during this initial term.

At the second step, your rate is adjusted and then may be fixed at that rate for the life of the loan. The new rate is tied to an economic index, usually the index plus the lender's margin, and sometimes has a rate cap, similar to an ARM. (For some loans, the loan is converted to an ARM during the second period of the loan.) Many loans have no caps after the initial term; instead, you pay the prevailing rate at that time.

With a two-step mortgage, the lender guarantees you the fixed-rate loan—that is, you don't have to requalify, and you don't have the expense of obtaining new financing at that time, although there is usually a conversion fee.

Table 14.2 shows an example of a 7/23 mortgage in which the buyer pays 6% for the initial seven years. Then the rate is adjusted, with a cap of 6%. The highest the payments could go (12%) is shown for years 8–23.

Table 14.2   A 7/23 Mortgage

Evaluating a Two-Step Mortgage

Loan Amount	$115,000		
Initial Rate	6%		
Lifetime Cap	6%		

Years	Rate	Explanation	Monthly Payment
Years 1-7	6%	Initial Rate	$689.48
years 8-23	12%	Adjusted Rate	1,182.90

Is the Two-Step for You?

The two-step mortgage offers a few key benefits. Because the initial payments are low during the first term of the loan, you may have an easier time qualifying for the loan.

Also, remember that the law of averages says that within five to seven years you're likely to sell your home. In this case, you may sell or be ready to sell just at the point where the rate will increase. You have the benefit of paying the lower rate during the time you lived in the house.

If you plan to move within a few years, the 5/25 or 7/23 might be ideal for your situation. If, on the other hand, you plan to stay in your home longer than the five to seven years, you may end up paying more than the fixed rates. The rate for the second term usually runs .75 to 1% higher than the prevailing fixed rates.

7/23 and 5/25 Balloons

You can also get 7/23 or 5/25 balloon mortgages. You pay a fixed rate for five or seven years. At the end of that term, a balloon payment is due—the balance of the loan.

If you don't want to pay off the balloon, you can convert to a fixed rate for the remainder of the term at the 60-day prevailing FNMA/FHLMC price plus .625%. Usually there is a conversion fee. Balloon loans are covered in more detail in Chapter 15.

The Least You Need to Know

Selecting an ARM can be tricky because you have to consider so many factors that affect the loan terms. As you're shopping around, keep these things in mind:

➤ An adjustable-rate mortgage (ARM) might be appropriate if you cannot qualify for a fixed-rate loan, if the interest rates are high, or if you plan to stay in your home only a short time (five to seven years).

➤ Many lenders offer a "teaser" rate to entice buyers to select an ARM. This low rate is only good for a short time; then your payments will most likely go up.

➤ The ARM's rate is tied to an economic index (for example, the sale of T-bills) and is usually the index rate plus a margin. When the index goes up, your payments go up. When the index goes down, your payments go down.

continues

continued

➤ Depending on the loan, the ARM may have one or more types of caps: a *lifetime cap*, which limits the amount the rate can increase or decrease over the life of the loan; a *periodic cap*, which limits the amount the rate can increase or decrease within one adjustment period; and a *payment cap*, which limits the amount your payment can increase. Payment caps are not a good idea because they can allow negative amortization.

➤ A two-step mortgage is like a fixed-rate and an adjustable-rate mortgage combined. During the first step, the buyer has a fixed-rate mortgage for that period. For a 5/25 loan, the period is five years. For a 7/23, the period is seven years. After the initial period, the rate is recalculated based on an index, margin, and any caps in effect. For the remaining term of the loan, this rate is used.

Chapter 15

Understanding Other Financing

In This Chapter

➤ VA loans

➤ Assumable Mortgages

➤ Balloon mortgages

➤ Seller financing

➤ Interest rate buy downs

➤ Land contracts

➤ Leasing with the option to buy

The majority of residential loans are either fixed-rate or adjustable-rate mortgages. Other types of loans are available, though, depending on your circumstances. For example, if you're a veteran, you may qualify for a VA loan. If the seller is amenable, you could have the seller provide financing. These and other financial options are described in this chapter.

VA Loans

In addition to the FHA loans, the government sponsors another type of loan for veterans. These loans are guaranteed by the Veteran's Administration and are available to any veteran who has served either 180 active days since September 16, 1940 or 90 days service during a war. If you enlisted after September 7, 1980, you must have two years' service. If you are no longer with the armed forces, you must have received an honorable discharge. ROTC members may also qualify. You must plan to live at the residence, and the property must pass a VA appraisal.

Why are VA loans attractive? For one, a VA loan is probably the *only* loan that you can get with little or no down payment. They also provide competitive interest rates with lower closing costs. (The structure of VA loans has recently changed. Before 1993, the VA would allow the buyer to pay only one point.) You can expect to pay discount points, appraisal fee, credit report, survey, title search, recording fees, plus a VA funding fee. You should not be charged a brokerage fee.

You can get a VA loan for up to $184,000, although this limit may soon be raised. You can prepay the loan without penalty, and the loan is assumable.

For more information about VA loans, contact the Veteran's Administration. The address is listed in Appendix B.

Assumptions

Certain mortgages are *assumable,* which means the buyer can just assume the responsibilities of the mortgage. Some benefits of an assumable mortgage are that the buyer doesn't have the expense of obtaining a new mortgage and waiting for approval, and, if the mortgage has a lower-than-market or reasonable interest rate, can save a lot of money on interest.

For example, suppose that a seller has a 7% fixed-rate mortgage and has a buyer that is interested in assuming the payments on this loan. If the loan is freely assumable, the buyer can save the costs of applying for a loan and other associated costs; instead, an assumption agreement is made between the buyer and seller. (Most new loans are qualified assumptions, meaning that the buyer must still qualify for the loan.)

The buyer assumes payment on the existing mortgage and pays the difference between the mortgage balance and the selling price. For example, if the seller sold the home for $100,000 and still owed $80,000, the buyer would assume the $80,000 mortgage and pay the seller $20,000. You can see that even if you don't have the expense of closing on a loan, you may still have to come up with a considerable sum of cash.

There could be liability factors in allowing a purchaser to assume a loan. The person who originally received the loan could be responsible if the new buyer defaults.

You may not want to assume a mortgage, but you'll want to ask whether the mortgage you're securing is assumable. An assumable mortgage may be more attractive to buyers when you sell your home.

Balloon Mortgages

A *balloon mortgage* is a type of financing that keeps the initial payments low for a certain period by financing the loan over a long term. The loan doesn't run the full term, though; instead the full balance is due in one lump sum at the end of the initial period.

For example, you may secure a seven-year balloon mortgage for $115,000 at 10 percent. For the first seven years, your payments would be the same as if you secured a fixed-rate mortgage for 30 years. Nearly all of these payments go toward the interest; the principal is reduced some, but not a lot. You may owe, for instance, $103,500 at the end of the seven years. At this time, the remaining balance (the $103,500) is due. This is the balloon payment. *Pop!*

In most cases, the purchaser doesn't expect to receive a windfall for the balloon payment. Instead, the purchaser may secure another loan for the remaining balance. At this point, the buyer has some equity, plus a record of making payments. Or the buyer may decide to sell the house sometime before the balloon payment is due.

Takebacks, Second Mortgages, and Similar Alternatives

The sellers are most likely in a better position to secure financing than you are; after all, they own a home. For this reason, some sellers may be willing to provide the financing for you. This process is called different things depending on how the financing is arranged. For instance, the seller may take out a second mortgage to help you make the down payment. Or the seller may provide all the financing—this is called a *seller takeback* or *purchase money mortgage.*

In a takeback situation, the seller agrees to take back a mortgage for the purchase price of the home, minus the down payment. You, as buyer, agree to make monthly payments to the seller at a certain interest rate. Basically, the seller takes the role of the bank.

This type of financing can be beneficial to both the seller and the buyer. The seller sells the home and makes a decent return on the investment. The buyer buys the home and doesn't have to worry with the hassles and costs associated with securing a traditional loan. It is advantageous to people who might not otherwise qualify for a normal loan.

In any type of agreement between buyer and seller, you should have a real estate attorney review the details. You want to be sure you understand the agreement and that the agreement is not unfair to you.

Buy-Downs

Takebacks, buy-downs, rollovers—as you review the terms of financing, you may get the sense that you're in some sort of police drama. All the words are so *active!* A buy-down isn't anything thrilling, though. A buy-down occurs when a seller pays a fee in order for the buyer to receive financing at a lower interest rate. This type of financing is often found with builders or developers.

For example, suppose that the interest rate is 10%, but you cannot qualify for a loan at this rate. Instead the buyer pays the lender 2% for the agreed-upon term, say two years. During those two years, you pay 8% interest. At the end of two years, you take over the entire 10% interest payment, or you can renegotiate the loan.

Who makes out on buy-downs? Usually the sellers, because they most likely will increase the price of the home to cover the money they pay in interest, plus usually make a profit or at least break even.

Land Contracts or Layaway Payments

Land contracts may be appropriate for individuals who cannot secure a bank loan. A land contract works like a layaway plan. You live in the house, make payments to the seller, make repairs, and generally live in the home as if it were yours. But the home isn't yours until the deed is transferred.

Depending on the agreement, the title may be transferred when you make the last payment or when you have a certain amount of equity in the property. It's a good idea to hire a real estate attorney and have this person carefully review the contract before you sign.

Remember that you don't hold the title to the property. If you miss a payment, the lender can get back the property without any foreclosure.

Lease Options

A lease agreement is similar to a land contract. You live in the home and make the agreed-upon payments. Unlike a land contract, though, you're not obliged to buy the property. Usually, you're given the right to purchase the home at a certain price within a certain time period. At that time, you can buy or continue to lease.

If you enter into one of these agreements, be sure to find out who pays for certain expenses. If the roof is damaged, who pays? Who pays for insurance?

Also, check to see whether the payments you make go towards the purchase price of the home. Hire a real estate attorney to go over the contract carefully before signing this type of agreement. The terms of a lease contract can vary a great deal. You want to make sure you understand all the provisions first.

You may also consider a *lease purchase*. You agree to purchase the property at a given time, but you pay rent in the interim.

Other Options

In rural areas, you can get a mortgage from the **Farmer's Home Administration (FHA)** if your income is within a certain range. See Appendix B for the address.

You may secure a loan from a **private individual**—for instance, a family member. Keep in mind that the IRS discourages low- or no-interest loans. Generally, the IRS looks favorably on 9% loans or loans at the applicable federal rate, an index published by the government. If you secure a loan at a lower rate, the IRS may tax the lender on the interest he *should* have received, even if he didn't.

For some mortgages, you can arrange for a **graduated payment plan**, which allows you to make a lower payment for a certain period, then gradually higher payments over the life of the loan. Your monthly payment is increased at preset intervals. Beware—this type of mortgage allows for negative amortization (see Chapter 14).

If you can secure the help of an investor, you may want to look into **shared-equity mortgages**. With this type of mortgage, an investor helps the buyer with a down payment and/or monthly payments. In return, the investor owns a percentage of the home or is entitled to a percentage of the profit when the home is sold. As a buyer, you pay the mortgage on your percentage of the loan, plus you may have to pay the investor rent on his percentage of the property.

If you cannot qualify for a loan by yourself, you may consider asking someone to **co-sign** with you. When an individual co-signs a loan, that person assumes the responsibility for repaying that loan. Some lenders will allow co-signers; some will make certain restrictions on the use of a co-signer. Keep in mind that the co-signer has to qualify just as the primary borrower does.

To make housing available in certain communities, many communities issue **bond-backed** or **municipal mortgages**. The government issues bonds, which are purchased by investors. The investors receive a good return on the investment, plus some tax advantages. The money raised by the bond sales is then made available to first-time homebuyers. For information about bond-backed mortgages, check with your local governmental agencies. You may also want to ask your agent.

The Least You Need to Know

Although fixed-rate and adjustable-rate mortgages are the most common ways to finance the purchase of a home, there are other financing options:

➤ If you're a veteran, you may qualify for a *VA loan*. See Appendix B for the address.

➤ If the seller has an *assumable loan*, you can take over the mortgage and make payments on the loan as if you had secured it. Older loans may be freely assumable, while newer loans are qualified assumptions.

➤ With a *balloon mortgage*, payments are amortized over a long period of time so that your initial payments are low and go mostly towards interest. At the end of the term, the entire balance of the mortgage, the balloon payment, is due.

➤ Sometimes the seller will act as the bank and give you a loan for the home. This type of arrangement is called a *seller takeback* or *seller financing*.

➤ Another form of financial help from the seller is the *buy down*, in which the seller (often a builder or developer) pays a certain part of the interest for a certain period of time. For example, on a 10% loan, the seller may pay 2% for two years. You pay 8% for two years and then the full 10% after two years.

➤ *Land contracts* and *lease purchase options* enable you to live on a property and make payments. With a land contract, you don't get the deed to the property until you make all the payments or until you reach a certain equity amount. With a lease option, you're not obligated to buy the property, but at a certain time and price, you **can** buy the property.

Live within your income, even if you have to borrow money to do so.

—Josh Billings

Chapter 16

Selecting a Lender

In This Chapter

➤ Understanding the different types of lenders

➤ Finding a lender

➤ Asking a lender questions

➤ Comparing fixed-rate loans

➤ Comparing adjustable-rate mortgages

I think a lot of buyers are grateful that someone is willing to lend them the money to buy a home, so they don't realize that they need to shop around for a lender. Although a lender may make you feel differently, you are a customer. You're giving them your business, and as such, you should be sure to select the lender that offers you the best deal and best service. The mortgage process can make or break a transaction. Purchasing a home can be exciting or it can be a nightmare. The mortgage process determines which it will be. This chapter teaches you how to select a lender, so that your home-buying experience will not be a nightmare.

Types of Lenders

Who's got money to lend? Who will lend it to you? There are many sources of loans in the U.S.

Who's Got the Money?

It can get confusing when you apply for a loan because you can be dealing with any number of types of lenders. Perhaps you have a mortgage broker who takes your paperwork but then submits it to another lender. Perhaps you use your local town bank and secure a loan from this source. Here are some common sources of loans:

Savings and loans. S & Ls are responsible for more than half of all mortgage loans in the United States.

The S & L Crisis

You'd have to have been living under a rock not to have heard of the recent S&L scandal. In the past, savings and loans collected deposits and then used this money to make loans, mostly to local borrowers and mostly for homes.

Then some—not all—S&Ls decided to venture into other types of loans—loans for office buildings, shopping centers, and so on. These types of loans can be riskier, which the bankers found out and then tried to hide. Many S&L companies have folded or been bought out.

Does this mean you shouldn't get a loan from an S&L? No. Savings and loans provide most of the financing for residential homes. The banks that were not involved in the crisis are operating fine. If you find an S&L with a good mortgage opportunity, you should take it.

Commercial banks. Though they make loans mostly for commercial ventures, in some cases a commercial bank may lend money for real estate sales, especially in a small town where the bank knows whether Jerome is good for the loan. *Credit unions* are another good source of loans.

Mortgage brokers. Acting as a middleman, a mortgage broker takes your loan application, processes the papers, then submits the loan to a lender who underwrites and closes the loan.

Mortgage bankers. Different from a broker, a mortgage banker both originates and serves the loan.

Originate? Underwrite?

Lenders must have a penchant for official-sounding words, hence, originate and underwrite. **Originate** means to process the loan, gathering all the paperwork. Once the paperwork is collected, it is sent to the underwriter who decides whether or not to give the loan. **Underwrite** is the same as *approve*.

Builders and developers. Some builders and developers also provide loans. Doing so makes it easy to sell and finance the home in one process.

Government agencies. Government agencies, such as the FHA and VA, don't actually give you a loan, but they do encourage loans that don't meet the conventional loan standards. Doing so makes you, as a potential borrower, more attractive to the lender.

The Secondary Market, or the Business of Selling Mortgages

Money-lending is a business, which to me is sometimes hard to remember. Some investors deal in pork bellies, some in stocks and bonds, and some in money. Here's how it works.

An investor isn't interested in your puny $100,000 mortgage. That's not enough to trifle with. But if you put several $100,000 loans together, that makes quite an attractive package. And that's what some lenders do. They combine several mortgages into a package or bundle and then sell the bundle to a secondary market, a group of investors who invest in mortgages. Banks, pension funds, and insurance companies, for example, often invest in mortgages.

183

If the lender where you apply for a loan plans to sell your loan, they will let you know. It doesn't mean too much to you as the borrower, just that you may be dealing with a different mortgage company at some time during the term of the loan. In some cases, the original lender continues to service the loan (sends you your payment books). In other cases the new lender takes over servicing; you'll receive a letter telling you where to send new payments.

Ginnie Mae, Fannie Mae, and Bobby Sue

The government has set up agencies specifically for buying mortgages. They have names that sound like the girls on "Petticoat Junction"—Fannie Mae (Federal National Mortgage Association), Freddie Mac (Federal Home Loan Mortgage Corporation), and Ginnie Mae (Government National Mortgage Association).

Because the original lender is interested in selling the loan packages and because Fannie Mae and the gang are avid purchasers, lenders follow the guidelines set out by the government agencies. This means that most lenders have the same limits on the amount they'll lend, and most check over your income using the same criteria—the criteria set forth by the government agency.

Portfolio and Jumbo Loans

In some cases, the rules of Fannie Mae and crew can cause you problems, and you may have to find a different type of lender. For example, if the lender is planning on packaging your loan to sell and you can't meet those requirements, you're going to have to find a different type of lender. You're shopping for a lender that provides a *portfolio loan*. Portfolio loans aren't structured to be sold to the secondary market, so they don't have to meet the requirements.

If the amount of money you want to borrow is beyond the limit of Fannie Mae, Freddie Mac, and/or Ginnie Mae, you need to find a lender that offers *jumbo loans*.

Where to Find a Lender

Depending on the market, you may have to look hard to find a lender, or the lender may be calling you! In a down market where money is tight, a lender has many customers vying for loans. In this type of market, the lender doesn't have to chase the customer.

In an up market where money is moving, a lender is more aggressive in searching out clients. You might, for instance, get calls asking you if you want to refinance your house or offering to give you a home equity loan. These calls indicate the lender is looking for customers.

Finding a Lender

No matter what the market, you can find lenders from several sources. Your real estate agent may recommend a lender or may be able to help you locate a lender. You can also ask friends and relatives to recommend a lender. Perhaps someone in your family or someone that you work with has recently purchased a home. Ask that person what his experiences were with the lender.

Read the paper. Many lenders advertise their current lending rates. You can call and interview the lenders yourself. The section later in this chapter, titled "What Questions to Ask a Lender," will help you with this interview. The next section explains how to read an advertisement. Ads are often deceptive. The advertised rates may no longer be available when you call. Don't base your decision on a lender only on advertised rates.

Check your local banks, savings and loans, credit unions. They may offer real estate loans, and if they do, they probably have some free literature that explains the services they provide.

You can enlist the help of a mortgage search company. This type of company uses a computerized network to find the best loan opportunities in your area. The search company will take your financial information and then match it up with the available lending services. One firm, HSH Associates, will provide a survey of 20 to 50 lenders in the area for a fee of around $20. (Their address is in Appendix B.)

Getting Help from Your Agent

Since 1974, it has been illegal for a real estate broker to receive a kickback or finder fee from referrals. If your agent sends you to a particular lender, you don't have to worry that the agent does so because he is receiving a payment for the referral.

Recently the Department of Housing and Urban Development (HUD) has allowed changes. If an agent searches out potential lenders by a computerized database, the agent can charge for the service. Advocates insist that this service will provide the convenience of one-stop shopping for buyers.

Others don't agree. For example, the rule does not say how many lenders have to be included in the database and how much the agent can charge. Also, new HUD provisions allow a brokerage to pay agents who recommend loan companies or settlement companies owned by the brokerage. This means you could be charged a fee that is too high for a "service" that the agent is being paid to do anyway. Also, the recommended company might not be the one with the best deal.

What should you do? If your agent offers to help you find a lender, be sure you understand what the agent gains from doing so. Some have always checked for loans and are doing so as a courtesy. If the agents are charging a fee, make sure that you know that up front.

Reviewing a Mortgage Advertisement

You may find a large advertisement in the real estate section of the paper that lists mortgage companies as well as their interest rates (see the following figure). To decode the ads, remember that a fixed-rate loan is interest, plus points. In comparing adjustable-rate mortgages, you want to know the initial rate, true rate, adjustment intervals, caps, and points.

The ad will list the name of the mortgage company, the phone number, and maybe the address.

For fixed-rate mortgages, the ad usually lists the term (30- or 15-year), the interest rate, the number of points, the down payment required, the length of the lock, and the application fee. In the example, Capital Mortgage has a 30-year mortgage at 8.75% interest. This loan requires no points and 5% down. You can lock in the rate for 45 days, and the application fee is $325.

For ARMs, the ad usually lists the type of ARM (for instance, one year), the interest rate, the number of points, the down payment required, the length of the lock, and the caps. In the example, King Mortgage has a one-year ARM at 5.25% interest and no points. This loan requires a 10% down payment. You can lock in the rate for 30 days. There's a 2% periodic cap and a lifetime cap of 6%.

186

A-1 Mortgage					800-555-0991
30 yr FIX	8.75	0.5	5%	60 day	$325
15 yr FIX	8.25	0.5	5%	60 day	$325
1 yr ARM/FHA	5.875	0.5	5%	60 day	2/6
6 mo. ARM	5.25	0.5	5%	60 day	1/6
King Mortgage					800-555-1211
30 yr FIX	8.625	0	5%	30 day	$300
15 yr FIX	8.25	0	5%	30 day	$300
1 yr ARM	5.25	0	10%	30 day	2/6
Capital Mortgage					800-555-6091
30 yr FIX	8.75	0	5%	45 day	$325
15 yr FIX	8.375	0	5%	45 day	$325
1 yr ARM	6.375	0.5	5%	45 day	2/6
7/23 balloon	8.25	0	10%	45 day	$325

A sample advertisement.

Questions to Ask Lenders

If you decide to shop for a lender yourself, you'll need to be prepared to interview the lender. You'll need to find out what types of loans they offer, at what interest, and at what terms. Even if you let your agent shop for you, you may want to call the lender to be sure you are comfortable. You want a lender you can trust. You should be prepared to tell the lender the selling price of the home, the down payment you can afford, and any other financial information needed to give the lender a general idea of your situation. Here are some questions to ask a potential lender or to find out by reading advertisements:

What types of loans are offered? Fixed rate and ARM? Other types? What payment schedules are offered? Does the lender offer, for instance, 15-year loans or biweekly payment schedules?

What is the current interest rate for a 30-year, fixed-rate loan? For a one-year ARM? Keep in mind that rates vary daily. When you're shopping for a home, you may want to keep your eye on the paper and watch the rates. When you're ready to apply for the loan, the rate for that *day* applies. You can lock in the rate or float the rate until closing. Also, you may want to tailor this question for the specific type of loan you're interested in. For example, if you're shopping for a 7/23 loan, ask for the rates on that type of loan.

187

How many points are charged for a particular rate? If you pay one more point, how much does the interest rate decrease? If you pay one less point, how much does the rate increase? Points also fluctuate. Does the lender charge an origination fee? You can get a good idea of the points charged from calls or from advertisements. Again, the points you pay will depend on when you apply and which package you select.

Don't be afraid to negotiate the fees. Many fees charged are *fluff fees*—unnecessary charges. Your agent can help you sort out what you can expect to pay, what you don't have to pay, and what you can negotiate *not* paying.

What application fees are charged? How much is the application fee? Credit report fee? Does the lender charge a loan origination fee? What nonstandard fees are charged by the lender?

Does the loan require mortgage insurance? If so, how much does it cost? Can you finance the insurance? How long is the insurance required? If it is required only until a set time or until equity reaches a certain point, what is the process for dropping the insurance?

Can you lock in the rates? If so, when are the rates locked—at application or approval? How long is the lock? Does the lock include both the interest rate and the points? Is there a charge for locking in a rate? If the rates drop and you're locked in at a higher rate, can you close at the lower rate?

Can you prepay on a loan without prepayment penalties?

What are the escrow requirements? How many months' insurance must you prepay? How many months of taxes do you have to prepay?

What is the processing time for the loan? An average processing time is 30 to 60 days. If you're working under a set deadline, you might ask whether the loan can be closed by a certain date.

What is the fee for late payments?

If you have a problem or question, whom should you call? You don't want to select a lender based just on the best deal. You also want a lender that is service-oriented.

Use the two checklists on the following page to compare fixed-rate and adjustable-rate mortgages.

Comparing Fixed-Rate Loans

Name of lender: _____

Type of loan: _____

Down payment: _____

Interest rate: _____

Points: _____

    ❏   Mortgage insurance required?

    Co: _____

    ❏   Can you prepay?

    ❏   Is there a prepayment penalty?

Payment schedule: ❏ 30-year   ❏ 30-year biweekly

                     ❏ 15-year   ❏ Other

Comparing ARMs

Name of lender: _____

Type of lender: _____

Down payment: _____

Interest rate: _____

Points: _____

Initial interest rate: _____

Term: _____

Today's true rate: _____

Index used: _____

Margin: _____

    ❏   Lifetime cap on rate

        Rate: _____

        Based on: _____

    ❏   Periodic cap on rate

        Rate: _____

    ❏   Payment cap

        Cap: _____

Readjustment interval: ❏ 6 months   ❏ 5 years

                           ❏ 1 year   ❏ Can you convert?

                           ❏ 2 years   ❏ Other

                           ❏ 3 years

Cost: _____

    ❏   Can you prepay?

Prepayment penalties: _____

    ❏   Does the loan allow negative amortization?

The Least You Need to Know

It is in your best interest as a home buyer to shop around for a lender. Ideally, you want the lender that offers you the lowest interest rates, points, and fees. You also want a lender that is committed to service.

➤ There are many sources for loans, including savings and loans, credit unions, mortgage brokers, and mortgage bankers.

➤ Many loans are combined into a package and then sold to a secondary market (investors). Several government agencies were set up specifically to purchase home loans—Fannie Mae, Freddie Mac, and Ginnie Mae.

➤ You can find a lender by asking your real estate agent for a referral, by checking your local paper, or by asking friends and family for recommendations.

➤ When shopping for a loan, ask the lender about the rate, points charged, and fees for processing the loan. You may also want to ask about the processing time as well as other factors, such as whether you can lock in the interest rate.

THE PLAYERS

STARRING

GREG WEINSTEIN
AS
THE LOAN ORIGINATOR

KARA WOODRUFF
AS
THE LOAN PROCESSOR

AND
BRAD MELTZER
AS
THE UNDERWRITER

Chapter 17

Applying for the Mortgage

In This Chapter

➤ Understanding who's who in the loan game

➤ Understanding how a lender qualifies you for a loan

➤ Applying for the loan

➤ What to do if you can't get a loan

Once you select a lender, you face the agonizing process of applying for the loan. Why "agonizing," you ask?

First, you have to gather and complete so much information. You may think you need everything from your second grade report card to your library card in order to secure a loan. This chapter helps you prepare for what you need so that you aren't shocked when the lender asks for the equivalent of one box of documentation.

Second, you're bombarded with foreign terms and concepts dealing with financing. You should be a step ahead here, though. This chapter—in fact, this entire Part—should help you prepare for understanding the financial world and all its lingo. When lenders talk about underwriters and origination fees, you'll know what they mean.

Third, you have to wait. Waiting for approval is the worst. This chapter gives you pointers on how to help speed along the loan process.

The Players

Depending on the type of lender you get your mortgage from, you can expect to deal with any of several loan people. Here's the roster:

Loan originator or Loan Officer This person is responsible for taking down all your financial information and is usually your primary contact at the lending company. This person makes sure that all the needed information is ready for review.

Loan processor This person handles the processing of the loan, making sure all the steps are followed. For example, this person will order the appraisal, order the credit report, and so on.

Underwriter This person is the decision maker. He or she takes all the information the other two have collected and decides whether you get the loan or not. (You don't have any contact with this person.) The next section explains how the underwriter makes this decision.

How the Lender Decides Whether to Lend You Money

How does an underwriter decide that Buyer A gets the loan, but Buyer B is rejected? The lender will look at a number of factors, including your current financial situation, your payment history, the current lending guidelines, and the property being purchased.

Here's the basic process the lender goes through: the lender takes your application, verifies your employment and income information and source of down payment, orders and checks your credit report and appraisal, and finally approves or rejects the loan.

Taking the Application

In the application process, the lender will ask you to provide a lot of information about your financial situation, such as your current income, your current debt obligations, and more. (The section "Applying for a Loan," later in this chapter, explains in detail the documentation you're asked to provide.)

Verifying Information

The lender then reviews and verifies your information. Have you been employed at the place you listed for the amount of time you said? Is your salary what you say it is? Do you have any serious criminal records? Do you have the money you say you do in your bank or other accounts?

Accuracy is the key. The lender is looking first to be sure the information is accurate, and second, to be sure that the information is honest (so if you want the loan, it's best to tell the truth).

Credit Report

In addition to verifying your income and employment, the lender will order a credit report. This report will tell the lender about your credit rating and credit history. How have you managed past debts? Have you recently filed for bankruptcy? The lender will look for any trouble signs, such as a history of late or missed payments, and will check to see whether you listed all your debts. Not including some debts on an application can raise a red flag to the lender.

Finally, the lender will check to be sure you don't have *too much* credit available. Lenders may think that too much credit can be too tempting.

It's a good idea to check and clean up any credit problems before you apply for a loan. This topic is covered in Chapter 3. Also, most lenders run two credit checks—an initial check at the time of application and one later right before closing. For this reason, it's not a good idea to take on any new debt during the loan process. That debt is likely to show up on your second credit report.

If you have more than enough assets, you may not want to list them all. If you do, the lender will have to validate each asset you list, which can be time-consuming. Instead, list only enough to qualify for the loan and down payment you want. If it turns out you need additional assets to qualify, you can always mention them later.

Getting an Appraisal

In addition to checking out *you*, the lender will also check out the property you intend to purchase. You may be silly enough to pay $125,000 for a house that is worth only $75,000, but the lender isn't going to loan you the money to do it. All loans require an independent appraisal, which you as buyer usually pay for. The appraiser determines the market value of the home.

Request a copy of the appraisal in writing from the lender at the time of the application. This appraisal can give you solid information that backs up the value of the home. Note that you cannot get the appraisal until the closing.

To determine the value, the appraiser will look at the neighborhood. How many homes are currently on the market? How desirable is the area? The appraiser will also look closely at the house—the condition of the home, the size and number of rooms, the type of construction, and the condition of the property. After reviewing the home and property, the appraiser will provide a value as well as supporting information on how that value was reached.

Usually, the lender hires the services of the appraiser, and you pay for the appraisal through the lender. Appendix B lists the phone numbers for the American Society of Appraisers and the Appraisers Association of America, both of which can give you a referral.

Approving or Denying the Loan

Once all the details are in—your income information, credit history, appraisal, and so on—the loan underwriter will decide whether to give you the loan. If the loan is going to be sold to a secondary market, the underwriter will make sure the loan complies with the guidelines for that market (for example, the Fannie Mae guidelines). The underwriter will also use the qualifying ratios (discussed in Chapter 3) to determine whether you're a good risk for the loan. If you require mortgage insurance, you'll also have to get the approval of the insurer.

WHOA!

The Four Cs of Lending

If you have ever shopped for a diamond, you may know that the four Cs determine a diamond's worth. Lenders also use four Cs to qualify an individual for a loan:

Capacity. Will you be able to repay the debt? Lenders base the answer to this question on your current income and employment record. Lenders also look at your other financial obligations.

Credit history. Being *able* to repay the debt doesn't mean you *will* repay the debt. Lenders look at your past record of making payments. Did you make them on time?

Capital. How much money do you have right now? The lender will look at your assets. For instance, do you have money for the down payment? Do you have enough money after paying the down payment and closing costs or will you have to scrape by for a few months?

Collateral. What can the lender get from you if you default on the loan? The house, of course, but lenders want to ensure the house is worth the amount you're paying, hence the appraisal.

If the loan is approved, you should receive a commitment letter stating the terms of the loan—the loan amount, the term or length of the loan, points, interest rates, and the monthly payment amount. If you agree to these terms, you sign the letter; that is, you accept all the terms and conditions of the loan. The letter will give you a set amount of time to sign and then close the loan. Often you close very shortly after loan approval, and you don't get the letter until closing. Read the commitment letter carefully. Lenders sometimes make mistakes. You'll want to be sure the terms are exactly as you intended. If the letter is not accurate, do not sign it.

If the loan is not approved, your loan officer will let you know. See the section "What to Do If Your Loan Is Not Approved."

Applying for the Loan

You now know what's going to happen once the wheel starts turning. This section explains how to get the wheel started—how to apply for the loan.

Spilling Your Financial Guts

When you apply for a loan, you'll most likely be interviewed by the loan officer. That officer will either ask you to complete the loan application or ask you questions and complete the application for you.

In addition to the application, the loan officer will ask you to provide documentation. Here are some of the things you will be expected to provide:

➤ Copies of all bank statements (savings and checking) for the past three months. If an account shows a large deposit in the past few months, be prepared to provide an explanation of where this money came from.

➤ Copies of all stock accounts, 401K, IRA, and other assets (life insurance).

➤ Your most recent pay stubs as well as the names and addresses of your past employers.

➤ Your W2 forms for the past two years.

➤ Your tax returns for the past two years. If you're self-employed, you'll need to provide additional tax returns and all your schedules, including profit and loss statements for past years as well as year-to-date.

➤ A copy of purchase agreement. You may also need a copy of the front and back of the check for the earnest money.

➤ A check. You'll have to pay some up-front fees for the application process, usually an application fee and possibly fees for the appraisal and credit report. Some lenders also charge a loan origination fee, a charge to prepare the loan.

➤ If you're selling your residence, you need to bring a copy of the listing agreement. If you have sold your house, bring a copy of the purchase agreement.

➤ If you're paying for the down payment with money given to you as a gift, you may be required to bring a gift letter, which states the money is a gift and does not have to be repaid.

➤ It's a good idea to bring a list of your addresses for the past five to 10 years. You'll be asked to complete this information on the application.

➤ Collect the addresses and account numbers for all credit cards and other debts. For example, if you have a car loan, you'll want to know the lender's name, account number, and address. You should also know the monthly payments and balance owed.

➤ If you're renting, bring in copies of the past 12 months' rent checks.

➤ If you have credit problems, be prepared to explain them.

See the sample three-page "Uniform Residential Loan Application" at the end of this chapter.

Shop around for lenders. Different lenders charge different fees. For example, you may find a lender that doesn't charge the loan origination fee. Or you may want to use a lender that has a cheaper application fee.

Once you sign the loan application, you may be required to accept the loan stated in that application. Be sure the terms and amounts are what you want.

Locking In an Interest Rate

When you apply for the loan, you'll want to decide whether you want to lock in the interest rate or let it float. Interest rates change daily. A rate of 8.25% today could jump to 8.5% tomorrow or go down to 8%.

If you're worried about the interest rates going up, locking into a rate may be a good idea. Locking in a rate guarantees that rate for a

Rates change daily. It would be wise to follow business and financial news closely during this process, even if you don't normally pay attention to it. If you find that you've locked into a rate, and rates actually drop, you might try stalling until the lock expires so you can get the lower rate.

certain period of time. For example, you can lock in the 8% rate for 60 days.

If you do lock in the rate, you'll want to make sure of a few things. First, be sure to get the commitment in writing. Don't take the lender's word that the rate is locked. Second, you'll want to be sure that the rate is locked for a long enough period of time for you to close on the loan. If you lock for five days, but can't close within those five days, the lock is worthless. Most locks run 30 to 60 days, on average. Third, you'll want to ask the lender whether you have to pay a fee for locking in the rate. Some lenders will charge a commitment fee. Finally, find out whether the lock includes both the rate and the points paid.

If you're not worried about the interest rates changing or if you think the rates may drop, you may want to float the rate. You can float the rate until the time of settlement, or you may float and then lock in later, depending on your lender.

Estimating Closing Costs

As part of the loan application process, the lender is required by federal law (the Real Estate Settlement Procedures Act, or RESPA) to give you a *good faith estimate* of closing costs (see the sample "Good Faith Estimate of Settlement Charges" at the end of this chapter). The lender will estimate your closing costs based on his or her experience in that type of loan. The estimate should be close to what you really pay, but it may be significantly different. The estimate will include costs for points, appraisal, title search, title insurance, survey, recording fees, attorney fees, and so on. The lender must give you this estimate within three business days. If you don't receive one, you should complain. You should also ask that a copy be sent to your real estate agent so that he can go over the charges. Chapter 2 explains some of the fees you can expect to pay.

Estimating Interest Rates

In addition, the lender is required to send you a Truth-in-Lending statement that tells you the annual percentage rate (APR) for the loan. Remember that the rate you're quoted and the "real" rate are different. The APR takes into consideration all the costs of obtaining the loan—points, application fees, and so on. See the sample "Federal Truth-in-Lending Statement" at the end of this chapter.

This statement should also show the finance charge (amount you'll be expected to pay over the life of the loan), amount financed (the mortgage amount minus any prepaid expenses you pay at or before closing), total of payments, schedule of payments, late payment charges, and other information pertaining to the loan. If all the information is not available for the Truth-in-Lending statement, you'll receive an estimate from the lender. You'll then receive a second statement at the time of closing.

Finally, you should receive a government publication that discusses settlement costs.

Ensuring a Smooth Process

You may feel as if the entire loan process is out of your hands. That out-of-control feeling can be uncomfortable when so much is at stake. There are some things that you can do to ensure a smooth loan process:

Clean up your credit report. Be sure to clear up any credit problems *before* you apply for a loan. If any problems turn up later, a lender won't want to hear your explanation after the fact.

Provide all the requested information quickly. If the loan officer asks you for a pay stub, get the stub to her as quickly as possible. You can hold up the process if the loan processor is waiting on something from you.

Get copies of everything to protect yourself. For instance, if you locked in a rate, but have no proof of that, you're going to have a hard time if the lender says you *didn't* lock in a rate or that you locked in a different rate.

Call your loan officer periodically to check on the progress. If there are problems, you'll want to know immediately, not at the end of 60 days. Perhaps the lender requires additional documentation. You should make sure that there are no holdups that you're responsible for.

Don't make any big purchases right before or during the loan process. If you go out and buy a new car right before you apply for a loan, that debt is going to show up on your record. If you buy the car after you apply, the debt may also show up because most lenders run *two* credit checks: one when you apply and one right before the closing. So, if you're contemplating a big purchase, it's best to wait till after your loan is approved.

What to Do If You Can't Get a Loan

If you're denied a loan, the lender is required to explain the decision in writing. You should talk to the loan officer and find out what went wrong. If you can clear up the problem, you may be able to be reconsidered. If not, you may have to secure other financing.

Ask the loan officer for suggestions on how to improve your chances of getting approved. A loan officer has experience dealing with many successful and unsuccessful loans. He may be able to give you some advice on improving your chances.

The following section discusses some of the problems that can cause a loan to be denied.

Income Problems

If you don't have enough income to qualify for that loan, you can try the following to correct this situation:

Secure other financing. If you cannot obtain financing through a traditional lender, you may want to try a different type of financing— for example, maybe the seller can help you with financing. Chapter 15 discusses other types of financing. Also, you should ask your agent for suggestions.

Point out extenuating circumstances to the lender. For example, if you're about to get a raise, you may ask your employer to give the lender a letter saying so. This may improve your financial picture enough to qualify.

Shop for a less expensive home. If you cannot qualify for the home of your dreams, perhaps you can qualify for a less expensive home and then trade up when you're more financially secure.

Start a savings program. If you don't have enough for the down payment, start saving now. You may not be able to afford a house today, but you don't want that to hold true forever. Create a budget and start saving money for your home. You could even consider taking a second job temporarily. You could set an amount that you have to save for a down payment, then deposit each paycheck from your second job directly into your savings account. When you've reached your savings goal, quit your second job and start looking for that dream home!

Examine your current debts. If that dream home is important enough to you, try lowering your existing debts by making some sacrifices. You could trade your car in for a less expensive model; you could sell one car if your family has more than one, then carpool or ride public transportation; you could consolidate some outstanding loans—your debt would still be as high, but your monthly payments would be lower. Be creative and brutal. Trim the fat. If you're spending a lot each month on concerts, movies, or eating out, cut back. You'll be surprised how quickly all of this adds up.

Credit Problems

If your credit report comes back with problems, you should ask to see a copy of the credit report. If there are errors, have them corrected. If there are problems, correct them or add your explanation. Doing so may or may not change the lender's mind.

If you have too much debt to qualify for a loan, consider paying off some of the debts if you're able. If you're not able, but have a good credit history, ask the lender to reconsider.

If you have serious debt-management problems, consider getting some financial counseling.

Appraisal Problems

Most lenders will only give you a loan for a certain percentage of the appraised value—for example, 95%. If the appraisal is higher than what you're paying, you won't have to worry. If the appraisal is less, you'll only be able to get a mortgage for the given percentage. In this case, you can try to come up with a larger down payment to cover the difference. Or, if you made the sale contingent on an acceptable appraisal and the appraisal is low, you may be able to renegotiate the price.

Sometimes an appraisal will be low because the house needs some type of repair. For example, maybe the home needs to be painted, or it needs a new roof. Ask the owner to fix the problem or set aside the funds to do the repair.

Discrimination

You cannot be turned down for a loan based on race, religion, age, color, national origin, receipt of public assistance funds, sex, or marital status. If you think you've been denied a loan for one of these reasons, you should file a complaint with the U.S. Department of Housing and Urban Development. The address and phone number are listed in Appendix B.

The Least You Need to Know

Getting a loan can be a tense situation. You'll want the process to go as smoothly as possible. Once the loan comes back approved, you have only a few more steps until you can move into your new home! Keeping these following points in mind can help you through the loan process:

➤ The loan officer takes your loan application and is your primary contact at the lender's office. The loan processor orders the credit check and appraisal and makes sure all the documentation is together. The underwriter decides whether to approve or deny the loan.

➤ The application process goes like this: You apply for the loan. The lender verifies the information, checks your credit history, orders and checks an appraisal on the property, then approves or denies the loan.

➤ You'll most likely be charged a fee for an appraisal. The appraiser will look at the home and property and determine its current market value.

➤ In qualifying you for a loan, the lender will decide whether you can and will pay. The lender will also look at the cash you have now and the collateral you'll have in case you default on the loan.

➤ A loan may not be approved for one of several reasons, including: insufficient income, bad credit report, or low appraisal.

Uniform Residential Loan Application

This application is designed to be completed by the applicant(s) with the lender's assistance. Applicants should complete this form as "Borrower" or "Co-Borrower", as applicable. Co-Borrower information must also be provided (and the appropriate box checked) when ☐ the income or assets of a person other than the "Borrower" (including the Borrower's spouse) will be used as a basis for loan qualification or ☐ the income or assets of the Borrower's spouse will not be used as a basis for loan qualification, but his or her liabilities must be considered because the Borrower resides in a community property state, the security property is located in a community property state, or the Borrower is relying on other property located in a community property state as a basis for repayment of the loan.

I. TYPE OF MORTGAGE AND TERMS OF LOAN

Mortgage Applied for:	☐ V.A. ☐ Conventional ☐ Other: ☐ FHA ☐ FmHA	Agency Case Number	Lender Case Number
Amount $	Interest Rate %	No. of Months	Amortization Type: ☐ Fixed Rate ☐ Other (explain): ☐ GPM ☐ ARM (type):

II. PROPERTY INFORMATION AND PURPOSE OF LOAN

Subject Property Address (street, city, state, ZIP)	No. of Units

Legal Description of Subject Property (attach description if necessary)	Year Built

Purpose of Loan ☐ Purchase ☐ Construction ☐ Other (explain): ☐ Refinance ☐ Construction-Permanent	Property will be: ☐ Primary Residence ☐ Secondary Residence ☐ Investment

Complete this line if construction or construction-permanent loan.

Year Lot Acquired	Original Cost $	Amount Existing Liens $	(a) Present Value of Lot $	(b) Cost of Improvements $	Total (a + b) $

Complete this line if this is a refinance loan.

Year Acquired	Original Cost $	Amount Existing Liens $	Purpose of Refinance	Describe Improvements ☐ made ☐ to be made
				Cost: $

Title will be held in what Name(s)	Manner in which Title will be held	Estate will be held in: ☐ Fee Simple ☐ Leasehold (show expiration date)

Source of Down Payment, Settlement Charges and/or Subordinate Financing (explain)	

III. BORROWER INFORMATION

Borrower	Co-Borrower
Borrower's Name (include Jr. or Sr. if applicable)	Co-Borrower's Name (include Jr. or Sr. if applicable)
Social Security Number / Home Phone (incl. area code) / Age / Yrs. School	Social Security Number / Home Phone (incl. area code) / Age / Yrs. School
☐ Married ☐ Unmarried (include single, divorced, widowed) ☐ Separated / Dependents (not listed by Co-Borrower) no. ages	☐ Married ☐ Unmarried (include single, divorced, widowed) ☐ Separated / Dependents (not listed by Borrower) no. ages
Present Address (street, city, state, ZIP) ☐ Own ☐ Rent ____ No. Yrs.	Present Address (street, city, state, ZIP) ☐ Own ☐ Rent ____ No. Yrs.

If residing at present address for less than two years, complete the following:

Former Address (street, city, state, ZIP) ☐ Own ☐ Rent ____ No. Yrs.	Former Address (street, city, state, ZIP) ☐ Own ☐ Rent ____ No. Yrs.
Former Address (street, city, state, ZIP) ☐ Own ☐ Rent ____ No. Yrs.	Former Address (street, city, state, ZIP) ☐ Own ☐ Rent ____ No. Yrs.

IV. EMPLOYMENT INFORMATION

Borrower	Co-Borrower
Name & Address of Employer ☐ Self Employed / Yrs. on this job	Name & Address of Employer ☐ Self Employed / Yrs. on this job
	Yrs. employed in this line of work/profession		Yrs. employed in this line of work/profession
Position/Title/Type of Business / Business Phone (incl. area code)	Position/Title/Type of Business / Business Phone (incl. area code)

If employed in current position for less than two years or if currently employed in more than one position, complete the following:

Name & Address of Employer ☐ Self Employed / Dates (from - to)	Name & Address of Employer ☐ Self Employed / Dates (from - to)
	Monthly Income $		Monthly Income $
Position/Title/Type of Business / Business Phone (incl. area code)	Position/Title/Type of Business / Business Phone (incl. area code)
Name & Address of Employer ☐ Self Employed / Dates (from - to)	Name & Address of Employer ☐ Self Employed / Dates (from - to)
	Monthly Income $		Monthly Income $
Position/Title/Type of Business / Business Phone (incl. area code)	Position/Title/Type of Business / Business Phone (incl. area code)

Freddie Mac Form 65 10/92   Fannie Mae Form 1003 10/92

VMP-21 (9210)   Page 1 of 4   Printed on Recycled Paper
VMP MORTGAGE FORMS • (313)293-8100 • (800)521-7291

A typical loan application, page one.

V. MONTHLY INCOME AND COMBINED HOUSING EXPENSE INFORMATION

Gross Monthly Income	Borrower	Co-Borrower	Total	Combined Monthly Housing Expense	Present	Proposed
Base Empl. Income *	$	$	$	Rent	$	
Overtime				First Mortgage (P&I)		$
Bonuses				Other Financing (P&I)		
Commissions				Hazard Insurance		
Dividends/Interest				Real Estate Taxes		
Net Rental Income				Mortgage Insurance		
Other (before completing, see the notice in "describe other income," below)				Homeowner Assn. Dues		
				Other:		
Total	$	$	$	Total	$	$

* Self Employed Borrower(s) may be required to provide additional documentation such as tax returns and financial statements.

	Describe Other Income *Notice:* Alimony, child support, or separate maintenance income need not be revealed if the Borrower (B) or Co-Borrower (C) does not choose to have it considered for repaying this loan.	Monthly Amount
B/C		$

VI. ASSETS AND LIABILITIES

This Statement and any applicable supporting schedules may be completed jointly by both married and unmarried Co-Borrowers if their assets and liabilities are sufficiently joined so that the Statement can be meaningfully and fairly presented on a combined basis; otherwise separate Statements and Schedules are required. If the Co-Borrower section was completed about a spouse, this Statement and supporting schedules must be completed about that spouse also.   Completed ☐ Jointly ☐ Not Jointly

ASSETS — Description	Cash or Market Value	Liabilities and Pledged Assets. List the creditor's name, address and account number for all outstanding debts, including automobile loans, revolving charge accounts, real estate loans, alimony, child support, stock pledges, etc. Use continuation sheet, if necessary. Indicate by (*) those liabilities which will be satisfied upon sale of real estate owned or upon refinancing of the subject property.		
Cash deposit toward purchase held by:	$	**LIABILITIES**	Monthly Pmt. & Mos. Left to Pay	Unpaid Balance
		Name and address of Company	$ Pmt./Mos.	$
List checking and savings accounts below				
Name and address of Bank, S&L, or Credit Union				
		Acct. no.		
		Name and address of Company	$ Pmt./Mos.	$
Acct. no.	$			
Name and address of Bank, S&L, or Credit Union				
		Acct. no.		
		Name and address of Company	$ Pmt./Mos.	$
Acct. no.	$			
Name and address of Bank, S&L, or Credit Union				
		Acct. no.		
		Name and address of Company	$ Pmt./Mos.	$
Acct. no.	$			
Name and address of Bank, S&L, or Credit Union				
		Acct. no.		
		Name and address of Company	$ Pmt./Mos.	$
Acct. no.	$			
Stocks & Bonds (Company name/number & description)	$			
		Acct. no.		
		Name and address of Company	$ Pmt./Mos.	$
Life insurance net cash value	$			
Face amount: $				
Subtotal Liquid Assets	$			
Real estate owned (enter market value from schedule of real estate owned)	$	Acct. no.		
Vested interest in retirement fund	$	Name and address of Company	$ Pmt./Mos.	$
Net worth of business(es) owned (attach financial statement)	$			
Automobiles owned (make and year)	$			
		Acct. no.		
		Alimony/Child Support/Separate Maintenance Payments Owed to:	$	
Other Assets (itemize)	$	Job Related Expense (child care, union dues, etc.)	$	
		Total Monthly Payments	$	
Total Assets a.	$	**Net Worth (a minus b)** ► $	**Total Liabilities b.**	$

Freddie Mac Form 65 10/92   Page 2 of 4   Fannie Mae Form 1003 10/92

A typical loan application, page two.

VI. ASSETS AND LIABILITIES (cont.)

Schedule of Real Estate Owned (If additional properties are owned, use continuation sheet.)

Property Address (enter S if sold, PS if pending sale or R if rental being held for income)	Type of Property	Present Market Value	Amount of Mortgages & Liens	Gross Rental Income	Mortgage Payments	Insurance, Maintenance, Taxes & Misc.	Net Rental Income
		$	$	$	$	$	$
Totals		$	$	$	$	$	$

List any additional names under which credit has previously been received and indicate appropriate creditor name(s) and account number(s):

Alternate Name	Creditor Name	Account Number

VII. DETAILS OF TRANSACTION

a. Purchase price	$
b. Alterations, improvements, repairs	
c. Land (if acquired separately)	
d. Refinance (incl. debts to be paid off)	
e. Estimated prepaid items	
f. Estimated closing costs	
g. PMI, MIP, Funding Fee	
h. Discount (if Borrower will pay)	
i. Total Costs (add items a through h)	
j. Subordinate financing	
k. Borrower's closing costs paid by Seller	
l. Other Credits (explain)	
m. Loan amount (exclude PMI, MIP, Funding Fee financed)	
n. PMI, MIP, Funding Fee financed	
o. Loan amount (add m & n)	
p. Cash from/to Borrower (subtract j, k, l & o from i)	

VIII. DECLARATIONS

If you answer "Yes" to any questions a through i, please use continuation sheet for explanation.

Borrower Yes/No — Co-Borrower Yes/No

a. Are there any outstanding judgments against you?

b. Have you been declared bankrupt within the past 7 years?

c. Have you had property foreclosed upon or given title or deed in lieu thereof in the last 7 years?

d. Are you a party to a lawsuit?

e. Have you directly or indirectly been obligated on any loan which resulted in foreclosure, transfer of title in lieu of foreclosure, or judgment? (This would include such loans as home mortgage loans, SBA loans, home improvement loans, educational loans, manufactured (mobile) home loans, any mortgage, financial obligation, bond, or loan guarantee. If "Yes," provide details, including date, name and address of Lender, FHA or V.A. case number, if any, and reasons for the action.)

f. Are you presently delinquent or in default on any Federal debt or any other loan, mortgage, financial obligation, bond, or loan guarantee? If "Yes," give details as described in the preceding question.

g. Are you obligated to pay alimony, child support, or separate maintenance?

h. Is any part of the down payment borrowed?

i. Are you a co-maker or endorser on a note?

j. Are you a U.S. citizen?

k. Are you a permanent resident alien?

l. Do you intend to occupy the property as your primary residence? If "Yes," complete question m below.

m. Have you had an ownership interest in a property in the last three years?

(1) What type of property did you own—principal residence (PR), second home (SH), or investment property (IP)?

(2) How did you hold title to the home—solely by yourself (S), jointly with your spouse (SP), or jointly with another person (O)?

IX. ACKNOWLEDGEMENT AND AGREEMENT

The undersigned specifically acknowledge(s) and agree(s) that: (1) the loan requested by this application will be secured by a first mortgage or deed of trust on the property described herein; (2) the property will not be used for any illegal or prohibited purpose or use; (3) all statements made in this application are made for the purpose of obtaining the loan indicated herein; (4) occupation of the property will be as indicated above; (5) verification or reverification of any information contained in the application may be made at any time by the Lender, its agents, successors and assigns, either directly or through a credit reporting agency, from any source named in this application, and the original copy of this application will be retained by the Lender, even if the loan is not approved; (6) the Lender, its agents, successors and assigns will rely on the information contained in the application and I/we have a continuing obligation to amend and/or supplement the information provided in this application if any of the material facts which I/we have represented herein should change prior to closing; (7) in the event my/our payments on the loan indicated in this application become delinquent, the Lender, its agents, successors and assigns, may, in addition to all their other rights and remedies, report my/our name(s) and account information to a credit reporting agency; (8) ownership of the loan may be transferred to successor or assign of the Lender without notice to me and/or the administration of the loan account may be transferred to an agent, successor or assign of the Lender with prior notice to me; (9) the Lender, its agents, successors and assigns make no representations or warranties, express or implied, to the Borrower(s) regarding the property, the condition of the property, or the value of the property. **Certification:** I/We certify that the information provided in this application is true and correct as of the date set forth opposite my/our signature(s) on this application and acknowledge my/our understanding that any intentional or negligent misrepresentation(s) of the information contained in this application may result in civil liability and/or criminal penalties including, but not limited to, fine or imprisonment or both under the provisions of Title 18, United States Code, Section 1001, et seq. and liability for monetary damages to the Lender, its agents, successors and assigns, insurers and any other person who may suffer any loss due to reliance upon any misrepresentation which I/we have made on this application.

Borrower's Signature _____ Date _____ X

Co-Borrower's Signature _____ Date _____ X

X. INFORMATION FOR GOVERNMENT MONITORING PURPOSES

The following information is requested by the Federal Government for certain types of loans related to a dwelling, in order to monitor the Lender's compliance with equal credit opportunity, fair housing and home mortgage disclosure laws. You are not required to furnish this information, but are encouraged to do so. The law provides that a Lender may neither discriminate on the basis of this information, nor on whether you choose to furnish it. However, if you choose not to furnish it, under Federal regulations this Lender is required to note race and sex on the basis of visual observation or surname. If you do not wish to furnish the above information, please check the box below. (Lender must review the above material to assure that the disclosures satisfy all requirements to which the Lender is subject under applicable state law for the particular type of loan applied for.)

BORROWER — I do not wish to furnish this information

Race/National Origin: American Indian or Alaskan Native; Asian or Pacific Islander; White, not of Hispanic Origin; Black, not of Hispanic origin; Hispanic; Other (specify)

Sex: Female / Male

CO-BORROWER — I do not wish to furnish this information

Race/National Origin: American Indian or Alaskan Native; Asian or Pacific Islander; White, not of Hispanic Origin; Black, not of Hispanic origin; Hispanic; Other (specify)

Sex: Female / Male

To be Completed by Interviewer

This application was taken by: face-to-face interview / by mail / by telephone

Interviewer's Name (print or type)

Interviewer's Signature _____ Date

Interviewer's Phone Number (incl. area code)

Freddie Mac Form 65 10/92 — Page 3 of 4 — Fannie Mae Form 1003 10/92

A typical loan application, page three.

MORTGAGE CORPORATION OF AMERICA
GOOD FAITH ESTIMATE OF SETTLEMENT CHARGES

Date	Applicant(s)
7/16/94	San B. Buyer

Address of Property	City	State	Zip
126 E. Main St.	Indpls	IN	46220

Sale Price	Mortgage Amount	Mtg. with MIP/VA F.F.	Term (Months)	Rate	Loan Type
94,000	70,500		360	9.0%	CONV

Margin	Index	Caps

Listed below is the Good Faith Estimate of Settlement Charges made pursuant to the requirements of the Real Estate Settlement Procedures Act (RESPA). These figures are only estimates and the actual charge due at settlement may be different.

GOOD FAITH ESTIMATE OF CLOSING COSTS

801	Loan Origination Fee	0
802	Loan Discount ____ %	0
803	Appraisal Fee	250
804	Credit Report Fee	50
805	Inspection Fee	
807	Assumption Fee	
808	Mortgage Broker Fee	
809	CLO Access Fee	
810	Tax Related Service Fee	56
811	Underwriting Fee	125
902	FHA MIP/VA Funding Fee (can be financed)	( )
902	FHA MIP/VA Funding Fee paid in cash	
902	Mtg. Ins. Prem. (CONV)	
1101	Title Company Closing Fee	250
1105	Document Prep Fee	95
1108	Title Insurance	95
1201	Recording Fees	25
1301	Survey	110
1302	Pest Inspections	
	Reservation Fee	
	ARM Conversion Fee	
	ESTIMATED TOTAL CLOSING COSTS	1,056

ESTIMATED PREPAIDS

901	Interest Adjustment* (30 day) 5 days	264.38
1003/		
1004	Tax Escrow and Prorations (14 mo.)	195.34
903	Hazard Ins. Premium (prior to closing) 1yr	(300.00)
1001	Hazard Escrow 2 mo.	50.00
1002	Mortgage Insurance Escrow	
904	Flood Ins. Premium (prior to closing)	
1006	Flood Ins. Escrow	
	ESTIMATED TOTAL PREPAIDS:	509.72

*This amount represents the greatest amount of interest you could be required to pay at closing. The actual charge is determined by the day of the month on which your closing occurs, and will be based on a daily interest charge of $ 17.63 .

DETAILS OF PURCHASE

Sales Price/Mtg. Balance on Refi	94,000
Total Closing Costs (Est.)	1,056
Prepaid Escrows (Est.)	509.72
TOTAL	95,565.72
Amount this Mortgage	70,500
Amount Paid at Application	50
Amount on Deposit with Realtor	
Closing Costs Paid by Seller	
Cash Required for Closing (Est.) (1379.86)	25,015.72
Plus Two Month's Payment Reserves	26,395.58

The sum of $ 50 which is paid to the Lender with this application is to cover the Lender's expense of obtaining an appraisal and a written credit report. If the expense of obtaining the appraisal and credit report has been incurred by the Lender and this loan application is canceled by applicants or denied by the Lender, the sum indicated above shall not be refunded.

I/WE HEREBY ACKNOWLEDGE RECEIPT OF THIS DISCLOSURE AND THE HUD GUIDE FOR THE HOME BUYER

Borrower	Date	Co-Borrower	Date

Lottie Lender	7/16/94
Mortgage Originator	Date

PROPOSED MONTHLY PAYMENT

Principal and Interest	567.26
Tax Reserve	97.67
Hazard Ins. Reserve	25.00
Flood Ins. Reserve	
Mortgage Ins. Reserve	
TOTAL MONTHLY PAYMENT	689.93

INFORMATION REQUIRED

____ Current paystubs
____ W-2's for 19___ & 19___
____ 1040's with attached schedules for 19___ & 19___
____ 19___ year to date profit and loss statement
____ Corporate tax returns for 19___ and 19___
____ Account numbers for

____ Current stock and bond verification of value
____ Gift letter completely executed and donor's verification
____ Listing agreement/PA for the sale of your present home
____ Most recent account statement for

____ Divorce Decree and Friend of Court verification
____ Bankruptcy Discharge and Petition
____ Certificate of Eligibility/dd214
____ PA fully executed
____ Private Road documentation
____ Well and Septic Cert./Current
____ Land Contract and Payment ledger
____ Personal statements concerning:

Other:

Express Processing: 3 most recent savings, checking and money investment statements, 12-month mortgage payment history or canceled checks, last 2 years' W-2s, and 30 days pay stubs.

A good faith estimate of closing costs.

FEDERAL TRUTH-IN LENDING STATEMENT
(THIS IS NEITHER A CONTRACT NOR A COMMITMENT TO LEND)

Creditor:

Date: 07-13-94   Loan Number:

Check box if applicable:

ANNUAL PERCENTAGE RATE	FINANCE CHARGE	Amount Financed	Total of Payments	☐ Total Sale Price
The cost of your credit as a yearly rate.	The dollar amount the credit will cost you.	The amount of credit provided to you or on your behalf.	The amount you will have paid after you have made all payments as scheduled.	The Total cost of your purchase on credit including your down-payment of $
9.085* %	$ 133892.94*	$ 70319.00*	$ 204211.94*	$

☐ REQUIRED DEPOSIT: The annual percentage rate does not take into account your required deposit.

PAYMENTS: Your payment schedule will be:

Number of Payments	Amount of Payments	When Payments Are Due	Number of Payments	Amount of Payments	When Payments Are Due	Number of Payments	Amount of Payments	When Payments Are Due
		Monthly Beginning:			Monthly Beginning:			Monthly Beginning:
359	567.26	00-00-00						
1	565.60	11-00-29						

☐ DEMAND FEATURE: This obligation has a demand feature.

☐ VARIABLE RATE: This loan has a Variable Rate Feature. Variable Rate Disclosures have been provided to you earlier.

You are also required to pay 1/12th of the insurance & taxes in your monthly payment.

INSURANCE: The following insurance is required to obtain credit:

☐ Credit life insurance and credit disability   ☒ Property Insurance $ 70500.00 ☐ Flood Insurance

You may obtain the insurance from anyone you want that is acceptable to creditor.

☐ If you purchase ☐ property ☐ flood insurance from creditor you will pay $ _____ for a one year term.

SECURITY: You are giving a security interest in: 126 E. 86TH ST. INDPLS, IN 46240

☒ The goods or property being purchased   ☐ Real property you already own.

FILING FEES: $ 25.00

LATE CHARGE: If a payment is more than   15 days late, you will be charged   5.0   % of the payment.

PREPAYMENT: If you pay off early, you

☐ may   ☒ will not   have to pay a penalty.

☐ may   ☒ will not   be entitled to a refund of part of the finance charge.

ASSUMPTION: Someone buying your property

☐ may   ☐ may, subject to conditions   ☒ may not   assume the remainder of your loan on the original terms:

See your contract documents for any additional information about nonpayment, default, any required repayment in full before the scheduled date and prepayment refunds and penalties.

* means an estimate   ☒ all dates and numerical disclosures except the late payment disclosures are estimates.

The undersigned acknowledge receiving and reading a completed copy of this disclosure.

Neither you nor the creditor previously has become obligated to make or accept this loan, nor is any such obligation made by the delivery or signing of this disclosure.

_____ _____ _____ _____

(Applicant)   (Date)   (Applicant)   (Date)

_____ _____ _____ _____

(Applicant)   (Date)   (Applicant)   (Date)

NOTE: Payments shown above do not include reserve deposits for taxes, assessments, and property or flood insurance.

VMP -784 (9607).02   KAR/KML   VMP MORTGAGE FORMS - (800)521-7291   7/88

A Truth-in-Lending statement.

Part IV
Close on the House

The final step in buying a house is the closing. This part covers the key steps you need to follow in getting to that final goal—owning your home. In particular, you need to arrange for insurance, have an inspection done, sign lots and lots of documents (be sure to read the fine print), hand over all your money, then finally, finally get the keys to your new house.

Insurance

When I started to write this chapter, I thought about the things that can happen to a home and then like most people, I figured that home damage wasn't all that common.

Then I started researching what is covered and what isn't covered in a policy, and I thought about articles in the local paper in the past year or so. Someone's house burnt down. Someone drove his car into a person's living room. A plane landed on a house. Hail broke out the windows in a house. Accidents do happen, even though we don't like to think that they will happen to us.

Insurance protects you from many different kinds of risks. When you purchase a home, you'll need to purchase a different type of insurance for each of these risks, as covered in this chapter.

Understanding the Types of Insurance

On a home, you probably immediately think of homeowner's insurance, but there are actually several types of insurance—two that you'll definitely need and one that may be required by the lender:

Homeowner's insurance covers your home, your possessions, and people on your property. It is required by the lender.

Mortgage insurance protects the lender in case you default on the loan. Depending on your financial situation, you may have to pay for this type of premium.

Title insurance protects you against any problems with your claim to ownership. It is required by the lender.

Getting Home Insurance

Someone once tried to sell my husband and me life insurance when we were in our 20s. We declined, and the salesperson starting telling us, "You could die any day. Even though you're only 26, you could drop dead tomorrow." Then the salesperson started quoting statistics on untimely deaths. Great sales technique, huh?

Most people don't like to think about bad things happening, and rightly so. Still, things happen, and you should be prepared. And your lender will *require* that you be prepared.

All lenders require fire, theft, and liability insurance. Depending on where you live, the lender may also require other types of insurance. For example, if you live in a flood plain, you may have to have flood insurance.

What Insurance Covers

When you purchase insurance on your home, you purchase a homeowner's policy that includes two types of protection. With *casualty insurance* (also called *property protection* or *hazard insurance),* you're covered for losses or damages to the house and contents caused by fire, theft, and certain weather-related hazards. *Personal liability* insurance protects you if you're sued by someone who is injured on your property. For example, if your Aunt Sunny has a few too many and falls off the porch, you're covered. Family members may also be covered if they are away from home.

Your lender will require both types of coverages, but the extent of the coverage is up to you. You can select different types of insurance, as described next.

Types of Insurance

A homeowner's policy includes several different kinds of insurance together in one package. Table 18.1 on the following page lists the types of coverages. HO-1 is the cheapest and covers the least, HO-2 is more expensive but covers more than HO-1, and so on.

The 11 Common Perils

The most basic policy, HO-1, covers what are known as the 11 common perils. More expensive policies cover these basics, plus some.

➤ Fire or lightning

➤ Loss of property because of fire or other perils

➤ Windstorm or hail

➤ Explosion

➤ Riots and other civil commotions

➤ Aircraft

➤ Vehicles

➤ Smoke

➤ Vandalism and malicious mischief

➤ Theft

➤ Breakage of glass that constitutes a part of the building.

Table 18.1 Types of Insurance Coverage

Type of Insurance	Type of Policy	Coverage
HO-1	Basic Policy	Covers fire, windstorm, explosion, smoke, broken glass, and other perils including theft, vandalism, and liability.
HO-2	Broad Form	Covers the same as HO-1 but adds several items. For instance, this type of policy may protect against damage from burst pipes, exploding furnaces, collapse of building, and falling objects.
HO-3	All-Risk Form	Covers everything not specifically excluded. May cover features that are part of the structure (for example, wall-to-wall carpeting).
HO-4	Renter's Policy	Protects renter's personal possessions.
HO-5	Comprehensive	Covers everything in HO-3, plus some. Exclusions are specifically listed. This is the most expensive type of insurance.
HO-6	Condo or Co-op	Insurance used for condominiums and co-ops.

How Much Do You Need?

When you are deciding how much coverage you need, consider a few things. First, ask your lender how much is required. The lender will require a minimum amount (usually purchase price less land value), but you may want to get additional coverage.

The amount of insurance you need (and the amount you pay) is based on the cost of replacing the entire structure and a value on personal property. For example, you may have a $120,000 policy for replacement value and personal property covered up to $75,000.

You want to insure your house for full replacement value. The *current market value* is what you can sell your house for today. The *replacement value* is the cost to replace your home.

To estimate the replacement costs, figure the square footage of floor space and then multiply this figure by the current construction cost per square foot for similar homes. You can find the construction cost by asking a local builder's association.

To cover your possessions, make an inventory. You can do this with pen and paper, a video camera, or a computer program. Once you figure a value for your possessions, find an appropriate insurance value. Keep in mind that there are certain monetary limits for specific items. For example, there may be a $1,000 limit on jewelry and furs. If you want additional insurance for specific items, you may have to pay more.

According to the Insurance Information Institute, eight out of 10 homeowners carry too little insurance. Be sure you have enough coverage in case something does happen. Also, update your insurance if the market changes, if you have more or fewer possessions, or if you make a major improvement to the home. Table 18.2 shows an example of an insurance policy.

Table 18.2 A Sample Insurance Policy

Section I		
A	Dwelling	$111,100
	Dwelling Extension	11,110
B	Personal Property	75,000
C	Loss of Use	Actual Loss Sustained

Section II		
L	Personal Liability	$ 300,000
	Damage to Property of Others	500
M	Medical Payments/each person	1,000
	Replacement Cost	
	Inflation Coverage Index	125.1%
	Deductibles	250
	Policy Premium	389

Tips on Insurance

Shopping for insurance can be a headache. You should make sure you have enough coverage, that you keep your coverage up-to-date, and that you get the best bargain. Don't be tempted to save money and get the least amount of coverage. This is your home! If you want to save money, don't scrimp on the policy. Instead, get a higher deductible. Doing so can lower the premium cost.

It's easy to put off getting insurance until the last minute. Then, since you have to have the policy at closing, you may just call the first company you think of. It's better not to wait until the last minute. Shop around and get quotes from several companies. Rates can vary significantly from area to area and from company to company.

If you make a new purchase, keep your receipts and add the item to your inventory of possessions. Having receipts will help you if you have to file a claim. A standard policy will not cover business assets. If you work from your home, you may need additional coverage.

Ask about discounts. You may get a discount from some insurers if you have both home and car insurance with the same company. Also, you may receive a discount if you have a smoke or burglar alarm or a newer home.

Check about changing the policy. Can you raise the coverage later? Some policies are tied to the Consumer Price Index and rise accordingly. You may have to pay extra for this feature.

Find out what is *not* covered. If the pipe in your basement bursts and you have water damage, is it covered? What about earthquakes (usually not covered)? Find out how damages are paid. You want the full replacement cost. If your roof is damaged, you want the insurer to cover entire payment for a new roof—not a partial fee.

How Payments Are Made

When you purchase a home, the lender usually requires that you pay for a one-year policy up front. You should ask your lender when the policy has to be delivered. Usually you must do so at or before closing. You'll most likely be asked to bring a paid receipt with the insurance policy.

In addition to the prepaid policy, you'll most likely be required to make insurance payments as part of your monthly mortgage payment. The lender sets up an escrow account and each month collects 1/12 of the fees. When the bill comes due, it is sent to the lender, and the lender pays.

Comparing Insurance

Use the following list to compare insurance policies:

Company name: _____

Type of coverage: _____

What is covered: _____

What is not covered: _____

Cost: _____

Deductible: _____

Liability limits: _____

Getting Mortgage Insurance

Mortgage insurance is required by lenders if you get an FHA loan or if you have a down payment less than 20%. Some states have laws that prohibit an 80% LTV (loan-to-value) ratio without insurance. Also, the secondary market may not purchase this type of loan without insurance. Your lender will set up and purchase this type of insurance.

 Don't confuse this type of mortgage insurance with the kind that pays off the house in case of the death of purchaser. You'll be bombarded with offers of this type of insurance when you close on the house. Don't be tempted—there is usually a better and cheaper way to provide the same protection.

For FHA loans, your loan is backed by an insurance program; this means you must pay the insurance premium. This type of mortgage is called *mortgage insurance premium,* or MIP.

Conventional loans require *private mortgage insurance* (flip the initials and you get PMI) when you put less than 20% down. They both work the same way; they help the lender recover the cost of selling your home if you default on the loan.

Paying Mortgage Insurance

With an FHA loan, you pay 3% of the loan amount at the closing, plus a monthly fee. This premium provides insurance for the life of the loan and can be financed. If you sell or refinance an FHA loan, you may be entitled to a refund. Ask your lender.

For private mortgage insurance, you usually pay one year up front, plus a monthly charge, or you can pay a lump-sum payment. The amount depends on the down payment, the coverage required by the lender and the type of loan (fixed or ARM). The premium may be higher for ARMs, for example.

Usually the first year rate is higher than subsequent years. For example, you may pay 1% the first year (up front) and then .5% each year afterward. The insurance is added onto your monthly mortgage. In the following example, if you borrowed $100,000, you would need to pay an up-front PMI insurance of $1,000. The next year's premium would be $500 at .5%. This fee would be divided by 12 and added to your monthly payment. Table 18.3 breaks down the costs of private mortgage insurance.

Table 18.3   The Cost of Private Mortgage Insurance

Description	Amount
Loan amount	$100,000
First year premium (1%)	$1,000
Following year premium (.5%)	$500
Added to monthly payment	$42

Canceling Mortgage Insurance

Depending on the loan agreement, you may be able to cancel the insurance once you reach a certain equity. If you have 20% equity (the loan value is below 80%), you may be able to stop paying insurance.

Check with the lender about how and when you can cancel. You have to request the cancellation in writing; the lender won't cancel automatically. The lender may require an appraisal if the property has been improved, a clean payment history (for instance, no more than one 30-days-late payment in 24 months and one 15-day-late payment in 12 months), and a minimum payment history (for example, two years). Finally, the property must still be occupied by the original owner.

Ask your lender to shop around on rates for private mortgage insurance. The cheapest is best for you!

Getting Title Insurance

More insurance! I can hear you groan. Yes, there is a third type of insurance that is required on all homes—title insurance. This type of insurance is purchased at the closing and insures a clear and trouble-free ownership. Trouble-free ownership doesn't guarantee that the plumbing is not going to go haywire or the roof isn't going to cave in. It does insure against any losses you might incur if the seller's long-lost Uncle Bob shows up with a solid claim to ownershhip of the house.

The Title Search

The lender does two things to guard against claims. First, it does a title search, which the seller usually pays for. Second, it requires title insurance.

In a title search, someone searches all the records and traces the history of ownership. The searcher starts with the current seller and works backwards from owner to owner until the very beginning (when the land was originally granted or sold). This person usually looks manually through many, many public records: deaths, divorces, court judgments, liens, taxes, wills, deeds, tax assessor's information, surveyor's information, and more.

A title search uncovers not only the chain of owners, but also whether there are any unpaid taxes on the property, easements, or encroachments. An *easement* is a permanent right to use another's property. For example, the phone company may have an easement to put up phone lines or poles. The same goes for other utility companies. You may also have an easement if you share a driveway.

The title search also uncovers any *encroachments*. It makes sure that nothing of yours is actually on your neighbor's property, and that nothing of the neighbor's is on your property.

If during the title search, a cloud appears on the horizon, it has to be cleared up. Either the person with the claim can release the debt lien or sign a quit claim deed. A quit claim deed releases any right to the property. Or if there is a record-keeping error, it can be corrected.

> **WHOA!**
>
> ### Partly Cloudy, Chance of Thunderstorms
>
> Someone in the title business must have been a frustrated meteorologist; that would explain all the weather terms. You want a **clear** title. If it's not clear, it has a **cloud** on it, which indicates a problem with the title. For example, any claims made against a property by a person or any tax assessment for payment of a debt could cloud up a title.

What Title Insurance Protects

The title search is intended to uncover any problems, but it is not guaranteed. That's why the lender requires title insurance. There are two types of policies. A *lender's policy* is required by the lender. It protects the lender against any losses if any parties challenge your ownership. (You can think of this type of policy as "cover our butts first.") You can also purchase an *owner's policy* which protects *you* from loss if anyone challenges the title search.

The cost of title insurance will vary depending on the area. You make a single payment up front that is good for the entire time you own the house. Usually the cost of the title search and title insurance are shared by you and the seller. Here sellers pay the bulk of the cost, and you pay a fixed amount. Still you may want to shop around for title insurance. The prices can vary.

Also, some locations don't require title insurance, but use another form of guarantee for the title, such as a title abstract.

The Least You Need to Know

Your lender considers himself a partner in your home, and, to protect his investment, requires you to have several types of insurance.

➤ Your lender will require a certain amount of homeowner's insurance. Don't get the minimum amount. Be sure to get enough to cover the replacement value of the home, plus your possessions.

➤ If you want to save money on your homeowner's policy, don't scrimp on the coverage. Instead, get a higher deductible, shop around among insurers, and ask about any discounts.

➤ At or before the closing, you'll have to show a one-year, paid homeowner's policy. Your lender will also collect insurance money each month to put in an escrow account. When your insurance comes due, the lender will then use this money to pay for the policy renewal.

➤ If you have an FHA loan or a loan with less than 20% down, you'll be required to pay for mortgage insurance. For FHA loans, the cost is a percentage of the loan value and is paid up front, plus a monthly premium. You can finance this fee. For conventional loans, you usually pay for a one-year policy up front, then make monthly payments for the following years.

➤ In some cases, you can cancel your mortgage insurance once you have a certain percentage equity in your home.

➤ Title insurance backs up the title search and protects the lender against losses if a claim does arise. If you have both a lender's and owner's policy, *you're* protected against claims as well. The fees for the title search and title insurance are usually shared between the buyer and seller.

Chapter 19

Having the Home Inspected

In This Chapter

➤ Understanding seller disclosure

➤ Scheduling an inspection

➤ What the inspector checks

➤ Reading the inspection report

➤ Handling any problems

Fear buying a house, moving in, and then finding out the house has termites? Or finding out the roof is ready to cave in? Or turning on the shower only to see black goo ooze out? You probably don't want to relive *The Money Pit*. And while you should look carefully at the house before you make an offer, it is imperative that you have a professional inspector look through the house.

Understanding Seller Disclosure

Recently the laws have changed regarding what the seller must disclose or tell you about a home's problems. The seller must disclose any known defects in the property that affect the value of the home.

Depending on the law in your area, the seller may be required to complete a seller disclosure form. Even if the law does not require this form, you can ask the seller to complete it. Basically, the form asks the seller to disclose any problems with the roof, pests, structure, basement, attic, heating and cooling, electrical system, toxic substances, and other matters. For a discussion of seller disclosure laws and a sample seller disclosure form, see Chapter 22.

Usually, the seller will say that the current price takes into consideration the problems listed on the seller disclosure. Or the seller may provide a certain amount to take care of needed repairs.

Even with a seller disclosure, you should still have a professional inspection done.

Why Get an Inspection?

When you are adding up all the costs associated with buying a home, you may want to skimp on some fees. For example, you may want to ask your Uncle Charlie to take a look at the house. Even though he sells mattresses now, he once built homes and knows a little about home construction.

Not a good idea.

You should hire a professional inspector and make your offer contingent upon a satisfactory inspection. An inspection can help you identify problems before you purchase a home. If there are problems, the inspection can help you negotiate an adjustment in purchase price or get sellers to pay for needed repairs. If the problems are big, the inspection report may enable you to withdraw your offer. If there aren't problems, the inspection will make you feel more secure in your decision to purchase the home.

Scheduling an Inspection

If you have made the offer contingent on an inspection, you usually have a certain time period in which to schedule the inspection. You'll want to do so early on so that you have time to review the findings and make any changes, if necessary.

You can find a good inspector by asking friends and relatives for referrals, by asking your agent, or by looking in the Yellow Pages. You can also contact the American Society of Home Inspectors (ASHI) for a referral. Inspectors affiliated with ASHI have completed a minimum number of home inspections, testing, and training. The address of ASHI is listed in Appendix B.

Ask to see a sample report. By looking over the report, you can tell what the inspector normally checks for and how thoroughly the house will be inspected.

When you are shopping around for an inspector, ask about the inspector's training and background. How long has he been in the business? What certification does he have? (The National Institute of Building Inspectors, NIBI, certifies inspectors and can tell you whether an inspector is certified. Again, the address is in Appendix B.)

Find out the cost for the inspection. You can expect to pay from $200 to $400. You may also have to pay additional fees if you want certain tests done, such as a water test, radon test, or termite certification.

What the Inspector Checks

An inspector does *not* determine the value of the home; that's an appraiser's job. Instead, an inspector evaluates the condition of the property. The inspector visually checks the home and then completes a report.

It's a good idea to accompany the inspector during the inspection. In fact, the inspector will encourage you to do so. If you go along for the inspection, you are in a better position to understand the report. You can also ask questions and you can see how extensively the inspector looks at the house. He should crawl down in the crawlspace, get up on the roof, poke around in the insulation, turn on all the faucets, and more. Expect to spend about two hours for a home inspection.

What the Inspector Should Check

At the minimum, the inspector should visually examine the following:

➤ **Foundation**   Will carefully check for cracks and any separation in the foundation.

➤ **Doors and windows**   Will make sure all the windows and doors open and close properly.

➤ **Roofing, chimney, gutters, vents, and fans**   Will determine whether the gutters drain properly and are in good condition, and whether the roof system needs to be replaced or repaired.

➤ **Plumbing**   Will check to see how well the sinks drain, how strong the water pressure is, whether there are any signs of leaks, and that the water heater is in good condition.

➤ **Electrical system**   Will check the wiring connection to fuses or circuit breakers and groundings. Will also check whether there is proper and safe wiring at outlets and switches.

➤ **Heating and cooling systems**   Will check the condition and operation of the furnace, and note any apparent unsafe conditions. If you buy a house in the winter, the inspector will make a note that the air conditioning was not checked.

➤ **Ceilings, walls, and floors**   Will note any cracks, moisture problems, or significantly uneven floors or walls.

➤ **Insulation and ventilation**

➤ **Septic tanks, wells, or sewer lines**   Usually, you get a separate report on septic and well water because the water must be tested for bacteria.

➤ **Exterior (decks, doors, windows)**   Will check for signs of rot and determine whether the house needs to be repainted or not.

➤ **Property**   Will check the drainage of the yard, garage, fences, paved areas, and other outside facilities.

➤ **Basement and attic**   Will check to see if the basement is wet, and if the basement or attic shows signs of current or past water damage. Is there mold on the walls or attic framing, for instance?

The lender will usually require a termite inspection that the inspector may do and may charge an additional fee for. Usually, the seller pays for the termite inspection on VA loans, while the buyer pays for termite inspections when applying for conventional loans.

In addition to the routine inspection, you can ask for other tests to be performed. Some states *require* these tests. For example, you may want to test for radon, lead paint, asbestos, hazardous waste, and other environmental concerns. You may be charged extra for these tests.

What the Inspector Doesn't Check

The inspector does not check the cosmetic features of the home, such as the carpeting and wall coverings. Also, keep in mind that the inspector does not warrant the home against any problems. He is just reporting on existing problems. Finally, most inspectors are generalists. If they uncover a problem, they may recommend a specialist. For instance, if the electricity is troublesome, the inspector may recommend having an electrician take a look.

What the Inspector Shouldn't Do

During the inspection, the inspector shouldn't tell you what the house is worth. Also, the inspector shouldn't give you advice on whether you should buy the house. Finally, the inspector shouldn't offer to make repairs on the house and shouldn't refer you to someone to make the repairs.

Reading the Inspection Report

After the inspector has flipped on all your light switches, crawled around in your attic, climbed up on the roof, and checked how well all your sinks drain, he will write up an inspection report (see figure on the following page for an example). This report will include general information about your property as well as information about when the inspection took place—for instance, the weather conditions.

Why include the weather conditions? If an inspector inspects during the middle of winter, he may not be able to check the air conditioning. In this case, he may make a note to do so later. Also, the inspector may not be able to check all components due to inclement weather. In some cases, he may make a return trip to fully inspect the house. There is usually a charge for the return trip.

SECURITY HOME INSPECTIONS, INC. - PROPERTY ADDRESS _____ 7

VI. INTERIOR ELECTRICAL SYSTEM

A. SYSTEM __100__ AMPS __240__ VOLTS GENERAL CONDITION: __Satisfactory at time of inspection__

NO. OF CIRCUITS __18__

NOTES: _____

_____

_____

_____

_____

_____

B. COMPONENTS

1. MAIN SERVICE PANEL	breakers	CONDITION:	Satisfactory at time of inspection
2. SUBPANEL(S)	breakers	CONDITION:	Satisfactory at time of inspection
3. MAIN SERVICE WIRE	aluminum	CONDITION:	Satisfactory at time of inspection
4. VISIBLE BRANCH WIRE	copper	CONDITION:	Satisfactory at time of inspection
5. SWITCHES & RECEPTACLES		CONDITION:	SEE NOTES #1 & #2
6. LIGHT FIXTURES		CONDITION:	SEE NOTES #3 & #4
7. DOOR BELL		CONDITION:	NOT APPLICABLE
8. SMOKE DETECTOR(S)		CONDITION:	SEE NOTE #5

NOTES:

1. Receptacle on south wall of kitchen is wired with reverse polarity.
2. G.F.I. receptacle in master bath is wired with reverse polarity. Also, receptacle does not function as a G.F.I. Repairs are needed.
3. Light fixtures in master bath are not installed.
4. Globe is missing from ceiling light in south bedroom.
5. A working smoke detector should be installed on each level.

A sample page from an inspection report.

The report will then cover each element of the home, broken down into categories. The categories and format of the report will vary. An ASHI inspector, for instance, will generally have reporting areas for the basement, crawlspace, slab, central heating, cooling, electrical system, plumbing system, interior structure, attic, doors and windows, garage, exterior structure, grounds, and appliances.

Usually the report includes a description of each system. For example, for an electrical system, the inspector may note the system amps and volts. The inspector may note whether the system is satisfactory, not applicable, or may note a problem.

Handling Any Problems

If the inspection report turns up any problems, which it most likely will, you'll need to decide whether the problem needs to be fixed prior to closing or after you move in. If you had a contingency relating to inspection, you can handle problems in any of the following ways:

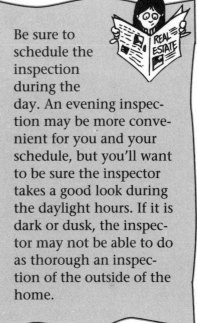

Be sure to schedule the inspection during the day. An evening inspection may be more convenient for you and your schedule, but you'll want to be sure the inspector takes a good look during the daylight hours. If it is dark or dusk, the inspector may not be able to do as thorough an inspection of the outside of the home.

If the problem is minor, you may choose to ignore it. For instance, you probably aren't going to have a big fit if one window screen is missing or if the porch light doesn't work.

If the problem is significant, you'll want to make a response to the inspection (see the "Inspection Amendment" at the end of this chapter for an example of how this is done). In this response, you may ask the seller to renegotiate the price. For example, if you have to pay $6,000 for a new roof, you may ask the seller to lower the price by $6,000 or some percentage of $6,000.

Instead of lowering the price, you may ask the seller to make certain repairs or to set aside money to have repairs done. For example, you may ask the seller to fix the roof or to set aside the $6,000 to have this work done after the closing.

If the problem is of such magnitude that you are reconsidering the purchase, you may be able to withdraw the offer. Usually, you must give the sellers a chance to make the repairs, though.

Generally, you ask sellers to make repairs to items that affect habitability. The seller has the option of making the repairs, or allowing you to withdraw your offer. In some areas, purchase agreements specify an amount of money up to which the seller agrees to make repairs. After that, it is at the buyer's option.

If you have found that the seller or agent has grossly misrepresented the home, you should withdraw the offer.

The Least You Need to Know

Having the home inspected by a professional inspector is a must. You'll want the utmost assurance that the house does not have problems. If it does have problems, you'll want to know about them before the closing.

➤ The seller must disclose any known defects in the home. In some states, the seller is required to complete a seller disclosure form.

➤ When you make a sales offer, be sure to include a contingency for an inspection. You should be sure that you state in the offer that the inspection must meet your satisfaction.

➤ To find an inspector, ask your agent or other friends and relatives for a referral. You can also contact the American Society of Home Inspectors (ASHI).

➤ The inspector should check the foundation, doors, windows, roof, chimney, gutters, plumbing, electrical system, heating and cooling, ceilings, walls, floors, insulation, ventilation, septic tanks, wells, sewer lines, exterior of the house, and property.

➤ After the inspection, the inspector will give you an inspection report. Usually the seller receives a copy of this report as well. If the inspection uncovers problems, you can choose to ignore the problem, ask the seller to renegotiate the price, ask the seller to fix the problem, or in extreme cases, withdraw the offer.

INSPECTION AMENDMENT

(Mark applicable box below)

☐ WAIVER OF INSPECTION(S)
☒ RESPONSE TO INSPECTION REPORT(S)

1. Purchaser (has) (has not) received an Inspection Report from *The Inspection Co*
2. on the property known as *8169 Ashwood Ct*
3. in *Pike* Township, *Marion* County, *Naples*, Indiana,
4. which is legally known as *Lot 131 Crooked Creek Heights*
5. and agrees to: *(circle applicable box)*
6. ☐1 Waive Inspection(s) and rely upon the condition of the property based upon his own examination.
7. ☐2 Accept the property in the condition reported in said Inspection Report(s).
8. ☒ Accept the property provided Seller corrects the following condition(s) on or before _____ 6 _____ (AM) (PM) (Noon) (Midnight)
9. *7/31* , 19 *94* , or within *3* days after *loan approval* , whichever is later,
10. and the Purchaser shall have the right to inspect and accept Seller's repairs (prior to closing) (within _____ 2 _____ days after
11. *notice of completed repairs.*):
12.
13. *① Seller shall put electrical system in good working order to*
14. *meet code - work to be done by licensed electrician.*
15. *② Broken floor of master bathroom shower to be replaced.*
16. *③ Missing shingles on roof to be replaced*
17.
18.
19. The Seller shall respond to this (Waiver Of Inspection) (Response To Inspection Report) on or before _____ 6 _____ (AM) (PM)
20. (Noon) (Midnight) *7/8/94* , 19 _____.
21. After compliance with selected item above, the Purchaser hereby releases the Seller, Brokers, REALTORS, named in said Purchase Agreement
22. dated *7/10/94* from any and all liability relating to any defect, except for latent defect(s)
23. affecting said real estate, which shall survive the closing of the transaction.
24. This Agreement may be executed simultaneously or in two or more counterparts, each of which shall be deemed an original, but all of
25. which together shall constitute one and the same instrument.

26. x *Michael True* *7/15/94* x *Terry True* *7/15/94*
27. PURCHASER SIGNATURE DATE PURCHASE SIGNATURE DATE

28. Seller responds as follows: *(circle applicable box)*
29. ☒ Seller agrees to correct condition(s) contained in Item 3 above.
30. ☐2 Seller is unable or unwilling to make the corrections requested by Purchaser.
31. ☐3 Seller agrees to correct the following condition(s) at Seller's expense (prior to closing the transaction)
32. (within _____ days after _____), whichever is later.
33. *work to be completed no later than 7/25/94*
34.
35.
36.
37.
38. If item #3 is selected, the Purchaser shall respond on or before _____ (AM) (PM) (Noon) (Midnight) _____, 19 _____.
39. This Agreement may be executed simultaneously or in two or more counterparts, each of which shall be deemed an original, but all of which
40. together shall constitute one and the same instrument. Delivery of this document may be accomplished by electronic facsimile reproduction
41. (FAX); if (FAX) delivery is utilized, the original document shall be promptly executed and/or delivered, if requested.

42. x *Richard Wright* *7/16/94* *Sandra Wright* *7/16/94*
43. SELLER SIGNATURE DATE SELLER SIGNATURE DATE

44. ACCEPTED BY PURCHASER:

45.
46. PURCHASER SIGNATURE DATE PURCHASER SIGNATURE DATE

Ⓡ REALTOR®   Approved by and restricted to use by members of the Metropolitan Indianapolis Board Of REALTORS
This is a legally binding contract, if not understood seek legal advice   © MIBOR 1992   (Form No. 230-01/92)   ⌂ EQUAL HOUSING OPPORTUNITY

5-92/P-212A

A response to an inspection report.

**Cross a termite with a praying mantis
and you get a bug that says grace
before eating your house.**

—Unknown

Handling the Closing: Buyer's Point of View

Finally! The big day has arrived. The last step in buying a home is the closing. At the closing, you'll sign document after document after document, turn over all your money, then get the much-anticipated keys to your new house. This chapter tells you what to expect at closing.

What Has to Happen Before the Closing

Getting to the closing is a kind of race. You have to pass over several hurdles before you cross the finish line. Here are the hurdles you can expect to jump.

Don't wait until the last minute to get insurance. Once the closing is approaching, you may be so excited that you'll sign up with the first insurance company available. It makes more sense to shop around and get several quotes so that you get the best deal.

First, you must obtain financing. This topic is the subject of Part III. Unless you are paying cash for the house, you have to have the backing from your lender. Backing comes in the form of a commitment letter from the lender. Once you receive this commitment letter, you have the money to buy the house. You've jumped hurdle one.

Second, the lender will require that you have a homeowner's insurance policy on the house. Before the closing you'll need to arrange for insurance. Usually, you must show a one-year paid policy. Insurance is covered in Chapter 18.

Third, there may be other requirements that you or the seller must meet before the closing. For instance, if you are getting an FHA loan, the lender may require certain repairs to be made before the loan is closed. Or if your home lies in a flood plain, you may be required to get flood insurance. Any other requirements of the lender will be spelled out in the commitment letter.

The final two things that must be done—deciding how to hold the title and having the final walk-through—are described here.

Who Owns the House?

As part of the closing, you'll be asked how you want to "hold the title." An appropriate response is not: "In my hands." Holding the title refers to the ownership. Do you own the house alone? Do you own it with a partner? How is the property shared? You spell out the ownership by selecting how to hold the title. Here are the most common ways:

Sole ownership   You are the only owner. If you are buying the house alone, you'll probably select this.

Tenancy by the entirety   Available for married couples only. With this type of ownership, both owners have to agree before the house can be sold or refinanced. If one spouse dies, the other automatically gets the house without going through probate (the legal process of settling a will).

Joint tenancy   Used when two or more people purchase a house. The owners agree that during their lifetimes, any of the owners can sell their interest to whomever they want without any type of approval from the others. When one owner dies, the surviving owner automatically gets the deceased's share.

Tenancy in common   The property is owned jointly. If one owner dies, his or her share goes to his or her heirs.

The Final Walk-Through

As part of the contract, you may stipulate that you want a final walk-through. Final walk-throughs are a good idea to ensure that the property is in the same condition it was in when you made the offer on the home. You may want to make sure that all the systems are in working order and that no damage has been done to the house.

As part of the purchase agreement, the seller agrees to turn the property over in the same condition as it was. If the house has been inspected and you have removed the inspection contingency, then you have agreed you are satisfied with the property. A final walk-through is just to be sure that there have been no major changes since that time. If there have been, the transaction can be opened up for renegotiation.

If you want a final walk-through, be sure to say so in the contract. You should schedule the walk-through before the closing. Give yourself enough time to settle any problems that pop up. For instance, if you schedule the walk-through the morning of the closing and find problems, you won't have any time to resolve them.

During the final walk-through, check the major systems (electrical, plumbing, and so on) and check the appearance of the house.

Next, check the personal property in the house. Is property that is supposed to be there really there? For example, if you asked the sellers to leave the washer and dryer as part of the deal, are the washer and dryer still there? Are the curtains and other floor coverings still there? Is property that is supposed to be gone truly gone? For example, if the sellers had an old refrigerator in the basement that you wanted them to take with them, did they take it? Or did they leave it for you to haul out? Any disputes about personal property should be taken care of before you close.

Finally, make sure the sellers are out of the house (or ready to be out). When you take possession of a home depends on local customs.

235

In many places, the seller must be out before closing. In some places the seller must move out a week after closing. Also, in some special cases, the seller may have arranged to remain in the house and pay you rent after closing.

If the seller is supposed to be out before closing and is not out when you go through the final walk-through, you may have a problem. Packing up and moving an entire houseful of possessions isn't an afternoon's task. If you are going through the home and the sellers show no signs of budging, you are looking at trouble. You should insist the sellers are out before you close.

If the house is in the shape you expect and the sellers and all their worldly goods are moved out, you are ready to close.

What You Pay at Closing

Closing on a house can be exciting, because at the end of the proceedings you'll have the keys to your new home. You'll also have an empty pocketbook or wallet, because at the closing you'll be expected to have the money for your down payment and all the closing costs.

Don't Forget the Down Payment

At the closing, you'll need to pay the balance of the down payment on the house. The down payment amount will vary depending on the purchase price and the amount you are putting down. If you are buying a $100,000 home and putting 10% down, you must have $10,000 for the down payment. Keep in mind that your earnest money will be applied toward the down payment, in most cases. So if you gave the sellers $1,000 in earnest money, you'll need to come up with the remaining $9,000 for the down payment.

Closing Costs

In addition to the down payment, you'll have to pay closing costs. When you apply for the loan, the lender is required by law to give you a Truth-in-Lending estimate of your closing costs. The lender will base this estimate on local practice as well as your sales agreement with the seller.

The following sections list the fees you can expect to pay at closing. Keep in mind that some closing costs may be paid by the seller, and some will be paid *before* closing. For example, you probably paid a loan application fee, which is considered a closing cost. This fee, though, is paid at the time of application. You'll see these closing costs listed as *POC*, or *paid outside of closing*, on the settlement total.

Also, FHA loans and VA loans have different restrictions on what the buyers and sellers are allowed to pay.

Items Payable in Connection with the Loan

Points   Depending on the loan package you selected, you may have to pay points. One point is equal to one percent of the loan amount. Points are usually tax deductible in the year paid. In some cases, the seller may agree to pay points.

Loan origination fee   A loan origination fee is similar to a point; it is usually one percent of the loan amount. Loan origination fees are not tax deductible. In some agreements, the seller may pay this fee.

Assumption fee   If you are assuming a mortgage, you may have to pay an assumption fee.

Application fee   When you apply for the loan, you may be charged an application fee. This fee may run anywhere up to $350, and is paid at the time of application.

Credit report   At the time of application, you may be asked to pay the fee for checking your credit history. This fee can run from $40 to $60 and is POC. Sometimes this fee is included as part of the application fee.

Appraisal fee   Paid at application, this fee runs from $225 to $300.

House inspection   To have the home inspected, you'll most likely hire a professional inspector. This fee can run from $225 to $275 and is usually paid before closing (at the time of the inspection). A pest inspection will be required by the lender. You or the seller may have to pay this fee.

Processing fees   The lender may charge you various fees for processing the loan. These fees may include a mail or delivery fee, a document preparation fee, an underwriting fee, and other fees. You can expect to pay from $100 to $400 when all these fees are totaled.

Items Required by the Lender to Be Paid in Advance

Prepaid interest Depending on when you close on your house, you may have to prepay the interest for the month. See the sidebar on the next page to understand how house payments are made and why the interest is due.

Mortgage insurance If your loan requires mortgage insurance, you'll be required to pay the required amount at the time of closing. Mortgage insurance is covered in Chapter 18.

Insurance You'll be expected to have a one-year prepaid policy on your home. You usually pay this POC and show the receipt.

Reserves Deposited with the Lender

Insurance At the time of closing, you'll need to pay a few months' insurance payments for the escrow account. See the section "Escrow Accounts—Forced Payments," later in this chapter.

Mortgage insurance You may have to pay a few months' worth of mortgage insurance, if it is required by your lender.

Property taxes You may have to set aside money for the tax escrow. You may also have to pay for a tax service contract.

Title Charges

Settlement fee A fee may be charged for the services of the settlement company. This fee can run from $150 to $400.

Attorney If you have hired an attorney, you'll be responsible for the attorney's fees. Also, sometimes the lender charges you an attorney's fee for their attorney.

Title search and insurance The lender will require a title search and title insurance. Expect to be charged $170 to $300. Which party pays which fees varies depending on local custom. For example, in Indiana, the seller pays the major portion of this combined fee, and the buyer pays around $100. This charge may be payable by either the buyer or the seller.

Government Recording and Transfer Charges

Recording fees You may be charged a fee for recording the deed and the mortgage. This fee can run from $25 to $75.

Transfer charges Depending on the location, some local and state governments charge transfer taxes. You may have to pay county, city, and/or state tax stamps.

Additional Settlement Charges

Survey The lender requires an unstaked survey to see that there are no encroachments on your property.

Condo and Co-op fees You may be charged a move-in fee or association transfer fees.

Taxes You may owe money for tax prorations, or the seller may pay you money on the proration, depending on how taxes are paid. For example, if the sellers have prepaid taxes for six months, but lived in the house for only three months, they may ask for the fee to be prorated and for you to pay the three month's worth. Any prorations should be spelled out in the contract.

> **WHOA!** **When is My House Payment Due?**
>
> Remember, the way house payments are made is different from the way rent payments are made. You pay your house payment *in arrears*. That means your September 1st payment pays for the month of *August*—not September. When you close, you'll have to prepay for the remainder of the month that you close in. Then you'll skip a month and start paying on the house the following month. The calendar on the next page illustrates the way your first two house payments will probably be made.

AUGUST 1994						
SUN	**MON**	**TUES**	**WED**	**THURS**	**FRI**	**SAT**
	1	2	3	4	5	6
7	8	9	10	11	12	13
14	15 Closing Prepay	16	17	18	19	20
21	22	23	24	25	26	27
28	29	30	31			

SEPTEMBER 1994						
SUN	**MON**	**TUES**	**WED**	**THURS**	**FRI**	**SAT**
				1	2	3
4	5	6	7	8	9	10
11	12	13	14	15	16	17
18	19	20	21	22	23	24
25	26	27	28	29	30	

OCTOBER 1994						
SUN	**MON**	**TUES**	**WED**	**THURS**	**FRI**	**SAT**
						1 First Payment

Understanding when house payments are due.

Escrow Accounts—Forced Payments

Your lender wants to make sure that you pay your property taxes and insurance. To be sure you have the money to do so, the lender will usually require you to prepay your insurance a year in advance. For taxes and insurance, the lender will take the total bill and divide by 12 to get a monthly amount due for each. Then the lender will usually collect a few months' fees for taxes and insurance. (The number of months will vary, depending on when you close.) This money is put aside in an escrow account.

Each month when you make a payment, you pay principal and interest, plus 1/12 of your bill for taxes and insurance. The tax and insurance money is put into your escrow account. When the tax bill or insurance bill comes due, the lender pays it using the money in your escrow account.

Some buyers prefer to have the lender take care of the tax and insurance bills. But keep in mind that your money sits in the escrow account but doesn't earn interest. Because the account doesn't pay interest, there's been some controversy over the use of escrow accounts. You may see changes in the future.

The Total Comes to . . .

Before the actual closing, the lender will tell your agent (who in turn will tell you) the precise amount of money you must bring to closing. You have the right to review the settlement charges one business day before the closing. You often will not get much lead time with the "final" figures, but refusing to close only hurts the buyers and sellers. The settlement statement (shown in the next section) explains exactly which fees are paid by whom.

You'll need to bring a cashier's or certified check for the balance of the down payment and closing costs. It's a good idea to have the check made out to yourself. You can then endorse the check at the closing.

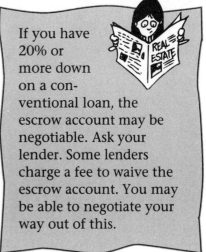

If you close on August 15, you have to prepay interest for the remaining days in August (16–31, or 16 days). The payment for September would be due October 1 and would pay for September 1 through 30. In essence, you skip a payment for September.

If you have 20% or more down on a conventional loan, the escrow account may be negotiable. Ask your lender. Some lenders charge a fee to waive the escrow account. You may be able to negotiate your way out of this.

What Happens at Closing

You can think of a closing as an invitation to a big event. Here are the juicy details:

Keep in mind that even if you get a fixed-rate mortgage, your payments can still go up. How? Taxes or insurance fees can be raised. If you don't have enough money in escrow to cover the new payment, you'll have to pay back any amount not covered, plus pay an increased amount, so that when the next tax bill comes due there will be enough.

Event: Depending on the location, closing can be referred to as *closing, settlement day,* whatever. This is the big day, the final step in buying a home.

Guests: Depending on local customs, different people may attend the closing. *You* definitely must attend. In addition, you may expect the sellers, sellers' agent, your agent, lender, attorneys, and a closing agent, depending on the circumstances.

When: After you receive your commitment letter for your loan or notice of your approval (which may be a phone call), you can set the date for the closing.

Where: Again, the location for closing depends on local practice. The closing may be held at the title company, attorney's office, escrow company, lending institute, or county courthouse.

Occasion: And finally, the reason for the closing: to sign papers and exchange money.

What You Should Bring to the Big Event

When you are preparing to attend the closing, you should expect to bring a cashier's check, as described in the section "The Total Comes To …," earlier in this chapter. You'll also need to bring a homeowner's insurance policy and one-year prepaid receipt as well as any other documentation required by the lender.

If you want, you can have your attorney attend with you. Your attorney can review and advise you on the documents you'll sign.

Signed, Sealed, and Delivered

One of the main purposes of the closing is to review and sign all the appropriate documents. You should carefully look over each document you are asked to sign before signing. If you notice any discrepancies, you should bring them to the attention of your agent, the lender, and the closing agent. You should also get a copy of every document.

During the closing, you can expect to review the following documents:

Truth-in-Lending statement   The lender is required by law to give you a copy of this document within three days of your loan application. This document will tell you the true APR, terms of the loan, finance charge, amount financed, and total payments required. Sometimes at application, the lender will give you an estimate. If the APR is different from the estimate given, the lender will give you another form at closing listing the true APR.

Note   This is your promise to pay and the terms of your payment. The document includes the terms of the loan, date on which your payments must be made, location where sent, penalties assessed, and other loan information.

Mortgage, or deed of trust   This document is the lien against your house held by the lender. This lien gives the lender claim to your property if you default. The document restates the information in the mortgage note.

Affidavits   Certain affidavits may be required by state law, the lender, or the secondary market agency. For instance, you may have to sign an affidavit stating that you'll use the property as your primary residence.

If you have locked in your rate, you should be sure to close before your lock expires. Don't let the lender or sellers drag out the closing, especially if rates have gone up. If rates have gone down, you may want to delay. Also, if your commitment expires on the 30th of the month, don't wait until the last day to close.

There generally isn't time to read the documents entirely at closing. If you want to read them, ask to have them prepared and ready for you a day in advance. This is what attorneys do.

If the lender is selling your mortgage, the lender should give you a name and phone number to call if you have trouble with your loan. If you have problems and the lender isn't involved anymore, you'll want to know who to contact.

Deed   The seller turns over property by means of a warranty deed. Sellers attest that they have not taken any new loans on the property. The deed should be properly signed and notarized. The transfer of the deed will be recorded at the registry of deeds or clerk's office.

IRS forms   You'll be asked to sign any forms required by the IRS for the sale or purchase of a home.

Disclosure statements   If the lender plans on selling your loan to the secondary market, the lender must disclose this information. In this case, you may be asked to sign a disclosure statement acknowledging that you received this information.

Compliance agreement   This document says you'll agree to re-sign documents if any error is made.

Sanity documents   You'll also be asked to sign other documents that state you have not been declared mentally incompetent, you are still employed at the same place, you are over 18, and so on.

Exchanging Money

In addition to signing documents, you'll exchange money. You'll pay the amount you owe, and the sellers will receive the amount they are due. The agent will receive his commission, and the loan company will receive its money.

To sort out who pays what and who gets what, you receive the RESPA HUD-1 statement (see the following figure), which breaks down the cost involved.

A.SETTLEMENT STATEMENT	U.S.DEPARTMENT OF HOUSING AND URBAN DEVELOPMENT		

ENTERPRISE TITLE
8440 Woodfield Crossing, #100
Indianapolis, IN 46240

OMB No. 2502-0265

B. TYPE OF LOAN

1. ☐ FHA 2. ☐ FmHA 3. ☒ CONV.UNINS. 4. ☐ VA 5. ☐ CONV.INS.

6. File Number:	7. Loan Number:	8. Mortgage Insurance Case Number:

C. NOTE: This form is furnished to give you a statement of actual settlement costs. Amounts paid to and by the settlement agent are shown. Items marked "(p.o.c)" were paid outside the closing; they are shown here for informational purposes and are not included in the totals.

D.NAME AND ADDRESS OF BORROWER:	E. NAME AND ADDRESS OF SELLER/TAX I.D.No.:	F. NAME AND ADDRESS OF LENDER:

G.PROPERTY LOCATION:	H.SETTLEMENT AGENT: Enterprise Title Services of Indiana Inc.

	PLACE OF SETTLEMENT: 8440 Woodfield Crossing, #100 Indianapolis, IN 46240	I.SETTLEMENT DATE: 07/18/94

J. SUMMARY OF BORROWER'S TRANSACTION		K. SUMMARY OF SELLER'S TRANSACTION	
100. GROSS AMOUNT DUE FROM BORROWER:		**400. GROSS AMOUNT DUE TO SELLER:**	
101. Contract Sales Price	124,900.00	401. Contract Sales Price	124,900.00
102. Personal property		402. Personal property	
103. Settlement charges to borrower (line 1400)	1,462.78	403.	
104.		404.	
105.		405.	
Adjustments for items paid by seller in advance		Adjustments for items paid by seller in advance	
106. City/town taxes to		406. City/town taxes to	
107. County taxes to		407. County taxes to	
108. Assessments to		408. Assessments to	
109.		409.	
110.		410.	
111.		411.	
112.		412.	
120. GROSS AMOUNT DUE FROM BORROWER	126,362.78	420. GROSS AMOUNT DUE TO SELLER	124,900.00
200. AMOUNTS PAID BY OR IN BEHALF OF BORROWER:		**500. REDUCTIONS IN AMOUNT DUE TO SELLER:**	
201. Deposit or earnest money	1,000.00	501. Excess deposit (see instructions)	
202. Principal amount of new loan(s)	91,900.00	502. Settlement charges to seller (line 1400)	9,339.00
203. Existing loan(s) taken subject to		503. Existing loan(s) taken subject to	
204. CUSTOMER DEPOSIT	1,319.00	504. Payoff of first mortgage loan 1st IND	80,209.43
205.		505. Payoff of second mortgage loan	
206.		506.	
207.		507.	
208.		508.	
209.		509.	
Adjustments for items unpaid by seller		Adjustments for items unpaid by seller	
210. City/town taxes to		510. City/town taxes to	
211. County taxes to		511. County taxes to	
212. Assessments to		512. Assessments to	
213.		513.	
214. NOVEMBER 1994 TAXES	630.65	514. NOVEMBER 1994 TAXES	630.65
215.		515.	
216.		516.	
217.		517.	
218.		518.	
219.		519.	
220. TOTAL PAID BY/FOR BORROWER	94,849.65	520. TOTAL REDUCTION AMOUNT DUE SELLER	90,179.08
300. CASH AT SETTLEMENT FROM/TO BORROWER		**600. CASH AT SETTLEMENT TO/FROM SELLER**	
301. Gross amount due from borrower (line 120)	126,362.78	601. Gross amount due to seller (line 420)	124,900.00
302. Less amounts paid by/for borrower (line 220)	94,849.65	602. Less reductions in amount due seller (line 520)	90,179.08
303. CASH (☒FROM) (☐TO) BORROWER	31,513.13	603. CASH (☒TO) (☐FROM) SELLER	34,720.92

Previous edition is obsolete.

HUD-1 (8-87)
RESPA, HB 4305.2

The front side of the HUD-1 statement.

-2-

L. SETTLEMENT CHARGES		PAID FROM BORROWER'S FUNDS AT SETTLEMENT	PAID FROM SELLER'S FUNDS AT SETTLEMENT
700. TOTAL SALES/BROKER'S COMMISSION			
based on price $ 124,900.00 @ 7.00 %= 8,743.00			
Division of Commission (line 700) as follows:			
701. $ 4,371.50 to			
702. $ 4,371.50 to			
703. Commission paid at Settlement			8,743.00
704.			
800. ITEMS PAYABLE IN CONNECTION WITH LOAN			
801. Loan Origination Fee %			
802. Loan Discount %			
803. Appraisal Fee to		275.00	
804. Credit Report to		108.00	
805. Lenders Inspection Fee			
806. Mortgage Insurance Application Fee to			
807. Assumption Fee			
808. PROCESSING FEE		125.00	
809. TAX/INS. VERIFICATIO		90.00	
810.			
811. MORTGAGE BROKERAGE FEE 1838.00			
900. ITEMS REQUIRED BY LENDER TO BE PAID IN ADVANCE			
901. Interest from 07/18/94 to 08/01/94 @$ 20.771918 /day		290.78	
902. Mortgage Insurance Premium for months to			
903. Hazard Insurance Premium for 1 years to STANDARD MUTUAL $321.00			
904. Flood Insurance Premium for years to			
905.			
1000. RESERVES DEPOSITED WITH LENDER			
1001. Hazard Insurance months @$ per month			
1002. Mortgage Insurance months @$ per month			
1003. City property taxes months @$ per month			
1004. County property taxes months @$ per month			
1005. Annual assessments months @$ per month			
1006. Flood insurance months @$ per month			
1007. months @$ per month			
1008. months @$ per month			
1100. TITLE CHARGES			
1101. Settlement or closing fee to ENTERPRISE TITLE		240.00	
1102. Abstract or title search to			
1103. Title examination to			
1104. Title insurance binder to			
1105. Document preparation to			
1106. Notary fees to			
1107. Attorney's fees to MICHAEL J. CURRY			35.00
(includes above items numbers:)			
1108. Title insurance to ENTERPRISE TITLE		95.00	550.00
(includes above items numbers:)			
1109. Lender's coverage $ 124,900.00 95.00			
1110. Owner's coverage $ 91,900.00 550.00			
1111. EXPRESS/PO ENTERPRISE TITLE			11.00
1112.			
1113.			
1200. GOVERNMENT RECORDING AND TRANSFER CHARGES			
1201. Recording fees: Deed $ 7.00 Mortgage $ 16.00 :Releases $		23.00	
1202. City/county tax stamps: Deed $:Mortgage $			
1203. State tax/stamps: Deed $:Mortgage $			
1204. DISCLOSURE FEE MARION COUNTY AUDITOR		5.00	
1205. MORTGAGE EXEMPTION MARION COUNTY AUDITOR		1.00	
1300. ADDITIONAL SETTLEMENT CHARGES			
1301. Survey to HAHN & ASSOCIATES		110.00	
1302. Pest inspection to			
1303.			
1304. SETTLEMENT TO NBDMC		100.00	
1305.			
1400. TOTAL SETTLEMENT CHARGES (enter on lines 103,Sect J and 502,Sect K)		1,462.78	9,339.00

I have carefully reviewed the HUD-1 Settlement Statement and to the best of my knowledge and belief it is a true and accurate statement of all receipts and disbursements made on my account or by me in this transaction. I further certify that I have received a copy of the HUD-1 Settlement Statement.

Marion E. Ayers   Marion L. Bugh

Borrowers Elizabeth Ayers Lathrop   Sellers Martha O. Bugh

The HUD-1 Settlement Statement which I have prepared is a true and accurate account of this transaction. I have caused or will cause the funds to be disbursed in accordance with this statement.

07/18/94

Settlement Agent Sarah Gregory   Date

Warning: It is a crime to knowingly make false statements to the United States on this or any similar form. Penalties upon conviction can include a fine and imprisonment. For details see: Title 18 U.S. Code Section 1001 and Section 1010.

The reverse side of the HUD-1 statement.

Side 1: The Totals

The front side of this statement lists the buyer's name and address, seller's name and address, lender's name and address, property location, settlement agent, place, and date.

The form is then split into two columns. The first column lists the money due from you (the buyer)—the sales price and the closing costs. Then the monies you have already paid and the monies being paid by someone else (for instance, the seller) are listed. Your credits are subtracted from the amount due to get the total due at closing.

The second column summarizes the seller's transactions and lists the sales price due to the seller as well as any reductions. For instance, your earnest money will be listed as a reduction as well as any closing costs paid for by the seller. The total amount due to the seller is listed on the bottom.

Side 2: The Closing Costs

The second side of the HUD-1 statement breaks down the closing costs. The first column lists the appropriate costs. Then there are two columns—one for you and one for the seller. If the fee is in your column, you owe the money. If the fee is in the seller's column, he owes the money. If the fee isn't due it isn't listed, and if the fee was paid before closing you'll see POC noted. Remember, POC stands for *paid outside of closing.*

The total closing costs for you and the seller are listed at the bottom of the form.

The Passing of the Keys

After all the documents have been signed and all the money exchanged, you are finally the proud owner of the home. The seller should give you all keys to the house, and you are ready to take possession. Congratulations!

Handling Problems

The closing is a hectic time for all involved. The seller is getting ready to move. The lender has to organize all the appropriate paperwork for the loan package. The settlement company has to be sure the event is orchestrated perfectly. You have to gather your money. Problems, both minor and major, can occur. This section describes some problems you might encounter.

Walk-Through Problems

If you have a final walk-through and find a problem, you'll need to decide how to handle it. If the problem is a minor one, you may decide to ignore it. If the problem is major, your course of action will depend on whether or not it was disclosed at the time of the sale. If the seller told you that the basement leaks, and you walk through and see water, you don't have much recourse. If the seller didn't tell you the basement leaks, and it is flooded, you should call your agent and seek to have the problem fixed. You may have legal recourse.

Money Problems

With all the number crunching, you may find that sometimes the numbers don't add up. For example, you may owe more than you originally thought. The lender should have prepared you for the total closing costs at the time of application; you should have received a written estimate. If that estimate is wildly incorrect, you can complain, but you may have to pay anyway. Remember that when you applied for the loan, you agreed to pay certain charges.

Be sure to get any mailbox keys or garage door openers. The seller may forget these items, but you'll wonder how *you* could have, when you need to pick up your mail or park your car.

There shouldn't be any disputes about what the seller is required to pay, because this information should be spelled out in the sales contract. If there are disputes, your agent may handle them, or you may need to have your attorney get involved.

Loan Problems

For the closing to take place, you need the loan package—the documents that spell out the terms of the loan. Without these documents, you cannot close on the house. If the documents are late, the lender may be able to send them by courier or overnight express. Or you may have to postpone the closing a day or two.

If there is disagreement about documents, you need to clear up any inaccuracies before the closing. For example, if the loan documents say you are paying 8.75% interest, but you had agreed to pay 8.5 percent interest and can prove that, the error must be corrected.

You don't close on a house very often, so the charges may seem confusing. Your agent is much more familiar with this part of the transaction. Be sure that he goes over the final charges in advance and agrees with them.

Title Problems

Remember that the title is your evidence that you own the house. To be sure the seller has the right to grant that title freely, a title search has been conducted and you have been required to take out title insurance. If a title problem pops up before the closing, it must be cleared up before you close.

Moving In!

At the end of the entire home-buying process, you may find yourself exhausted. So much has to be done before you get your dream house. So many problems, big and small, can make the entire process tense. Your satisfaction will come when you can finally move in. The dream of owning a home is then yours! Here are a few tips on getting ready for the move:

Don't take everything with you. Have a garage sale or give items away to charity. Moving is a great time to get rid of possessions you don't need or don't use.

Start saving newspapers and boxes as soon as you know that you'll be moving. You can use them when you pack your stuff.

If possible, do your redecorating before you move in. Painting or wallpapering a room that is full of furniture is more difficult than painting or wallpapering an empty room.

Put the utilities in your name. You should contact the phone company, gas company, electric company, water company, garbage collection company, recycling company, and any other utilities or services to put them in your name. Likewise, discontinue the utilities at your old residence.

Fill out a change-of-address card. Be sure to let the post office know your new address, and to send address-change postcards to friends, family, businesses, magazines, etc.

Meet the neighbors. As you move in, your neighbors are probably going to see the moving trucks and be curious. Now is a great time to say hello and get to know your new neighbors.

Start a house file. In this file, keep all the documents pertaining to the purchase of your home. You can deduct the interest paid as well as property taxes, so you'll want to keep a record for tax purposes. In some cases, you can deduct moving expenses. Also, keep a record of home improvements.

The Least You Need to Know

Closing on the house is the final step in purchasing a home. At this event, you sign the appropriate documents, exchange money, and get the keys to your new home.

➤ Before the closing, you need to have received loan approval, paid for a one-year insurance policy, and taken care of any other requirements spelled out in the commitment letter.

➤ If you want, you can do a final walk-through of the house to make sure it is in the same condition as when you made the offer. If you want a final walk-through, be sure to put it in the contract.

➤ At the closing, you must pay the remaining amount of the down payment (the down payment minus your earnest money). You should also be prepared to pay closing costs. You should have received an estimate of closing costs after application. Before closing, the lender will call and tell you the exact amount you need to bring. Bring a cashier's or certified check.

➤ The HUD-1 statement lists all the closing costs as well as which party is responsible for paying them.

➤ The closing is scheduled after you receive your loan commitment. It may be held at a title company, attorney's office, county courthouse, escrow company, or someplace else, depending on local custom.

➤ At the closing, you can expect to sign the mortgage note, the mortgage, affidavits, disclosures, and any other forms required by the lender.

**Home is the place where, when you go there,
They have to take you in.**

—Robert Frost

Part V
Sell Your House

*There are some people who buy one house and never leave. They never have to worry about the prospect of selling because they never intend to sell. Other people **think** they won't move, but they do. In fact, most people stay in their homes an average of five to seven years. That means that just when you finish all your remodeling projects, just when the house is exactly the way you want it to be, it's time to move on. A word of caution on those remodeling projects, though—be careful not to make your house look too eccentric. Remember, beauty **is** in the eye of the beholder.*

Chapter 21

Deciding To Sell Your Home

In This Chapter
➤ Understanding why you want to sell
➤ Timing the sale
➤ Understanding the costs involved in selling your home
➤ Knowing what to expect

Those of you reading this section have probably already endured the joys of being a homebuyer and a homeowner; now you're preparing for the delights available only to the home *seller*. Dozens of muddy-footed strangers trudging through your home, criticizing your wallpaper, your bathrooms, your wedding portrait. Weeks spent cleaning, polishing, repairing, till the house looks so good you may wonder why you're moving.

Why *are* you moving, anyway? Are you tired of standing in line outside the one bathroom, waiting for your turn to shower and shave every morning? Tired of hearing your teenage daughter complain about having to share a bedroom with her four-year-old brother? Or maybe you love your current residence but are being transferred to a new city and *must* move.

No matter what the reason, you have decided to sell your house. Unfortunately, you can't just stick a FOR SALE sign in the yard and hope for the best. Selling a home takes a lot of preparation. This chapter helps with the initial decision: Do you really want to sell?

Why Do You Want to Sell?

Before you decide to put that for-sale sign up and move on, you should take a careful look at *why* you want to move. It's easy to put your house on the market for the wrong reason. To avoid making a mistake, ask yourself why you want to sell.

If you have to move because of your job, you may not have to look into your motivation much further than that simple reason. If you are moving simply because you want a new house, that may not be a good enough reason. *Why* do you want a new house?

Likes, Dislikes, Wishes, and Wants

Before you decide to pack up and move to a new house, you want to be sure you aren't packing up your troubles and moving them with you. Maybe it's really your furniture that you hate. Maybe you love the house, but just need a few changes. It's a good idea to analyze what you like and dislike about your house.

What do you dislike about the house? If you're frustrated with your home, you can probably easily make a list of what you dislike. For example, suppose that it's July 1, 104°F outside, and you don't have central air conditioning. You may hate the house because it's hot.

After you make a list of what you don't like, look over your list and then note whether you can change any of the dislikes into likes. For example, if you could change the house, what would be different? Would you have more bedrooms? Central air? A bigger yard?

Some changes aren't possible. If you hate the location of the house, you simply cannot change that. If changes are possible—for instance, you can always add central air—consider the cost.

Next make a list of what you like about the house. Perhaps it has a nice view or you like the neighborhood. Maybe the house has built-in cabinets that you enjoy. Perhaps you like more than you think.

Once you have a good idea of what you like and dislike, you can take a better look at why you want to move. If you love the location, but simply need more room, you may want to add on a room rather than move. Or maybe you just need some redecorating or new furniture.

On the other hand, if the house can't be redone to suit your needs, you'll know you really do want to move. You'll also have a better understanding of what to look for in your next home.

You can use your list of likes and dislikes when you are shopping for a new home. Defining your dream home is covered in Chapter 5.

What Do You Hope to Gain?

In addition to reviewing the home's pluses and minuses, ask yourself what you hope to gain by moving. You may answer: a bigger home, more money, fewer commitments. Knowing what you hope to gain can help you plan your strategy.

Ask yourself how realistic your goals are. For example, suppose that it is currently a hot market for selling homes and you want to sell now so that you can make a profit. Making money is the primary reason you are selling. In this case, you'll want to keep in mind that you are still going to need someplace to live. If you sell in a seller's market, you'll most likely also have to buy in a seller's market. Will you really gain anything? Also, you'll want to consider the time, energy, and money involved in selling. Is the gain worth the pain? (The section "What Costs Are Involved?," later in this chapter, discusses the costs involved in selling a home.)

As another example, suppose that you have a large house, your children are grown and moved out, and you are retiring. You want to sell your house and buy a condominium so that you do not have the maintenance and expensive upkeep of a large home. You want to sell your house to another family that will enjoy the pleasures of your home. Your motivation here is a release from current commitments.

If you can verbalize your reasons, you can better plan when to sell and what is important when you do sell.

Timing the Sale

Timing the sale of your home depends on many factors. First you have to make up your mind that you are ready to sell. Then, in most cases, you have to coordinate the sale of your current home with the purchase of a new residence. This section discusses these timing issues.

When Is the Best Time to Sell?

There are no pat answers for this question. The best time to sell is when you are ready to sell. Many things can affect your readiness to sell.

One is your job. If you are being transferred, you may want to put your house on the market right away. If you have just been promoted and received a pay increase, you may be able to move up to a more expensive home. If you are retiring, you may be ready to sell the family home and retire to a home more suited to your needs.

Another thing that can affect readiness is your family situation. If you live in a two-bedroom house and are about to have your second child, you may be ready to move to a bigger home. If you are divorcing, you may want to sell the house. If you are taking in an elderly parent, you may be ready to look for a more accommodating house. If your last child has just moved out, you may not need the big four-bedroom home and may be ready for a smaller house.

The economy is another factor that can determine how ready you are to move. For example, if interest rates are sky high, you may have to stay in your current home, regardless of whether it meets your needs. If interest rates are low, you may want to take advantage of the situation and trade up to a more expensive home, as an alternative to refinancing.

Another good time to make a move up is in a buyer's market. You may have to sell your present house at a lower price, but you'll be in a stronger position to buy a more expensive house.

Only you can determine how ready you are to move. And when you are ready to move, you are ready to sell.

Buying Your Next Home

Timing the sale of your home with the purchase of a new home can be tricky. Should you buy first and then sell? Or should you buy and sell at the same time? Or should you sell and then buy? Each of these has its strengths and weaknesses.

Buy First

If you find your next house first and then purchase it, you know you have somewhere to live. You don't have to worry about being forced to find a house after you sell yours.

On the other hand, this strategy is risky. You don't want to end up with two houses and two mortgage payments, which could happen. To avoid doubling up on the mortgages, you can make the purchase of your new house contingent upon the sale of your existing house. Keep in mind that sellers don't usually like offers with this contingency. They don't know anything about your house. What if it is a dump and you never get rid of it? They may not want to tie up their property while yours is on the market. They may reject your offer.

Or the sellers may limit your contingency. For example, they may continue to keep their house on the market. If they get another offer, you have the right to remove your contingency (and buy the house) or withdraw your offer.

Also, this strategy puts pressure on you to sell. You may accept an offer that you wouldn't have if you weren't under the gun.

Buy and Sell Together

Most people put their home on the market and begin looking for a new house at the same time. This strategy could time out perfectly; you could close on your current home one day, and your new home the next day.

Sell First

Many sellers choose to sell their home first. Doing so puts them in a strong bargaining position. First, they don't have to include a contingency for selling their home. Second, they know how much money they have made (or lost) from the sale of their first home.

The danger in this strategy is that you'll end up with nowhere to live. If your new buyers want in and you haven't found a house, you may end up living in an apartment or with relatives for awhile.

259

What Costs Are Involved?

When you sell something, you usually focus on what you get. You have something to offer, and a buyer gives you something for that item. You may forget that you have to give something to get something. That is, selling a house is an involved process, and there are many costs involved in selling:

Repair expenses. As you get your home ready, you may find that certain repairs need to be made. You can do the repairs yourself or you can hire someone to complete them. Deciding which repairs to make is the topic of Chapter 22. Even if you think the house is in perfect condition, the buyer is most likely going to have your home professionally inspected. If the inspection report turns up problems, you may have to pay for repairs or lower the sales price.

Sales commission. If you list your house with an agent, you pay for the agent's commission, usually seven percent of the sales price. Negotiating commissions and selecting an agent is covered in Chapter 23. If you sell the home yourself, you don't pay the commission. Selling your home yourself is covered in Chapter 27.

Closing costs that you must pay. Some closing costs are customarily paid by the seller.

Closing costs that you offer to pay. As part of the negotiating process, you may offer to pay additional closing costs for the buyer. Deciding what you want to offer is covered in Chapter 24.

Moving expenses. Unless you have one duffel bag of stuff, moving your entire home is going to cost some money—even if you do it yourself. You may have to hire a moving company or rent a moving truck.

Costs for buying a new home. If you are buying a new home after selling your current one, don't forget to plan for the costs involved in buying a home. Chapter 2 gives you a preview of the costs you can expect to pay.

What to Expect When You Sell Your Home

The remaining chapters in Part V discuss all the aspects of selling a home. This section is intended to give you a preview of what to expect.

Step 1:   Getting the House Ready

When you decide to sell your house, you need to get it ready for selling. You need to decide what repairs to make and what information to collect.

As you get your house ready, expect to "undecorate." This advice is usually surprising to first-time sellers. "What? Put away all my family portraits? But that's what makes the home look like a home! Paint all the walls white? Where's the character in that?" The reason you want to undecorate your house and other strategies for getting ready are covered in Chapter 22.

Step 2:   Deciding Whether to Use an Agent

Deciding whether to sell your home yourself or use an agent is an important decision. You may be tempted to stick a FOR SALE sign in the front yard and BAM!—you save 7% commission. But are you prepared for the negotiating and haggling that must be done? And remember, most buyers will expect you to share your savings with them. Chapter 23 covers the benefits of using an agent and explains how to select one.

But what if it's a strong seller's market? If you notice a lot of FOR SALE signs going up and down quickly, chances are you can make out just fine without an agent. Chapter 23 covers the benefits and liabilities of selling your home yourself, and Chapter 27 teaches you how to do it.

Step 3:   Pricing and Marketing the House

Setting the price for your house can be tricky. The price will depend on the current market, what your house has to offer, and how quickly you want to sell. Your agent can help you come up with the listing price you want to start with. Pricing is covered in Chapter 24.

In addition to pricing, you should work on marketing the house—getting buyers to notice your house over all the other houses for sale in the area. If you have an agent, he will do most of the marketing, as covered in Chapter 24. If you are selling the house yourself, Chapter 27 includes marketing ideas.

You can also expect that just when you sit down to a wonderful dinner, your agent will call with a showing—that is, a buyer who wants to come by and tour the home. You'll have to put the food in the oven and drive around the block for 30–45 minutes. Expect to waste a lot of time driving around the block or sitting in the local McDonald's while potential buyers tour your home.

Also, expect criticism. You may love the red velvet wallpaper in the bathroom, but expect to hear criticism of that and every other aspect of the house. Don't let the criticism weigh you down. While one person may hate the wallpaper, another one may come along who loves it as much as you do.

Step 4: Negotiating Offers

If you are lucky, you'll have several offers on your house and you can pretty much dictate the terms. In most cases, though, you'll have to negotiate the terms. Negotiating means a little give and a little take. Your agent can help you negotiate offers; this topic is covered in Chapter 25.

Step 5: Closing on the House

Once you accept an offer and the buyer has done his job (getting financing, for example), you are ready to close on the house—take your money and hand over the keys. Closing is covered in Chapter 26.

Step 6: Buying a New House

Unless you are moving to an apartment, closing on the house is not the end of the process. Usually you'll buy a new house at the same time or soon after you sell your current house. In this case, it's back to square one, Chapter 1, to learn all you ever wanted to know about buying a house.

The Least You Need to Know

Before you decide to put your house on the market, examine your reasons for doing so. If you look at the reasons, you'll know what you hope to gain by selling and what you are looking for in a new house.

➤ Ask yourself what you like and dislike about your house. There are a lot of costs involved with selling. If you love the location, but just need more room, you may want to add on.

➤ Ask yourself what your motivation is for selling the home. What do you hope to gain? A better house? Money? Less commitment? Knowing what you hope to gain can help you plan your selling strategy.

➤ The best time to sell is when you are *ready* to sell. Readiness is affected by your family situation, your job, the economy, and other factors.

➤ Be prepared for the costs involved in selling your home—the sales commission, closing costs, moving expenses, repair expenses, plus the cost of buying a new home.

Lots of fellows think a home is only good to borrow money on.

—Kin Hubbard

Getting the House Ready

Once you've decided to put your house on the market, you have to get it ready. If your home is in perfect condition, getting it ready may just involve straightening up. If your home is like most, though, you may need to do some repairs. Got a leaky faucet? Better fix it. Roof need repair? You can have it repaired or take the repairs into consideration when you price the house.

In addition to cleaning and repairing, you should start to collect the information you'll need to sell the house. Buyers will want to know about maintenance and upkeep. For example, what does the electric bill run a month? When was the furnace last checked? This chapter helps you prepare for the sale of your home.

Doing Repairs

There are several types of do-it-yourselfers. There's the ideal Mr. and Ms. Fixit who love to work on the home, do a perfect job, and finish all the work they start. On the far end of the scale, there's the handyman who's not handy at all and doesn't even attempt repair work. He hires someone to do the repairs. If either of these descriptions fits you or your spouse, you're lucky—for the most part you won't have problems with the repairs.

If you want to be super-prepared, you can hire a professional home inspector. This will allow you to make any major adjustments before the buyer's inspector shows up.

A dangerous type of do-it-yourselfer is the one who can do the work, but gets bored or preoccupied halfway through the job and starts something new. (That would be my husband.) Another dangerous type *thinks* he or she can do repairs, attempts to do the work, and then has to hire someone to clean up. You usually pay twice as much money for a muddled job. If you or your spouse is a danger to your home, you may have problems.

This section helps you decide what repairs to make.

Inspecting the House

To start, you should do a thorough inspection of your house. Look through each and every room as if you were a buyer. What problems do you see? What sticks out? If you were a buyer, what would you notice? Take a clipboard and note any problems. You may be tempted to leave off some problems. For example, you may think that the buyer won't notice the missing tile in the bathroom. But if you noticed it, the buyer will notice it. Put the problem on your list.

Once you have a complete list of the problems, you can decide what you can fix yourself, what you need to hire someone to fix, and what you can let go. Here are some areas to check:

Check all your floors. Do you have any missing tiles? Are the baseboards in good shape? Do they need to be cleaned? Does the floor creak anywhere? Check the stairs for loose handrails.

Check all the walls and ceilings. Is the paint and wallpaper in good shape? Do any holes or cracks need to be fixed? Do rooms need to be repainted? Is wallpaper peeling in spots? Do your children have posters on the walls?

Check all the doors and windows. Do they open smoothly? Do they shut completely? Any door knobs missing? Any loose hinges? Are the windows caulked? Any broken or cracked panes? You could combine checking and cleaning in one process and wash the windows as you check. Clean windows make a good impression. Repair any broken doors or windows.

Inspect the bathrooms. Are the tiles clean and caulked? Any missing tiles? Do the faucets leak? You should replace damaged tiles in the kitchen and bath and fix any leaking faucets. Does the toilet flush properly? What about the walls? Does the bathroom need to be painted or wallpapered? Check the water pressure. Make sure the water drains properly.

Take a close look at your kitchen. Do all the appliances work? Is the floor clean and free of missing tiles or cracked linoleum? What about the cabinets? Paint or wallpaper? What about the sink? Does it drain okay? Any leaks?

If you have to repaint or repaper, select a neutral color. White or off-white are good choices. They may not do much to set off your tiger-striped couch, zebra chairs, and beaded doorways, but not everyone will have your tastes. It's better to stick with something neutral.

A quick coat of paint on painted cabinets will make the entire kitchen brighter. Also, new knobs on the cabinets go a long way to update a kitchen.

Examine your basement or attic. Clean out stored stuff (see "Eliminating Clutter," later in this chapter). In the basement, check pipes for leaks and check for any sign of dampness.

Make sure the electrical system is in good shape. Do you have any outlets that don't work? Any broken switches?

Check the heating and cooling systems. Make any necessary repairs. Replace dirty air filters. You may want to have the heating and cooling systems professionally serviced.

Check the roof, gutters, exterior walls, driveway, garage, and yard. Does the roof need repairs? If so, make them. Does the outside need to be painted? Is the yard in good shape? Check for overgrown bushes, tree limbs touching roof, gutters. Repair any missing siding.

After you do your inspection tour, you may become depressed. You may see problems that you never noticed before. Don't fret. Break down the list into what are essentially cleaning tasks, what are repair tasks you can do, what are repair tasks you need to hire someone to do, and what are repairs you are going to ignore.

You'll uncover some problems on your inspection tour that are simply cleaning tasks. No one likes to scrub the bathroom floor until it shines, but maybe that's all it needs. Mark all the cleaning tasks and save them for later. Cleaning is covered in the next section. This section focuses on repairs.

 Big Problems

A survey of the American Society of Home Inspection memberships came up with the following list of sale-killing problems:

➤ Water in the basement or crawlspace

➤ Bad wiring

➤ Damaged roofs

➤ Heating system problems

➤ Poor overall maintenance (untrimmed shrubs, loose doors, dirty paint).

You may not notice these problems, but an inspector will. So fix them before they turn away prospective buyers.

Deciding What Repairs to Make

As you review the repairs on your list, first decide which ones really need to be made. If you notice, for instance, that the roof needs to be repaired, you can choose to have it repaired and pay for the new roof. Or you may note that the roof needs to be repaired and then price the house accordingly. For example, if you do not have the money to have the roof repaired, you may want to use the second strategy—lower your selling price. In this case, you'll want to get estimates for the repair so that you can adjust the price accordingly. You should submit this estimate with your disclosure statement.

Do It Yourself or Hire Someone?

Once you decide the repair has to be made, the next decision is whether you are going to do it yourself or whether you need to hire someone. Some repairs are easy enough. For instance, most people can paint. Other repairs are going to require a professional. If you need to rewire outlets, unless you are an electrician, you'll probably want to hire someone.

Be realistic when deciding what you can and cannot do. You may want to save money by doing the repairs yourself, but if you don't have the time or talent, hire someone. You'll save money in the long run.

Also, keep in mind that most people overestimate the costs for minor repairs; they may not be as bad as you think.

Should You Remodel?

When you think about the repairs in your home, don't get carried away with remodeling. For example, you may want to redo the entire bathroom. Keep in mind a few cautions.

It's hard to recoup money on extensive remodeling and renovations. You may think that adding a deck will add a huge value to your home, but that's unlikely. (Kitchen remodeling is one thing that does add a great value.) It's better to leave the remodeling to the buyer.

The most cost-effective improvements are to the kitchen or bathroom. For instance, if you convert a one-bathroom house to a one-and-a-half or a one-and-a-half to a two-bathroom house, you'll expand your market of possible buyers.

Also, you'll not enjoy any of the benefits of the remodeling. You may have always dreamed of a greenhouse, so you add one in order to make the house more appealing. You won't ever get to enjoy the greenhouse, and the potential buyers might not share your enthusiasm for gardening.

It's also a mistake to think that you can make even more money by fixing up the house. Likely, there's a top price for a house with your amenities. You may get this top price, but you'll most likely get no more than that.

You may want to consider making changes if you have eccentric decor. Most buyers are not very imaginative. They cannot look past the decor of the house. If they hate the red velvet wallpaper, they may ignore the house, without realizing they can easily redo the wallpaper. If you have any out-of-the ordinary decorating touches, you may want to make them more subdued.

Cleaning Up

Does anyone really like to clean? Does anyone get up and think that they can't wait to tackle the grime in the oven today? I don't know anyone who actually enjoys cleaning, but there must be some freaks out there who do.

Hire professional cleaners to do the initial, thorough scrub-down. This will ensure that the house is in tip-top condition. If a house looks well-kept and clean, buyers are more apt to think it has been well-maintained also.

Cleaning is hard work, but it does give you a sense of satisfaction. When that oven sparkles, so do you. Cleaning your house in preparation for selling it is an ongoing process. First, you need to do a deep clean. Then you need to keep the house picked up so that when a potential buyer wants to stop by you don't have to run around sweeping and dusting and mopping. This section covers the deep clean.

First Impressions Count—Clean Up the Outside

Start with the outside. Stand back on the curb and take a look at your house. What do you notice? Are the hedges neat? Is the lawn over-grown? What is the first impression of the house?

The first impression of the house makes a big impact on the buyer. Even if the inside is their dream home, buyers are going to remember driving up and seeing fallen shutters and overgrown shrubs. They're going to remember trudging through the knee-high grass to get to the door—if they even get that far. Therefore, you should make the home look as inviting as possible from the outside.

Trim the hedges. Mow the lawn. Weed the walk. Plant flowers. Get rid of dead trees. Shovel the walk in the winter, rake the yard in the fall.

Also, repair any problems (such as a damaged roof) that you uncovered in your house inspection. Be sure to repaint the ceilings damaged by a leaky roof.

Flowers really make the outside of the house look inviting. If you're selling during the spring, plant flowers to make the yard look colorful and pleasant. You can plant them in the yard or in flower boxes. A pretty wreath on the door and a welcome mat are nice touches also.

Cleaning the Inside

Next, put away your hedge trimmers and lawn mower and get your mop, broom, bucket, and other supplies. It's time to start on the inside. Start with one room and clean it so that it passes the white-glove, mother-in-law test. Don't just do your normal once-over with the feather duster; *really* clean. Scrub the cabinets, wash the baseboards, remove all the stuff from the shelves and dust them, clean the walls.

Shampoo the carpets or have them professionally cleaned. Wash the drapes. Clean the walls, floors, and ceilings. Every room should sparkle when you finish with it. Then on to the next room, and the next room, and the next room.

Eliminating Clutter

When a buyer walks into your house, you don't want him or her to be taken with your collection of Amish cross-stitch samplers. Yes, they are beautiful, but the buyer isn't there to admire your possessions. He or she is there to buy the *house*, hopefully.

What you want the buyers to think about when they tour the house is where they will put their furniture. You want the buyer to mentally move in. To do so, you need to do two things. First, you need to get rid of any clutter. Second, you need to depersonalize the house. The house shouldn't look "lived in."

Put Everything Away!

The kitchen is the worst clutter culprit. You may have all your appliances on the counter, baskets of stuff on the table, little Mikey's artwork on the refrigerator, cookbooks on the shelves, coupons on the window sills. Get rid of all of it! Yep, put everything away. All surfaces should be clean and clear, including the kitchen desk if you have one. Clutter makes the buyer think the house is too small and doesn't have enough storage. Reducing the clutter will make the house look cleaner and more spacious—more room for those buyers to move in their artwork, cookbooks, and appliances.

You should unclutter each and every room in the house. You may be blind to clutter, so have someone follow you to point out the clutter—for example, your agent.

Also, unclutter places where clutter breeds—the basement, the attic, and closets. The basement is supposed to be a spot for clutter, but that doesn't mean you have to keep it. Now is a good time to take a look at all your possessions and get rid of stuff you don't need and don't use.

You'll find *lots* of excuses not to get rid of stuff. "I'm going to lose 50 pounds and then this outfit will be perfect." "I know I've never used that winemaking kit in the five years I've had it, but this year I am going to make some elderberry wine, really!" "The coffeemaker is fine; it just needs to be fixed." Will you really ever be able to wear those pants that you wore your freshman year in high school?

Be ruthless! If it doesn't fit, out with it. If you haven't used it in the last year, out with it. If it doesn't work, out with it.

Do something worthwhile with your clutter. Have a garage sale; donate it to charity; give it to Goodwill or the Salvation Army. Also, recycle old magazines and newspapers—nursing homes, women's shelters, and so on often love to get old magazines; those you can't give away, be sure to put in the recycling bin.

You can't unclutter by shoving everything in a drawer or cabinet because buyers like to peak in the drawers and cabinets. Therefore, for clutter you want to keep (old books, photo albums, baby clothes), pack them away neatly. If necessary, store them in a commercial storage area or a friend's house.

Be sure to put your valuables someplace safe. Most of the time, the agent will escort any potential buyers through your home, but you won't want to leave money or jewelry out in the open.

You may also want to get rid of furniture, especially if you have a lot. Consider rearranging the furniture so that the room is roomier. You want the house to look spacious.

Undecorating the House

Okay. You've gotten rid of the clutter. Almost. Now you need to be brutal. You need to declutter even more—get rid of things you may not think of as clutter. Remember that you want the buyer to focus on the house, not on how cute you have it decorated. It may pain you to do so, but you should depersonalize the house as much as possible.

Put away your family photos; you want the buyers to imagine *their* family pictures on the mantel. Put away knickknacks and other collectibles. Remember, you aren't striving for a house that looks lived in, but one that looks *ready* to be lived in.

Collecting Information

The buyer will be interested not only in how the house looks but also in the maintenance and upkeep of the house. Collect the following information:

Property tax statements. Know how much you pay for property tax as well as when you pay and how you pay. For example, if you have

273

prepaid for the next six months and then sell the house, you may ask for a proration of the taxes.

Utility bills. The buyer will want to know approximately what it costs to heat the house, how much the electric bill runs, what costs you pay for water and sewage. Collect a few months' utility bills for each service and have this information available.

Warranties. If you are leaving your appliances, collect all warranties for them. For example, if you have a new stove, the buyer will need the warranty information. You'll also want any warranties on repairs done on the home—for instance, if you redid the roof.

Maintenance information. It's a good idea to keep a record of the maintenance you have done on the home. A record indicates to the buyer that you have kept track of the maintenance. For example, they may want to know when you had the heating system serviced, the chimney cleaned, and so on.

Understanding Seller Disclosure

In the past, the rule of buying was *caveat emptor*—"let the buyer beware." If you bought a house, and there were problems, you were stuck. Recently, the rule has changed to more of a *caveat venditor*—"let the seller beware."

Since 1984, many states have passed laws requiring the seller to tell the buyer about substantial defects that the seller knows about. Real estate agents back the laws because if there are problems, agents don't want the finger pointed at them. If it clearly points at the seller, the real estate agent is free and clear.

Do You Have to Disclose?

Whether you have to disclose depends on where you live. Some states require disclosure. In some states, legislation is pending or in review regarding disclosure. Some states emphasize voluntary disclosure (Washington, Idaho, Nevada, Colorado, North Dakota, Minnesota, and Georgia). As of March 1994, only five states don't require disclosure (Arizona, Kansas, Tennessee, Alabama, and Massachusetts). In some cases, the buyer or real estate agent may ask you to disclose, even if the laws don't require it.

If disclosure is required, you should do so before the buyer makes an offer. You may want to include a disclosure form in your information sheets about your home.

What Must You Disclose?

Basically, you must disclose any physical defects that would change the buyer's assessment of the property value. About 18 states use a seller disclosure form which covers the areas a seller must respond to. See the "Seller's Residential Real Estate Sales Disclosure" form at the end of this chapter.

> If a potential buyer or agent asks a direct question, you must answer truthfully or be subject to a lawsuit.

This form covers water in the basement, mechanical systems, appliances, other systems, water supply, sewer system, roof, wood floors, and structures. In addition to these areas, you may also be required to disclose any environmental hazards—radon, lead, asbestos, ureaformaldehyde insulation, and so on.

Some states require that you disclose any potential problems in the area—for example, zoning changes or upcoming assessments.

What about *stigmatized* properties? If the house is believed to be haunted, do you have to tell the buyer? If someone has been murdered on the property, do you have to tell the buyer? The answer depends on the state.

Check with your agent or local state officials to find out exactly what you are required to disclose.

Completing a Seller Disclosure Form

When you are completing a disclosure form, remember that you are not providing a warranty for the home. You are not saying the water heater won't break, you are saying it works now and you don't know of any problem. Also, you don't necessarily have to fix any problems; you just have to let the seller know about any defects that could affect the home's value.

If there is a problem, be precise in describing it. For example, if the basement floods, how much does it flood and how often? If you don't know about a feature, say so. It's better to say "unknown" than to lie or guess about a feature.

If you want to be fully prepared for all problems, have the home inspected. An inspector can more easily spot problems. Also, an inspector puts another person in the blame circle. You can point your finger at the inspector if a problem turns up later on the house.

The Least You Need to Know

Getting your house ready for the market will involve first inspecting the home through the buyers' eyes and then doing any needed repairs and clean-up.

➤ Thoroughly examine every room and all major systems of your house and note any problems. Check for any sale-killing problems such as water in the basement, bad wiring, damaged roof, or heating problems.

➤ If you are planning extensive remodeling, keep in mind that it's hard to recoup that money. Buyers will consider the value of other homes in the area. If you have the only $200,000 home in a $115,000 area, you may not see the price you want.

➤ Clean up the outside and the inside of your home. You want a clean, clutter-free home that looks bright and spacious. As the buyers tour your home, they should imagine their furnishings in it, not notice yours.

➤ To prepare for the sale of your home, collect information on taxes, utilities, warranties, and maintenance.

➤ You may have to complete a seller disclosure form (see sample form on the following page). You are required by law to tell the buyer of any known defects that would affect the value of your home.

SELLER'S RESIDENTIAL REAL ESTATE SALES DISCLOSURE
State Form 46234 (R/1293)

Date *(month, day, year)*
6/30/94

Seller states that the information contained in this Disclosure is correct to the best of Seller's CURRENT ACTUAL KNOWLEDGE as of the above date. The prospective buyer and the owner may wish to obtain professional advice or inspections of the property and provide for appropriate provisions in a contract between them concerning any advice, inspections, defects, or warranties obtained on the property. The representations in this form are the representations of the owner and are not the representations of the agent, if any. This information is for disclosure only and is not intended to be a part of any contract between the buyer and the owner. Indiana law (IC 24-4.6-2) generally requires sellers of 1-4 unit residential property to complete this form regarding the known physical condition of the property. An owner must complete and sign the disclosure form and submit the form to a prospective buyer before an offer is accepted for the sale of the real estate.

Property address *(number and street, city, state, ZIP code)*
8169 Ashwood Court Indianapolis, In. 46268

1. The following are in the conditions indicated:

A. APPLIANCES	None/Not Included	Defective	Not Defective	Do Not Know
Built-in Vacuum System	X			
Clothes Dryer	X			
Clothes Washer	X			
Dishwasher			X	
Disposal			X	
Freezer	X			
Gas Grill	X			
Hood			X	
Microwave Oven			X	
Oven			X	
Range			X	
Refrigerator	X			
Room Air Conditioner(s)	X			
Trash Compactor	X			
TV Antenna / Dish	X			

C. WATER & SEWER SYSTEM	None/Not Included	Defective	Not Defective	Do Not Know
Cistern	X			
Septic Field / Bed	X			
Hot Tub	X			
Plumbing			X	
Aerator System	X			
Sump Pump	X			
Irrigation Systems	X			
Water Heater / Electric			X	NEW '9'
Water Heater / Gas	X			
Water Heater / Solar	X			
Water Purifier	X			
Water Softener	X			
Well	X			
Other Sewer System *(Explain)*			CITY	

	Yes	No	Do Not Know
Are the improvements connected to a public water system?	X		
Are the improvements connected to a public sewer system?	X		
Are the improvements connected to a private / community water system?		X	
Are the improvements connected to a private / community sewer system?		X	

B. ELECTRICAL SYSTEM	None/Not Included	Defective	Not Defective	Do Not Know
Air Purifier	X			
Burglar Alarm	X			
Ceiling Fan(s)			X	
Garage Door Opener / Controls			X	
Inside Telephone Wiring and Blocks / Jacks			X	
Intercom	X			
Light Fixtures			X	
Sauna	X			
Smoke / Fire Alarm(s)			X	
Switches and Outlets			X	
Vent Fan(s)			X	
60 / 100 / (200) Amp Service *(Circle one)*			X	

D. HEATING & COOLING SYSTEM	None/Not Included	Defective	Not Defective	Do Not Know
Attic Fan	X			
Central Air Conditioning			X	
Hot Water Heat	X			
Furnace Heat / Gas	X			
Furnace Heat / Electric *Ht Pump*			X	
Solar House-Heating	X			
Woodburning Stove	X			
Fireplace	X			
Fireplace Insert	X			
Air Cleaner	X			
Humidifier	X			
Propane Tank	X			

NOTE: "Defect" means a condition that would have a significant adverse effect on the value of the property that would significantly impair the health or safety of future occupants of the property, or that if not repaired, removed or replaced would significantly shorten or adversely affect the expected normal life of the premises.

6-94/L-137

Sample disclosure form, page one.

2. ROOF	YES	NO	DO NOT KNOW
Age. If known: ORIGINAL Years	X		
Does the roof leak?		X	
Is there present damage to the roof?		X	
Is there more than one roof on the house?		X	
If so how many? _____ roofs.			

3. HAZARDOUS CONDITIONS	YES	NO	DO NOT KNOW
Are there any existing hazardous conditions on the property, such as methane gas, lead paint, radon gas in house or well, radioactive material, landfill, mineshaft, expansive soil, toxic materials, asbestos insulation or PCB's?		X	

4. OTHER DISCLOSURES	YES	NO	DO NOT KNOW
Do improvements have aluminum wiring?			X
Are there any foundation problems with the improvements?		X	
Are there any encroachments?		X	
Are there any violations of zoning, building codes or restrictive covenants?		X	
Is the present use a non-conforming use? Explain:		X	
Have you received any notices by any governmental or quasi-governmental agencies affecting this property?		X	
Are there any structural problems with the buildings?		X	
Have any substantial additions or alterations been made without a required building permit?		X	
Are there moisture and/or water problems in the basement or crawl space area?		X	
Is there any damage due to wind, flood, termites or rodents?		X	
Are the furnace / woodstove / chimney / flue all in working order?	X		
Is the property in a flood plain?		X	
Do you currently pay flood insurance?		X	
Does the property contain underground storage tank(s)?		X	
Is the seller a licensed real estate salesperson or broker?		X	
Is there any threatened or existing litigation regarding the property?		X	
Is the property subject to covenants, conditions and / or restrictions of a homeowner's association?		X	
Is the property located within one (1) nautical mile of an airport?		X	

E. ADDITIONAL COMMENTS AND / OR EXPLANATIONS: *(Use additional pages if necessary.)*

The information contained in this Disclosure has been furnished by the Seller, who certifies to the truth thereof, based on the Seller's CURRENT ACTUAL KNOWLEDGE. A disclosure form is not a warranty by the owner or the owner's agent, if any, and the disclosure form may not be used as a substitute for any inspections or warranties that the prospective buyer or owner may later obtain. At or before settlement, the owner is required to disclose any material change in the physical condition of the property or certify to the purchaser at settlement that the condition of the property is substantially the same as it was when the disclosure form was provided. Seller and Purchaser hereby acknowledge receipt of this Disclosure by signing below:

Signature of Seller Irma Seller	Date 6/30/94	Signature of Buyer	Date
Signature of Seller John Seller	Date 6/30/94	Signature of Buyer	Date

Sample disclosure form, page two.

Chapter 23

Selecting an Agent

In This Chapter

➤ Deciding whether to use an agent

➤ Selecting an agent

➤ Understanding listing agreements

Remember all that you went through when you purchased a home? You have to go through that again, on the other side of the net, when you sell your home. Selling a home isn't as easy as placing an ad and then taking calls. You have to set the price, market the house, qualify buyers, and more. To help you handle all the details of selling, you may want to hire an agent. This chapter helps you decide whether to use an agent or not, then explains how to select a good agent.

If you decide to sell the home yourself, see Chapter 27 which covers FSBOs (for-sale-by-owners).

Should You Use an Agent or Sell Alone?

Why go without an agent? To save money. Many sellers don't want to pay the six- to seven-percent commission on the house. On a $100,000 house, you can save $6,000 to $7,000 if you sell the home yourself.

But that money is hard-earned. You have to be prepared mentally and psychologically for selling a home yourself. A lot of work and time are involved. First, consider what an agent can do for you. Then consider what it takes for you to sell your home yourself. After reviewing this information, you should be able to make your decision.

What an Agent Can Do for You

As you know from buying a home, there are a lot of *i*'s to dot and *t*'s to cross in the home-selling process. An agent has the experience both as a salesperson and as a real estate expert to help you through this. Here are some of the things an agent can do for you:

Help you set the listing price. You'll want the most money you can get from your home, but a home that is priced too high is just going to sit there. And you won't like it one little bit. Starting with a good price is the first step for a successful sale. The agent can help determine the asking price by looking at comparable homes in the area. If the house down the street sold for $115,000 and is nearly identical to yours, you know that you should be able to get at least $115,000. The agent can help you collect the sales data to back up your sales price.

Make suggestions on repairs and renovations. An agent knows what buyers look for when they tour a home. Does a deck really add value? Or do most buyers ignore it? An agent can turn an objective eye on your home and tell you what problems stick out and what changes you should consider making.

Screen potential buyers. Do you want to open your house to every Curious Carole and Nosey Ned? Or do you want to spend that time showing the home to buyers who are *really* interested? An agent can help screen buyers. Are the buyers serious? Is this house appropriate for them?

Help qualify buyers. You want buyers who are really looking for a home, and you also want buyers who can *afford* your home. Many home buyers don't know what they can afford. You don't want to waste time showing your house to anyone with two nickels. Instead, an agent can financially pre-qualify the buyers to be sure they can afford your home.

Market the house. An agent will add your home information to the multiple listing service (MLS), a computerized collection of all listed homes. Other agents use this service to find matches to their buyers.

For example, a couple may be looking for a home just like yours. If your home is listed and an agent searches the listing, your home will come up a match. This service helps bring buyers to your home. In addition to the MLS, the agent will have other strategies for marketing your home—open houses, ads, flyers, and so on. Some of the more motivated buyers are moving from out of town with only a weekend to look for a home. These buyers are usually working with an agent.

Handle negotiations. There's a lot of back and forth when a deal is being negotiated. A good agent should be an adept negotiator and can keep the deal alive. Often a buyer feels uncomfortable dealing directly with the seller. They think you'll be offended when they offer less than the list price, so rather than offer, they will walk away. An agent, on the other hand, is a mediator. The buyer won't have any qualms about telling the agent what's wrong with the house and what price *they* think the house is worth. Your agent has the resources to show the buyer the true market value of your home.

Oversee the closing process. Once an offer is accepted, there's still more work to be done—paperwork that has to be completed, inspections that have to be responded to, and more. An agent can help you manage the final hurdles up to and including the closing.

Going It Alone

If you read what an agent can do and said "I can do that," you may want to pursue selling your home yourself. Keep in mind that about 65% of for-sale-by-owner sales don't go through. The home is taken off the market, or the seller tries for a while and then signs an agent. That doesn't mean you should give up. It just means you should be prepared for the difficulties of selling your home yourself.

To successfully sell your own home, you should have experience with sales. If you don't like the sales game, you aren't going to enjoy selling your home. You should know the current real estate market, including details of other homes listed in your area. What is the asking price of these homes? What was the selling price of comparable homes in the area? You'll also need to know what is involved in buying a home. You should know about appraisals, inspections, sales contracts, and more. And you'll need some up-front money for advertising and for hiring consultants.

The best time to sell a home yourself is in a hot market, when homes in the area are selling quickly. The worst time to sell is in a slow market, when homes are not moving so well. Also, it's riskier to sell a home yourself when you have to move in a hurry because selling it yourself can take longer.

An agent usually helps a buyer arrange financing. Because there is no agent, you take on the role of financial expert. You need to be able to qualify buyers yourself. Can a buyer actually afford your home? Plus, you may have to educate the buyer about getting financing. The deal isn't done until the buyer has the loan, so you'll be motivated to get the buyer a loan. Are you comfortable asking the buyers how much they earn and how much they have in the bank?

Face-to-face negotiation is tough. You aren't going to like it when the buyer tells you the house is okay, but the decorating is crappy and will have to be redone. You have to be able to stand back from the process to negotiate successfully.

You'll need time to prepare for the sale— time to handle sales calls, and time to show the house. With an agent, you don't have to worry about daytime showings. Without an agent, you are most likely going to have to be available more than just weekends and evenings.

Selling your home will require a lot of work. You'll have to do research. You'll have to prepare buyer's qualification forms and information sheets about your house. You'll have to do the advertising, answer sales calls, show the property, and more. About your home, you should know how many square feet, how many rooms, when the furnace was put in, when the house was built, and more. You should be an expert about your home and your property.

Unless you are incredibly lucky, you aren't going to sell your house the first day it goes on the market. It may take awhile, and while you wait, you'll have to be patient. A buyer isn't going to want to come to the house if you're frustrated and growl into the telephone when he calls.

Using an Agent

Agents have a sixth sense when it comes to potential homes for sale. Before you even make up your mind, you may have several offers to list your home. It's a good idea to carefully select the agent that is going to sell your home. This person will have a lot of responsibility; you want someone who is committed to making the sale and someone you feel comfortable with.

A good way to find an agent is to ask friends and neighbors. Who sold their house? How long was it on the market? Did they get the asking price? Did the sellers think they could get more or did they think they got a good deal? Most sellers will remember bad experiences vividly; by asking around, you'll find out who *not* to use, and with luck, you'll also find out who *to* use.

You can also check your local paper for advertisements or visit a local broker's office.

Quizzing the Agent

Once you have a few agents in mind, you may want to call and talk to each one on the phone or set up a meeting. You can use the following checklist to interview the agent(s):

How long have you been a real estate agent? _____ years

What professional organizations do you belong to?

_____

_____

Do you belong to a franchise? ❑ Yᴇs ❑ No

Do you work as an agent full-time? ❑ Yᴇs ❑ No

How many homes have you listed in the past six months? _____

How many homes have you sold in the past six months? _____

Do you have access to the multiple listing service? ❑ Yᴇs ❑ No

Where do you advertise? _____

What is your commission?_____

References _____

_____

_____

Get the List

Ask for a list of past listings, call these sellers, and ask about their experiences with the agent. Your agent should be happy to give you some names. If he isn't, consider using a different agent.

Listing Presentation

A potential agent should also complete a detailed listing presentation. This presentation should include:

➤ Information about the agent.

➤ Information about the housing market, such as how many homes are for sale in your area.

➤ Information about your home. For example, the agent may make suggestions on what repairs should be made.

➤ A list of what the agent will do to sell the home. For example, how she will advertise the home; what additional information she will create, such as flyers or information sheets.

➤ All recent comparable sales (both sold and pending sales) in your area, including detailed listings of the home information—number of stories, number of bedrooms, number of baths, other rooms, other amenities (fireplace, basement, special features), the list date, list price, sales date, and sales price of the homes. May also include the MLS listings and pictures of the comparable homes.

Using the information from this report, the agent should then make a recommendation on an asking price for your home. The agent may give you a range. For example, he may give you a price for a 30-day sale, a 60-day sale, and a 90-day sale.

The agent should also provide a *net proceeds sheet* that shows you different scenarios for the different asking prices. This sheet should list the commission and closing costs you should expect to pay and give you a rough estimate of your net at closing. Table 23.1 shows you a sample net proceeds statement from a marketing report. Finally, the agent should give you an explanation of various listings.

Table 23.1 Net Proceeds Statement

Property	55 N. Main Street		
Date	8/14/94		
Prepared by	Agent O'Neil		
Sales Price	**$115,000**	**$112,500**	**$110,000**
1st Mortgage Payoff	$85,000	$85,000	$85,000
2nd Mortgage Payoff	_____	_____	_____
Brokerage Fee	8,050	7,875	7,700
Title Insurance	400	400	400
Mortgage Discount Points	_____	_____	_____
Origination Fee	_____	_____	_____
Deed and Affidavit	50	50	50
Document Preparation	_____	_____	_____
Taxes	249	249	249
Buyer's Closing Costs	_____	_____	_____
Closing Fee	_____	_____	_____
Assessments	_____	_____	_____
Inspections	_____	_____	_____
Termite Inspection	_____	_____	_____
Underwriting Fee	_____	_____	_____
Tax Service Fee	_____	_____	_____
Repairs	_____	_____	_____
Other	_____	_____	_____
Costs of Selling	8,749	8,574	8,399
Net at Closing	21,251	18,926	16,601

Signing a Listing Contract

Once you agree to use an agent, she will most likely ask you to sign a listing contract which gives her the right to list the home. This section teaches you about the different types of contracts and what a contract should include. See: "Listing Contract (Exclusive Right to Sell)" at the end of this chapter for an example of one of the most common types of contracts.

Types of Contracts

The contract basically spells out who gets the commission. Here are the most common:

Exclusive right to sell   Your agent will most likely push this type of contract because she will get the commission no matter who sells the property. If your brother Joe buys the house, your agent still gets the commission.

Exclusive agency   You don't pay the commission if you find your own buyer without help from the agent. For example, if it turns out your coworker is looking for a home just like yours, and you arrange for the coworker to buy the property, you don't pay the commission. This type of agreement may be a good idea if you know of someone who is interested in buying.

Open   You pay the commission to any agent who finds you a buyer. It's a free-for-all, and as such, many agents won't spend a lot of time working on selling your home. This type of agreement is useful for sellers who want to do the selling but want agents to bring buyers to the house. For example, you may see ads that say "Brokers welcome at 3%." This means the seller will pay the agent 3% for bringing a buyer.

What the Contract Should Include

Your listing agreement should state the following:

Length of the contract. Contracts usually range from 90 to 180 days, and you can extend them if you want. Be sure you don't sign a contract that is automatically extended. Also, a shorter contract may be better, because at the end of that time period, you can reevaluate. Why isn't the house selling? Do you need a different agent?

How long the agent is protected after the agreement is expired. If an agent has a buyer but the contract is expired, the agent is going to want the commission anyway. Usually, the agent is protected for 30–60 days after the expiration for any buyers that the agent brought to the home.

The commission rate. The commission is based on the sales price. Seven percent is common, but the commission rate is negotiable.

Your agent may give you a break on the commission if you use him to list your home *and* find your next home. It can't hurt to ask.

A statement of the condition of property. Are you selling the property as is? Or are you making repairs? If so, what will be repaired? What will be changed?

A marketing plan. The agreement should spell out how the agent plans to market the house. Where will the home be advertised? Will the agent hold open houses? If so, how often? What else will be done? Will the agent create flyers? Signs? How soon will the home be entered in the MLS listing? Will the agent schedule a showing from other agents?

A statement of the price and terms for the sale of the house. For example, the agreement should include the list price, the amount of deposit you require, and the terms of the sale you are willing to accept. Also, the agreement should list what is included in the sale—appliances, draperies, and so on.

Permissions. The agreement should grant explicit permission for the agent to do certain things such as use a lockbox, put a sign in the yard, and so on.

Getting Out of Listing

If you are unhappy with an agent, you can't just fire him. You have a signed agreement, remember. If you're not satisfied with the agent's performance, start by asking yourself what you are dissatisfied with. Are you unhappy because you haven't sold the house in the first month? Or are you unhappy because the house has been on the market for one month, but there's still no sign in the yard, and you haven't had a single showing?

You'll be anxious to sell, but you have to keep your expectations reasonable. If they aren't, you need to be more patient. If you have reasonable expectations that are unfulfilled, you should voice your concerns with the agent. Tell him what you expect to be done, then give him a second chance.

If you are still unsatisfied, ask for your listing back. The agent doesn't *have* to give the listing back, but may. If he doesn't, you may want to complain to the agent's broker, to the real estate board, and to the Better Business Bureau. If you become a nuisance, the agent may change his mind.

You also can't just take the house off the market for any reason. If you have a legitimate reason (for example, a death in the family), the agent will most likely be understanding. If you don't have a legitimate reason, for example, you want to take the house off the market because you found a seller yourself, the agent isn't likely to be as accommodating.

It's best to ask the agent up front in what cases you can take the house off the market.

The Least You Need to Know

Preparing for the sale of your home requires a lot of work and a lot of knowledge about sales and the real estate market. To help you with this task, you may want to hire an agent. An agent not only knows about sales, she should have much experience in the housing market.

➤ Your first decision should be whether you want to use an agent or not. An agent can help you set your list price, suggest which repairs to make, screen buyers, market the house, and negotiate the deal.

➤ Many sellers decide to sell their homes themselves to save the 7% commission to the agent. If you decide to sell your home yourself, you should have experience with sales, know about your house and the current market, have an understanding of financing a home, and have the time and patience to do the work and deal with potential buyers.

➤ You should ask for recommendations from friends and family when searching for an agent. Ask about an agent's background, experience, number of listings, number of homes sold, education, and more.

➤ The agent you select should prepare a marketing report for your home that includes information about comparable homes in your area (features of the home, listing price, sales price, date listed, and date sold). In addition, this report should include a recommendation on a list price for your home, a net proceeds sheet, and a description of what the agent will do to market your home.

➤ Your agent will require you to sign a listing agreement that gives him permission to list and sell your home. This agreement should include the length of the contract, the commission charged, the marketing plan for the home, the list price of your home, a description of what terms you'll accept, and other information.

GRAVES
REALTORS®

LISTING CONTRACT
(Exclusive Right to Sell)

1. In consideration of services to be performed by _____ A. H. M. GRAVES COMPANY, INC. _____
2. (Broker/Company, hereinafter referred to as "REALTOR") for *John & Irma Seller*
3. (SELLER), Seller hereby appoints REALTOR, as Seller's agent with irrevocable and exclusive right to sell the property known
4. as _____ *8169 Ashwood Ct Indpls, In* _____ Zip Code *46268*
5. for the price and upon the terms and conditions herein, or otherwise acceptable to Seller.
6. **LEGAL DESCRIPTION:** The property is legally described as *Lot 131 Crooked Creek Heights*
7. in *Pike* _____ Township, *Marion* _____ County, *Indpls.* _____ Indiana.
8. **FAIR HOUSING:** This property shall be offered, shown, and made available to all persons without regard to race, color, religion,
9. sex, handicap, familial status or national origin.
10. **TERM:** This contract begins on *June 30, 1994* _____ and expires at midnight
11. on *December 31, 1994* _____ unless extended in writing by all parties hereto. Provided, however, that if the
12. Seller and a Buyer sign a Purchase Agreement, Option to Purchase Real Estate, or the closing of the sale of the property will not
13. take place until after the term of this contract, then this contract shall automatically be extended to coincide with the closing date.
14. **PRICE:** The property will be offered at a price of $ *109,900* .
15. **ACCEPTABLE FINANCING:** Said property may be sold for cash or any of the following methods indicated below:
16. ___X___ Conventional Mortgage
17. ___X___ Insured Conventional Mortgage
18. _____ Assumption of Existing Mortgage Balance
19. _____ Conditional Sales Contract
20. _____ FHA
21. _____ VA
22. _____ Other
23. Seller agrees to pay costs associated with financing not to exceed *0 —*
24. **PROPERTY OFFERED FOR SALE:** The above sale price includes the property and all improvements and fixtures
25. permanently installed and affixed thereto, except *N/A*
26.
27. **SELLER DISCLOSURE OF PROPERTY CONDITION:** Seller represents to the best of Seller's knowledge and belief, the
28. property is structurally and mechanically sound and all equipment to be included in the sale is in good operating condition. Seller
29. agrees that maintaining the condition of the property and related equipment is Seller's responsibility during the period of this
30. contract and/or until Buyer's time of possession, whichever is later.
31. **PROPERTY DEFECTS:** Seller discloses the following known defects: *none known*
32.
33. **INDEMNITY:** If a dispute arises at any time concerning the condition of the property, the structures, improvements permanently
34. installed and affixed thereto, property defects, or health hazards, Seller agrees to indemnify and hold harmless the REALTOR,
35. cooperating Broker, and/or Metropolitan Indianapolis Board of REALTORS, Inc. (MIBOR) and MIBOR Service Corporation
36. (MSC) from and against any liabilities, judgments, damages, expenses, costs and/or reasonable attorney fees which they may
37. incur as a result of any such dispute.
38. **REALTOR SERVICES:**
39.   1. REALTOR warrants that REALTOR holds a valid Indiana real estate license.
40.   2. REALTOR will make an earnest and continued effort to sell the property in accordance with the terms and conditions of this
41.   contract.
42.   3. REALTOR is a member of MIBOR and the Multiple Listing Service (MLS).
43.   4. REALTOR will enter detailed information, a photo of the property, if available, and types of financing acceptable to Seller
44.   into the MLS computer system and all available MLS publications.
45.   5. Print-outs of this listing will be readily available to members of MLS by computer and will be provided to other REALTORS
46.   and Brokers upon request.
47.   6. REALTOR has given Seller a written estimate of selling expenses.
48.   7. REALTOR will cooperate with all other REALTORS and Brokers in an effort to procure a Buyer for the property.
49.   8. REALTOR may advertise the property and place a "For Sale" sign upon the premises. REALTOR may provide a lockbox
50.   for the keys to the property in order to facilitate showings. REALTOR will follow Seller's instructions for making
51.   appointments for the property to be shown.
52.   9. REALTOR will promptly present all Purchase Agreements received on the property for Seller's consideration. After a
53.   Purchase Agreement has been accepted by Seller, REALTOR will continue to present any offers received until the
54.   transaction is closed.
55. 10. REALTOR may place a "SOLD" or a "SALE PENDING" rider upon the sign after a Purchase Agreement has been
56.   accepted, and will remove all signs after the transaction has been closed.
57. 11. REALTOR will assist the Buyer in obtaining financing, if requested.
58. 12. REALTOR will make arrangements for closing time and place in cooperation with all parties.
59. **PROFESSIONAL SERVICE FEE:** The Professional Service Fee charged by the listing REALTOR for services rendered, with
60. respect to any listing, is solely a matter of negotiation between REALTOR and Seller and is not fixed, controlled, suggested,
61. recommended or maintained by MIBOR, the MLS or any person not a party to the contract.
62. Seller agrees to pay REALTOR a fee of *seven per cent of sales price,* _____ which shall be
63. paid upon the occurrence of any of the following events:
64.   1. At the time of closing the sale, when title to or an interest in the property is transferred to a Buyer; or
65.   2. At the time of default by Seller if, at that time, Seller and Buyer have entered into a fully executed, written Purchase
66.   Agreement; or
67.   3. At the time REALTOR procures a written offer to purchase from a Buyer who is ready, willing and able to purchase the
68.   property according to the terms herein, but the Seller refuses to accept the offer; or
69.   4. At the time Seller sells the property to a Buyer procured in whole or in part by the efforts of REALTOR, a cooperating
70.   Broker or the Seller during the term of this contract, if such sale occurs within 120 days after this contract terminates;
71.   however, this paragraph #4 shall not apply if this contract terminates and the property is listed exclusively with another
72.   licensed Broker.
73.   5. At the time of closing a sale on an Option to Purchase and/or Lease Option entered into during the term of this contract,
74.   even though the closing takes place after the expiration of this contract.
75. **AGENCY DISCLOSURE:** Seller acknowledges that REALTOR has advised the Seller that the property may be sold with the
76. assistance of a cooperating Broker, operating in either of the following capacities, and that the REALTOR'S policy is to
77. compensate such Broker as indicated by a check on the appropriate corresponding line:

1-94/L-100

Sample Listing Contract, page one.

78. __X__ Sub-Agents
79. Sub-Agents are licensees who procure buyers, but who agree to act as an agent of the listing REALTOR¹, are compensated
80. by the listing REALTOR¹, and who represent the interest of the Seller.
81. __X__ Buyer-Agents
82. Buyer-Agents are licensees who represent the interest of the buyer, even if compensated by the listing REALTOR¹. (NOTE:
83. Listing REALTOR¹ will always cooperate with Buyer-Agents compensated by the Buyer, even if this line is not checked.)

84. **POTENTIAL DUAL AGENCY:** Dual Agency exists when both Buyer and Seller are represented by the same person or
85. company in a transaction. When one of REALTOR'S¹ agents, acting as a Buyer-Agent, wishes to show the property, Seller will
86. be notified that there is a potential for dual agency. Only after full disclosure, and Seller's written consent for REALTOR¹ to act as
87. a dual agent in this instance, will a Purchase Agreement be written or negotiations begun.

88. **SELLER AUTHORIZATION AND COOPERATION:** Seller agrees to provide REALTOR¹ with the required information
89. necessary for entry into the MLS. The Seller will cooperate with REALTOR¹ by permitting the property to be shown at reasonable
90. times and authorizes REALTOR¹ to place "For Sale" and other signs on the property.
91. 1. Seller hereby authorizes REALTOR¹ to conduct or allow cooperating Brokers to conduct key-entry showings of the
92. property.
93. 2. Seller will provide REALTOR¹ with key(s) necessary to open the primary door of the property.
94. 3. Seller authorizes REALTOR¹ to have duplicate keys made for use in case of an emergency.
95. 4. Seller agrees not to rent or lease the property during the term of this contract without written notification to REALTOR¹.
96. 5. Seller agrees that REALTOR¹ may appoint or work with sub-agents and Buyer-Agents, to assist in performing
97. REALTOR'S¹ duties according to the terms of this contract.
98. 6. Seller authorizes REALTOR¹ to disseminate price and terms of financing on a closed sale to members of MIBOR, to
99. other Brokers upon request, and this information shall be published in the MIBOR MLS.
100. 7. Seller authorizes its lending institution to divulge all mortgage information to REALTOR¹ and to provide copies of the
101. note and mortgage, if requested. Seller's lending institution is _First Federal S. & L. Indpls._ and the
102. mortgage loan number is _0036754_. If Seller's mortgage is subject to a pre-payment penalty, Seller agrees
103. to give timely written notice to Seller's lender that the mortgage is to be pre-paid from the sale proceeds of the real
104. estate. It is acknowledged that Seller's failure to give said notice may result in a pre-payment penalty.

105. **LOCKBOX AUTHORIZATION/USE:** To facilitate showings of real estate, a lockbox installation (is __X__) (is not _____)
106. authorized, subject to the following acknowledgments/conditions:
107. 1. Seller will provide keys.
108. 2. Seller will safeguard valuables.
109. 3. Seller acknowledges REALTOR¹ is not an insurer of Seller's real estate and personal property and waives claims
110. against REALTOR¹ and REALTOR'S¹ authorized agents for loss and/or damage to such property pursuant to showing
111. the property. Seller further agrees to indemnify and hold harmless REALTOR¹ and all authorized agents from claims by
112. third parties from loss and/or damage pursuant to showing the property.
113. 4. Seller instructs REALTOR¹ to make reasonable efforts to notify Seller of showing requests. If Seller cannot be contacted
114. to schedule a showing, Seller (wants __X__) (does not want _____) REALTOR¹ to use the lockbox for access to the
115. property.
116. 5. Where a tenant/leasee occupies the Property, it is Seller's full responsibility to obtain tenant/leasee consent to allow the
117. use of a lockbox.

118. **EARNEST MONEY:** Earnest money, tendered with an accepted Purchase Agreement, shall be deposited immediately in listing
119. REALTOR'S¹ Escrow Account until the sale is closed. In the event the sale is not closed, the earnest money shall be disbursed
120. based on either the mutual agreement of the Seller and Buyer or upon court order. In the event that the Seller is to receive any
121. portion of the earnest money, Seller agrees that REALTOR¹ shall be entitled to retain any or all of Seller's portion of the earnest
122. money in payment of advertising and/or other expenses. In no event shall the amount retained exceed the amount of the
123. professional service fee had the transaction been closed.

124. **ADDITIONAL PROVISIONS:**
125. 1. Seller understands the terms of this contract, and has received a copy hereof.
126. 2. Seller acknowledges receipt of an estimate of selling expenses.
127. 3. Seller represents that Seller has the capacity to convey the property by a general Warranty Deed or by _____.
128. 4. Seller represents and warrants that Seller is not a "Foreign Person" (individual or entity) and therefore is not subject to
129. the Foreign Investment in Real Estate Property Tax Act.
130. 5. The parties to this contract agree that this contract contains the entire agreement of the parties and cannot be changed
131. except by their written consent.
132. 6. The parties to this contract agree that this contract is binding upon the parties hereto, their heirs, administrators,
133. executors, successors and assigns.
134. 7. The parties to this contract agree that if it becomes necessary for the REALTOR¹ to retain an attorney or initiate any
135. legal proceedings in order to secure compliance with this contract, then, in addition to all other sums to which the
136. REALTOR¹ may be entitled to recover, the REALTOR¹ shall also be entitled to recover court costs and reasonable
137. attorney fees.
138. 8. The parties to this contract further agree that this contract may be executed simultaneously or in two or more
139. counterparts, each of which shall be deemed an original, but all of which together constitute one and the same
140. instrument. Delivery of this document may be accomplished by electronic facsimile reproduction (FAX). If FAX delivery
141. is utilized, the original document shall be promptly executed and/or delivered, if requested.

142. **FURTHER CONDITIONS:** _____
143. _____
144. _____
145. _____

146. _Excellent Agent_
147. SALESPERSON/AGENT   INDIANA LICENSE #
148. A. H. M. GRAVES COMPANY, INC.   CO81297143
149. REALTOR¹/BROKER OR COMPANY NAME   INDIANA LICENSE #
150. _The Best Manager_
151. ACCEPTED BY: NAME AND TITLE
152. _6/30/94_
153. DATE

146. _John Seller_   _6/30/94_
147. SELLER   DATE
148. _304-12-3434_
149. SOCIAL SECURITY #/FED. I.D. #
150. _Ima Seller_   _6/30/94_
151. SELLER   DATE
152. _304-34-5656_
153. SOCIAL SECURITY #/FED. I.D. #
154. _8169 Astwood Ct Indpls In. 46268_
155. MAILING ADDRESS   ZIP CODE

R
REALTOR¹

Approved by and restricted to use by members of the Metropolitan Indianapolis Board of REALTORS®
This is a legally binding contract. If not understood seek legal advice. ©MIBOR 1994 (Form No. 250-01/94)

EQUAL HOUSING OPPORTUNITY

Sample Listing Contract, page two.

We often pay our debts not because it is only fair that we should, but to make future loans easier.

—François de La Roche Foucauld

Pricing and Marketing the House

Every year, there are approximately four million homes on the market. How many will sell? And how fast will they sell? The answers to these questions depend on a lot of factors—the most important being the price. This chapter first covers how to set the listing price for your home, then covers the marketing techniques for getting buyers to your house.

Setting the Listing Price

It's easy to make a mistake when thinking about the price to ask for your house. As a seller, you want to get the highest price you can, but you also want to avoid the many pitfalls.

Pitfall 1. Pricing the house as high as you can and worrying about lowering the price later. Mistake! When an agent and potential buyers see your overpriced house, they will most likely move on. By the time you wise up and set a more reasonable price, your house will have been on the market for a while. In this case, the property just sits, and the price is lowered and lowered and lowered until it finally sells. Buyers may think there is something wrong with the house since it has been on the market for so long.

Pitfall 2. Coming up with a reasonable price and setting the listing price there. Again, mistake. Most buyers *expect* to pay less than the asking price, except in very hot markets. You should leave room for negotiating.

In an active market, a reasonable asking price, near or at what other like homes have sold for, should attract many buyers. You'll be in a stronger negotiating position to hold to your price.

Pitfall 3. Determining the profit you need and setting the price accordingly. Another mistake. Of course, you should consider what you hope to gain from the sale. Doing so will enable you to plan for the next home you purchase. But you can only get for your house what someone is willing to pay. What you need and what you expect should not really factor into pricing the home.

Setting the price is a tricky balancing act. This chapter will give you some advice on setting the right price.

Studying Comparables

The best way to find out what a home like yours is worth is to look at what other similar homes have sold for in your area. It's key to compare like homes to like homes. The first determining factor is the area. You can't compare a home in one neighborhood to a similar house in a neighborhood across town. Remember: location, location, location.

The second determining factor is what the home has to offer—how many bedrooms, how many baths, number of other rooms (dining room, living room, family room), amenities (fireplace, hardwood floors, and so on). You may find some houses very similar to yours and some that are close.

Your agent's marketing report should contain a survey of homes that have recently sold or are on the market. Table 24.1 compares a seller's house to four comparable houses in the area that have recently sold, and to four comparable houses in the area that are still on the market. Features compared in the analysis are: Number of stories; number of bedrooms; number of bathrooms; whether or not the house has a dining room (DR), front room (FR), fireplace (FP), air conditioning (A/C), basement (BSMT); the age of the house; and any of the special features listed below.

HF = hardwood floors
NR = new roof
NF = new furnace
HO = home office
NC = new carpet
WD = wood deck
PO = porch
PA = patio

The listing also shows the list date and price for the properties still listed, and the sales date and price for the properties sold.

Table 24.1 Comparative Market Analysis

Address	Stories	Bdrm	Bath	DR	FR	FP	A/C	BSMT	AGE	Features
Your Property										
57 S. Riley	2	3	2	X	X	X	X	X	50	HF
Properties Sold										
55 S. Main	2	3	2	X	X	X	X	X	50	NR
79 N. Central	2	3	1.5	X	X	no	X	X	55	NF
77 S. New	1	3	2	X	X	X	X	no	40	HO
89 N. Greene	2	3	2	X	no	X	X	X	35	NC
Properties Now on Market										
89 N. Meridian	2	3	2	X	X	X	X	X	39	WD
45 N. Markey	2	3	2	X	X	X	X	no	40	PO
64 W. 55th	1	3	1.5	X	X	X	X	no	40	PA
80 E. 55th	2	3	2.5	X	X	no	X	X	35	HF

continues

Table 24.1 Comparative Market Analysis (Continued)

Address	List Date	List Price	Sales Date	Sales Price
Properties Sold				
55 S. Main	Jul-94	115,000	Sep-94	110,400
79 N. Central	May-94	112,000	Jul-94	108,640
77 S. New	Aug-94	113,000	Sep-94	109,610
89 N. Greene	Jun-94	116,000	Sep-94	109,040
Properties Now on Market				
89 N. Meridian	Jul-94	116,000		
45 N. Markey	Aug-94	115,000		
64 W. 55th	Aug-94	113,000		
80 E. 55th	Sep-94	112,000		

Figure the percentage spread of the listing price and selling price to gain an understanding of the market. For instance, houses selling for 95% of the list price means the market is hot, 80–90% means the market is weak. The difference, or spread, may vary depending on area.

Once you know what similar homes have sold for, you can compare your house and come up with a reasonable price. For instance, if one house has a little more to offer than your house, you may want to price your house a little under what that one sold for. Others will have less to offer and you can price your house a little over what they sold for. This method helps price your home based on market data—what people are willing to pay.

Looking at the list prices for houses that are currently on the market can be helpful, but keep in mind that these homes have not sold. The sales price could be significantly lower than the list price.

Getting an Appraisal

If you cannot come up with a listing price by looking at comparables, you may want to get an appraiser to help in setting the price. You can hire an independent appraiser for around $250 to $300 to provide you with a professional opinion on the market value of the home. The appraiser will study similar homes, look at your home, and come up with a value. You especially may want to get an appraisal if you and your agent are not in agreement on what the house is worth.

Getting the appraisal beforehand can help in another way. When a buyer applies for a loan, the lender is going to require an independent appraisal. If your home appraises for more than the asking price, the lender will not have any trouble approving the loan. If your home appraises for less, the lender may not give the buyer the loan for the entire amount. You may have to renegotiate the offer. It helps to find out what the house is worth *before* you start taking offers.

A lender cannot use an appraisal that you ordered. The lender must order an appraisal independently. So don't count on the lender to skip a second appraisal.

How the Market Affects Price

In a hot market, houses are in demand, and there are more buyers than sellers. What this means for you is that a buyer may be willing to overlook a few maintenance items, you may be able to get top price for your house, and your house may sell more quickly.

In a medium market, there are both a lot of buyers and a lot of sellers. In this market, you can expect to wait one to three months to sell your home, and the price and terms will be midrange. Because there are a lot of houses on the market, a buyer may use the condition of the house to make a decision. For example, if the buyer sees two similar houses; one in good condition and the other needing work, the buyer is likely to select the home in good condition.

In a cool market, there are a lot of sellers, but not a lot of buyers. You are going to have to work on adding incentives to entice the few buyers out there.

Deciding What Else to Offer

In addition to deciding the listing price, consider what else you want to offer the buyer. If you are selling in a hot market, you may not have to offer incentives. If you are selling in a slow market, on the other hand, you may want to entice buyers by offering them something extra.

297

For example, you may agree to pay some of the closing costs. You may pay one point for the buyer or agree to pay other closing fees. If the home needs repairs, you may offer the seller a repair allowance to have the repairs done rather than do the repairs yourself. Or you may want to offer a redecorating allowance. For instance, you might offer $1,000 dollars for new carpeting.

If you find a prospective buyer, but the buyer cannot get financing, you may want to help with financing. For example, you may want to buy down the mortgage rate or take back a mortgage. Creative financing choices such as these are covered in Chapter 15. Chapter 25 also covers some strategies for financing.

You may want to purchase a home warranty (around $300 a year) that protects the major systems and appliances in the house. This warranty may make an older home more attractive to the buyer.

You should have a good idea of what you want to offer the buyer so that you are prepared for the costs involved in selling.

Figuring Your Net Proceeds

When you sell your house, you'll most likely be buying another house. Therefore, you need to plan financially for what you can afford on your new house. This may depend on your proceeds from the sale of your existing home.

For this reason, you should consider several scenarios to determine your net profit (or loss). Again, your agent should give you a net proceeds statement as part of the market research (see Table 24.2 on the following page).

Consider different selling prices. Doing so may help you come up with the least amount you are willing to accept. Consider any repairs you must make. If you need a new roof, be sure to account for the expense. Know beforehand what other incentives you want to offer the seller. For example, if you plan to offer help with the closing costs, be sure to include these costs in your net proceeds estimate.

Know the closing costs you'll be responsible for. Some closing costs are traditionally paid for by the seller. For example, the seller usually pays for some part of the title search and/or insurance. You should get an estimate of the fees from your agent.

Taking a look at the financial aspect of the sale will help you evaluate the offers you receive. It gives you a game plan for negotiating.

Table 24.2   Net Proceeds Statement

| | Property | 55 N. Main Street | | |
| | Date | 8/14/94 | | |
	Prepared by	Agent O'Neil		
Sales Price		**$115,000**	**$112,500**	**$110,000**
1st Mortgage Payoff		85,000	85,000	85,000
2nd Mortgage Payoff				
Brokerage Fee		8,050	7,875	7,700
Title Insurance		400	400	400
Mortgage Discount Points				
Origination Fee				
Deed and Affidavit		50	50	50
Document Preparation				
Taxes		249	249	249
Buyer's Closing Costs				
Closing Fee				
Assessments				
Inspections				
Termite Inspection				
Underwriting Fee				
Tax Service Fee				
Repairs				
Other				
Costs of Selling		8,749	8,574	8,399
Net at Closing		21,251	18,926	16,601

Getting the Attention of Buyers

Your agent should provide you with a complete plan for marketing the house—that is, getting the attention of buyers. There are many strategies for doing so. The most obvious is the listing in the MLS database. Your agent will take down the key information about your home including the size of the rooms, age of the house, and so on. See the following figure for an example of an MLS entry.

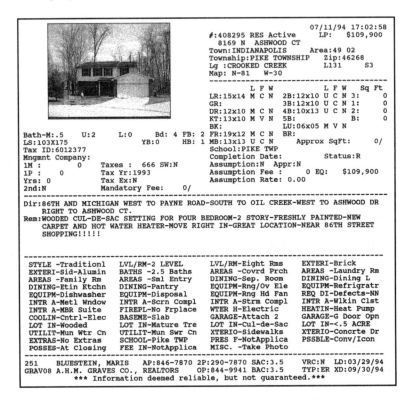

A sample MLS entry.

In addition to the MLS entry, your agent may also create information sheets to give to potential buyers. This information sheet may include a photo of the home, the address, and the listing price. In addition, the agent may write some inviting copy for the information sheet, such as "Great curb appeal!" Or "Beautiful mature trees. Great yard for dogs, kids, and cookouts!" The information will stress the most positive aspects of your house.

The agent may also schedule open houses (see the section "Holding an Open House," later in this chapter). For an open house, the agent will most likely put an advertisement in the paper as well as put up signs around the neighborhood.

The agent may use other means to advertise your house. For example, in some areas, there is a real estate show on TV on Saturday or Sunday mornings. Maybe your agent will showcase your home on the show. Also, your area may have fat booklets of homes for sale that are available free in grocery stores and other locations. Perhaps your agent will arrange for an entry in one of these books.

Have a flair for writing copy? You may want to make suggestions to the agent. After all, no one knows your house and its best features better than you. Feel free to tell the agent what you feel are the best selling points.

The agent may also have a good network of other agents, buyers, and associates. He may use his other contacts to get good word-of-mouth exposure for your home.

The types of advertising the agent does should be agreed upon when you sign the listing contract.

Showing Your Home

As part of the agent's services, he will arrange for showings. Or another agent may pull your listing from the MLS and arrange for a showing. This section covers the preparation for the showing—preparing the house and preparing yourself.

Scheduling a Showing

If you had to run home and unlock the house each time someone wanted to show it, you would quickly tire of running back and forth and back and forth. Usually the agent makes arrangements to make the home more convenient to show. For instance, the agent may put a lockbox on your front door with the keys inside. If another agent wants to visit the home, he calls your agent, who calls back to verify that the agent is really an agent and not some thief looking for a quick way into the house. Then your agent will tell the other agent the combination so that he can show the house.

If you don't use a lockbox, the agent will use another security measure for showing your house, but the idea is the same. Only agents can show the house.

Plan on having showings at the most inconvenient times. Just when you are sitting down to dinner. Just when you climb in the bath. You can always say no when your agent calls with a showing, but what if that person was *the* person to buy your house?

You can also stay during the showing, but your presence may make the buyer uncomfortable, and you want the buyer to feel as comfortable as possible. For this reason, you'll probably spend a lot of time driving aimlessly around your neighborhood or sitting at some fast food restaurant for an hour or so.

If you're like my husband and me, you may "spy" a little on the buyers; that is, try to catch a glimpse of them as they come to the house, or time how long they stay at the house by driving by and seeing whether the car is still there. The longer they stay, the more hopeful you may get.

Also, if you have a dog, you may have to arrange for the dog to be locked up during the day for showings or take him with you during showings in the evenings.

Getting the House Ready

When you get the call for a showing, you need to get the house ready as quickly as possible. This is another hassle of having your home on the market; you have to keep it clean and tidy all the time.

You should have done your major cleaning before the house went on the market (see Chapter 22). You just need to do a quick look-through for a showing. Put away any clutter that has crept out. Do a quick clean of each room.

Also, try to set the mood for the showing. For example, if it is winter, you may want to have a fire in the fireplace. You may want to simmer some potpourri so that the house smells nice. If the showing is during the day, open the windows and let the sunshine in. Turn on all the lights. You want the house to look bright and cheerful, not drab and dreary. Finally, put on some soft music.

Dealing with Criticism

After the potential buyers take a look through your house, their agent will most likely ask them what they thought about the house. Then their agent will call your agent and relay the news. "Loved the fireplace. Hated the small bathroom."

Be prepared to hear criticism. It's going to hurt, especially after you went to so much trouble, but you want to see the house through the buyers' eyes. If you have three buyers who say the carpeting in the living room is pathetic, you can do something about it.

Keep in mind that the buyers are going to critique the house, and they are going to nit-pick. You probably do too when you look at a house for sale. Don't take offense.

When you've had a lot of showings and no particularly bad comments, consider reducing the price. This may be the reason you haven't received any offers.

Holding an Open House

In addition to showings, your agent may schedule open houses, traditionally on Sundays. You can think of an open house as one long showing with more browsers than buyers.

If you are thinking an open house is a surefire way to sell your house and you'll have rooms and rooms full of buyers, think again. A 1991 survey of the National Association of Realtors found that just three percent of homeowners found their homes through an open house. Sometimes an agent finds a buyer through an open house, but more often the agent finds new clients through an open house. Does that mean that you shouldn't have open houses? No.

Be sure not to schedule too many open houses. Think about those reading the paper and seeing the house over and over. You don't want potential buyers to think your house is a loser. You don't want to overexpose the house.

Open houses, even if they attract mostly lookers, do call attention to the house. The agent will advertise the open house in the paper and will put up signs. If a potential buyer is looking through the paper or driving by, he may notice your house.

Also, even the lookers can be beneficial. Maybe they aren't in the market for a house, but they may know of someone who is. Word of mouth can't hurt.

The Least You Need to Know

How quickly you sell your house often depends on the listing price you set and how well you advertise. Your agent can help you come up with a reasonable listing price and will help you get buyers to your home.

➤ The best way to figure your listing price is to study data on comparable sales in your area. Check the listing price and sales price of these homes. Also, see when they were listed and when they were sold to find out how long they were on the market.

➤ After you decide on your listing price, also think about the terms you want to offer to the buyer. For example, will you help with loan discount points? You should have a good idea of what you'll pay for the buyer as well as what you'll be required to pay at closing.

➤ When you know the price and terms, you can come up with different scenarios that would work for you. Having a target bottom line will help you evaluate any offers you receive.

➤ Your agent will most likely market the house by entering the home information into the multiple listing service, by creating advertisements and flyers, by arranging for showings, and by holding open houses.

Negotiating Offers

All the cleaning, repairing, decision-making, marketing, and so on that you've done, has been with the explicit goal in mind of getting an offer on your house. All that work for one simple piece of paper that says, "Yes! I want to buy your home." What should you expect when you receive an offer? How can you decide whether you should accept an offer? What happens if you don't get any offers? This chapter covers these questions and more.

Dealing with Other Agents

When you sign an agreement with an agent, the agent agrees to do her best to sell your home at the price you decided on. The agent is entirely responsible to you and has only your interest in mind. Remember that getting the best price is in the agent's best interest. The higher the price, the more the agent stands to earn on commission.

The buyers will also most likely have an agent who represents them. In recent years, many buyers have elected to use a buyer's agent—an agent who represents the buyer and no one else. This agent is not required to pass along any confidential information and has only the buyer's interest in mind.

If the buyer doesn't use a buyer's agent, but uses a subagent, that agent actually works for you. (Chapter 4 describes the different types of agents in more detail.) Although the subagent is helping the buyers, he is being paid by you, and therefore, he owes his loyalty to you. A subagent should pass along all information regarding offers. If a buyer offers $100,000 but tells the agent he is willing to go to $105,000, the agent should let you know.

This means that when you receive an offer, you should ask what type of agent the buyer has. Depending on the type of agent, you can expect to receive different information from the agent.

Evaluating an Offer

Before you even think about evaluating an offer, you should spend some time thinking about what you want from the sale of your home. You should have in mind several scenarios of both price and terms, as described in Chapter 24. What is the lowest price you find acceptable? Which terms are okay? Which terms are not okay? You should discuss the price and terms with your agent so that she knows what is acceptable and what isn't.

Knowing your bottom line can help you evaluate any offers you receive. You can compare the offers to your different scenarios to see how they match up.

When potential buyers want to make an offer, they will sit down with their agent and draw up a sales agreement. Usually the buyer's agent will contact your agent and convey the offer, usually in person, sometimes on the phone. The buyer's agent will then give your agent the offer. You should accept only written offers accompanied by a check for earnest money. The following figure shows the front and back sides of a sample purchase agreement.

GRAVES
REALTORS®

Selling Broker *Graves Realtors* (#Dav8) By *Maria Bluestein* (#251)
Listing Broker *Ogii Real Estate Co* (#OTRE1) By *Charles Chuck* (#127)

PURCHASE AGREEMENT

1. Date: *July 12, 1994*
2. Buyer offers to buy real estate (the "Property") known as *3569 Camelot Lane*
3. in *Clay* Township, *Hamilton* County, *Carmel* Indiana *46033* Zip Code, which is
4. legally described as: *Lot 23 Brookstone Village Section 2*
5. in accordance with the terms and conditions set forth below:
6. **A.   PURCHASE PRICE:** Buyer agrees to pay $ *103,000—* for above Property.
7. **B.   IMPROVEMENTS AND FIXTURES:** The above price includes all improvements permanently installed and affixed, such as, but not limited
8.   to, electrical and/or gas fixtures, heating equipment and all attachments thereto, gas grills, incinerators, window shades, curtain rods,
9.   drapery poles and fixtures, awnings, TV antennas, all landscaping, mailbox, garage door opener with control(s), ceiling fans, smoke alarms,
10.   mini barns/storage sheds, satellite dish with control(s) and the following
11.   *all items as listed in MLS #418369 also include refrigerator in*
12.   *kitchen, fireplace screen and tools*
13.
14.   All items sold shall be fully paid for by Seller at time of closing the transaction.
15. **C.   METHOD OF PAYMENT:** *(Circle appropriate paragraph number)*
16.   1. **CASH:** The entire purchase price shall be paid in cash and no financing is required.
17.   2. **NEW MORTGAGE:** Completion of this transaction shall be contingent upon the Buyer's ability to obtain a (Conventional) (Insured)
18.   Conventional) (FHA) (VA) (Other _____) first mortgage loan
19.   for $ *90% of sale price* , payable in not less than *30* years, with an original rate of interest not to exceed *9%* %
20.   per annum. Buyer shall pay all costs of obtaining financing, except *seller shall pay 2 discount*
21.   *points for buyer*
22.   3. **ASSUMPTION:** Buyer shall pay (approximately) (exactly) $ _____ in cash and agrees to pay the unpaid balance of
23.   the note and to perform the provisions of the existing mortgage on the Property held by _____ .
24.   The Seller represents that the unpaid principal balance is [approximately] [exactly] $ _____ as of _____ ,
25.   19 _____ , payable at $ _____ per month including interest at a rate of _____ % per annum, and also
26.   including: (taxes) (insurance) (mortgage insurance). The exact balance including interest shall be computed through day of closing.
27.   Buyer shall pay the next payment due after closing. If the existing mortgage cannot be assumed by Buyer at the interest rate shown
28.   above, Buyer hereby agrees to accept an interest rate not to exceed _____ % per annum and if this is not available, at Buyer's
29.   option, this Agreement may be terminated. Seller agrees to pay any shortage in escrow account. Buyer agrees to pay all fees charged
30.   by mortgagee for assumption. The parties agree to (reimburse the Seller) (assign at no cost to Buyer) any escrow account balance on
31.   day of closing.
32.   4. **CONDITIONAL SALES CONTRACT:** Within _____ days after acceptance of this Agreement the parties hereto shall approve
33.   the Metropolitan Indianapolis Board of REALTORS Conditional Sales Contract form or another acceptable form embodying the terms
34.   contained herein:
35.   Cash down payment $ _____ , interest rate on the unpaid balance _____ % per annum calculated monthly and paid monthly
36.   in arrears; monthly principal and interest payment $ _____ ; first payment shall be due on _____ , 19 _____ ;
37.   interest shall commence the day after closing. Property taxes and insurance are to be paid (separately when due) (monthly) in addition
38.   to the monthly principal and interest payment; no prepayment penalty for early pay-off; a _____ day default period for any
39.   time provisions; forfeiture provisions are to be released by Seller when Buyer has paid more than $ _____ or (_____ %)
40.   of the purchase price. Contract shall be paid in full on or before _____ , 19 _____ .
41.   Special provisions: _____
42.
43.
44.   The Conditional Sales Contract is to be prepared by _____
45.   at _____ expense. Buyer shall only use the Property for _____
46. **D.   TIME FOR OBTAINING FINANCING:** Buyer agrees to make application for any financing necessary to complete this transaction, or for
47.   approval to assume the unpaid balance of the existing mortgage within *5* days after the acceptance of this Purchase
48.   Agreement and to make a diligent effort to obtain financing in cooperation with the Broker and Seller. No more than *30* days
49.   after the acceptance of the Purchase Agreement shall be allowed for obtaining favorable commitment(s) or mortgage assumption approval.
50.   If a commitment or approval is not obtained within the time specified above, this Agreement shall terminate unless an extension of time for
51.   this purpose is mutually agreed to in writing.
52. **E.   CLOSING DATE:** Closing date shall be on or before *August 15* , 19 *94* or within *3* days
53.   after *loan approval* , whichever is later.
54. **F.   POSSESSION:** Seller may retain possession of the Property up to 12 o'clock midnight on *August 18* , 19 *94*
55.   or 12 o'clock midnight *3* days after closing the transaction, whichever is later, and Seller's possession until that date shall be
56.   free of rent. If Seller does not deliver possession by that date, Seller shall pay Buyer $ *100.—* per day as liquidated damages
57.   until possession is delivered to Buyer; and Buyer shall have all other legal and equitable remedies available against the Seller.
58. **G.   INSPECTIONS:** *(#1 OR #2 MUST BE CIRCLED AND INITIALED)*
59.   1. Buyer reserves the right to have the Property inspected. All inspections shall be made within *10* days after *acceptance*
60.   with written reports delivered within SEVEN days thereafter to Buyer, Buyer Agent or Sub-Agent and Seller and/or Listing agent.
61.   Inspections are to be at Buyer's expense by qualified inspectors or contractors, selected by Buyer.
62.   If the Buyer does not make a written response to a report within FIVE days of its receipt, the Property shall be deemed to be acceptable.
63.   Inspections include, but are not limited to, heating, cooling, electrical, plumbing, roof, walls, ceilings, floors, foundation, basement, crawl
64.   space, well, septic, water analysis, wood eating insect infestation and radon. Other _____
65.   If the inspection report reveals a major problem affecting the Property, and the Seller is unable or unwilling to remedy the problem, then
66.   this Agreement may be terminated by the Buyer.
67.   It is agreed that any Property defect previously disclosed to Buyer, shall not be a basis for cancellation of this Purchase Agreement.
68.   Inspections required by FHA, VA or lender do not necessarily eliminate the need for other inspections.
69.   2. BUYER HAS BEEN MADE AWARE THAT INDEPENDENT INSPECTIONS DISCLOSING THE CONDITION OF THE PROPERTY ARE
70.   AVAILABLE AND HAS BEEN AFFORDED THE OPPORTUNITY TO REQUIRE AS A CONDITION OF THE AGREEMENT THE ABOVE
71.   MENTIONED INSPECTIONS. HOWEVER, BUYER HEREBY WAIVES INSPECTIONS AND RELIES UPON THE CONDITION OF THE
72.   PROPERTY BASED UPON BUYER'S OWN EXAMINATION AND RELEASES THE SELLER, BROKER, AND LISTING AGENT,
73.   BUYER AGENT AND/OR SUB-AGENT FROM ANY AND ALL LIABILITY RELATING TO ANY DEFECT OR DEFICIENCY AFFECTING
74.   THE PROPERTY, WHICH WAIVER SHALL SURVIVE THE CLOSING.
75. **H.   REAL ESTATE TAX:** BUYER shall pay all real estate property taxes, beginning with the installment due and payable in
76.   *May* , 19 *95* , and SELLER shall pay all real estate property taxes due prior thereto. In the event real
77.   estate taxes are unknown at time of closing, then the last installment of such taxes shall be used as a basis for any credits due Buyer. Buyer
78.   agrees that any variance between actual tax liability and the amount credited at closing shall be their sole responsibility, and Buyer agrees,
79.   if necessary, to escrow an amount necessary to satisfy the first installment of taxes due after closing. ("Real Estate Taxes" shall include all
80.   charges placed on Tax Bill for collection.)

1-94/P-200

I. **TITLE EVIDENCE:** Prior to closing, Buyer shall be furnished at Seller's expense, a commitment for title insurance in the amount of purchase price. Any encumbrances or defects in title must be removed from said commitment and subsequent title insurance policy issued free and clear of said encumbrances and title defects, with the exception of any mortgage assumed by Buyer. The final policy shall be subject only to taxes; easements and restrictive covenants of record, encumbrances of Buyer; and rights or claims of parties in possession, boundary line disputes, overlaps, encroachments and any other matters not shown by the public records which would be disclosed by an accurate survey and inspection of this Property. The commitment shall be ordered (immediately) (after mortgage approval) (other _____).

J. **SETTLEMENT/CLOSING FEE:** If the method of payment for this transaction is cash, assumption, or conditional sales contract, the settlement/closing fee shall be paid by _____.

K. **SURVEY/SURVEYOR LOCATION REPORT:** At Buyer's expense a (staked survey) (improvement location report) of the Property is required, which shall (1) be received prior to closing, (2) be reasonably satisfactory to Buyer, (3) be certified as of a current date, and (4) show the location of all improvements and easements.

L. **UTILITIES/MUNICIPAL SERVICES:** Seller shall pay for all municipal services and public utility charges through the day of possession.

M. **PUBLIC IMPROVEMENT ASSESSMENTS:** Seller warrants that Seller has no knowledge of any planned improvements which may result in assessments and that no governmental or private agency has served notice requiring repairs, alterations or corrections of any existing conditions. Public or municipal improvements which are not completed as of the date hereof but which will result in a lien or charge shall be paid by Buyer.

N. **RISK OF LOSS:** Seller shall be responsible for risk of loss and/or damage to the improvements on the Property until time of closing when title to or an interest in the Property is transferred to Buyer.

O. **MAINTENANCE OF PROPERTY:** Seller agrees that maintaining the condition of the Property and related equipment is his responsibility during the period of this Contract and/or until time of possession, whichever is later.

P. **TIME IS OF THE ESSENCE:** Time periods specified in this Agreement shall expire at midnight on the date stated unless the parties agree in writing to a different date and/or time.

Q. **EARNEST MONEY:** Buyer submits herewith $ 2500.00 as earnest money which shall be applied to the purchase price. Earnest money shall be deposited in the listing REALTOR's Escrow Account, immediately upon acceptance of the Purchase Agreement, and held until time of closing the transaction or termination of this Purchase Agreement. Earnest money shall be returned promptly in the event this offer is not accepted. If this offer is accepted and Buyer shall fail or refuse to close the transaction, without legal cause, the earnest money shall be forfeited by Buyer to Seller as liquidated damages, or Seller may pursue any other legal and equitable remedies. The Broker holding any earnest money is absolved from any responsibility to make payment to the Seller or Buyer, unless the parties enter into a Mutual Release or a Court of competent jurisdiction issues an Order for payment.

R. **HOMEOWNERS ASSOCIATION/CONDOMINIUM ASSOCIATION:** Documents for a MANDATORY membership association shall be delivered by the Seller to Buyer within _____ days after acceptance of this Agreement. If the Buyer does not make a written exception to the documents within _____ days after receipt, the documents shall be deemed acceptable. In the event the Buyer does not accept the provisions in the documents and such provisions cannot be waived, this Agreement may be terminated by the Buyer and the earnest money deposit shall be refunded to Buyer without delay. Any approval of sale required by the Association shall be obtained by the Seller, in writing, within _____ days after Buyer's approval of the documents.

S. **MISCELLANEOUS PROVISIONS:** The transaction shall be closed in accordance with the following:
1. Prorations for rent, association dues/assessments, or any other items shall be made and computed through the date of closing.
2. Notwithstanding any other provisions of this Agreement, any inspections and charges, which are required to be made and charged to Buyer or Seller by the lender, FHA, VA, Mortgage Insurer or closing agent, shall be made and charged in accordance with their prevailing rules or regulations and shall supersede any provisions of this Agreement.
3. Conveyance of this Property shall be by general Warranty Deed, or by _____ subject to taxes, easements, restrictive covenants and encumbrances of record, unless otherwise agreed to herein.
4. Seller agrees to pay the cost of obtaining all documents necessary to perfect title, so that marketable title can be conveyed.
5. If said title insurance is not available, Buyer shall be furnished, at SELLER'S expense, an abstract of title continued to date, showing a marketable title to said Property in OWNER'S name.
6. The price and terms of financing on a closed sale shall be disseminated to members of the Metropolitan Indianapolis Board of REALTORS', to other Brokers upon request, and shall be published in the MIBOR'S Multiple Listing Service.
7. The Professional Service fee payable to the Listing Broker is the obligation of Seller.
8. Seller represents and warrants that Seller is not a "Foreign Person" (individual or entity) and therefore is not subject to the Foreign Investment in Real Property Tax Act.
9. Any amounts payable by one party to the other, or by one party on behalf of the other party, shall not be payable until this transaction is closed.
10. Buyer hereby discloses to Seller that Buyer is licensed under the Indiana Real Estate Broker and Salesperson Licensing Act and holds License # _____

T. **FURTHER CONDITIONS:** *This offer is contingent upon the closing of purchasers house at 1024 Hampton Rd. Indianapolis IN for which an offer has been accepted and is expected to close no later that 8/15/94*

U. **EXPIRATION AND APPROVAL:** This Purchase Agreement is void if not accepted in writing on or before *12* (AM) (PM) (Noon) (Midnight) *July 13*, 19 *94*.

V. **TERMS BINDING:** All terms and conditions are included herein and no verbal agreements shall be binding.

W. **ACKNOWLEDGEMENTS:** Buyer and Seller acknowledge that each has received agency disclosure forms, have had their agency options explained, and now confirm their respective agency relations. They further acknowledge that they understand and accept agency relationships involved in this transaction. By signature below the parties verify that they understand and approve this Purchase Agreement and acknowledge receipt of a signed copy.

This Agreement may be executed simultaneously or in two or more counterparts, each of which shall be deemed an original, but all of which together shall constitute one and the same instrument. Delivery of this document may be accomplished by electronic facsimile reproduction (FAX); if FAX delivery is utilized, the original document shall be promptly executed and/or delivered, if requested.

Paul Pierce	7/1/94	*Paula Pierce*	7/2/94
BUYER'S SIGNATURE	DATE	BUYER'S SIGNATURE	DATE
PAUL PIERCE		PAULA PIERCE	
PRINTED		PRINTED	
108-03-4153		116-32-6498	
BUYER'S SOCIAL SECURITY # / FEDERAL I.D. #		BUYER'S SOCIAL SECURITY # / FEDERAL I.D. #	

ACCEPTANCE OF PURCHASE AGREEMENT

The above terms and conditions are accepted this _____ day of _____, 19 _____
at _____ (AM) (PM) (Noon) (Midnight).

SELLER'S SIGNATURE _____   SELLER'S SIGNATURE _____

PRINTED _____   PRINTED _____

SELLER'S SOCIAL SECURITY # / FEDERAL I.D. #   SELLER'S SOCIAL SECURITY # / FEDERAL I.D. #

Approved by and restricted to use by members of the Metropolitan Indianapolis Board Of REALTORS1
This is a legally binding contract. If not understood seek legal advice   ©MIBOR 1992   (Form No. 310-01/94)

The buyers will most likely give you a time for responding to the offer (usually one or two days). During that time, you and your agent can evaluate the offer, as described next.

What an Offer Should Include

You can expect an offer to include the following:

➤ The address and legal description of the property (lot, block, and square recorded in government records).

➤ The names of the brokers involved.

➤ The price, down payment, loan amount, and the amount of the deposit.

➤ A time limit for the response to the offer, for getting financing and closing on the house, and for moving in.

➤ Certain conditions, or *contingencies,* that must be met.

➤ Other provisions, such as what personal property is included; whether certain payments are prorated; how assumptions, damages, and other special circumstances are handled; and so on.

What Price and at What Terms?

The first thing you are going to want to know is, "How much?" How much did the seller offer? Unless you are in a really hot market, the buyer is most likely going to offer less. Before you tear up the offer, though, look at how much less. Is the price close enough? Also, look at the terms of the contract. If the buyer offered less, did he or she give more on the terms?

Next, look at the money you have in hand—the deposit. How much deposit did the buyer put down? Is it sufficient? Does the deposit show that the buyer is serious about purchasing the home?

Also, look at the down payment the buyer is offering. Is it sufficient? Does it show you that the buyer has the funds to purchase the home? Ask your agent if the buyer is well qualified.

Checking the Contingencies

Look through any contingencies the buyer has included in the contract. A contingency makes the sale conditional on something else. For instance, the buyer will most likely make the sale contingent on being able to get financing.

As you look through the contingencies, ask yourself whether they are acceptable. Are they reasonable? For example, a financing contingency is pretty common and pretty reasonable.

Look also at the limits of the contingency and note how they are removed. For instance, yes, the buyer has to have financing, but if the buyer doesn't specify how long he has to get financing or specifies outrageous terms (a loan with three-percent interest and no money down), the contingency may not be acceptable.

 If you can't move out by the date specified and the buyer isn't in a hurry to move in, you may be able to make arrangements for a rental agreement. You sell the house to the buyers but then rent from them for a few months until you can move out. Some buyers will agree to this arrangement.

Commonly, the sale is contingent on the buyers getting financing. You should be sure the buyers specify a time frame to apply for the loan. Also, you will want to know whether the buyers are likely to qualify for a loan—they should be prequalified by their agent or yours. Also, you should make sure you know when the buyers obtain financing, and you should know what happens if they don't get financing.

The sale is often contingent on a satisfactory inspection. The buyers usually want a thorough inspection of your home. If you did your job in preparing the house, you should know where the problems are. Make sure that the buyer has a certain time frame in which to have the house inspected, that you get a copy of the report, and that the buyers use an independent inspector.

The sale may also be contingent on the buyers selling their home. This contingency should give you serious pause. Do you really want to tie up your home sale with the sale of an unknown home? If you agree to this contingency, you may want to ask your agent to evaluate the current home at the price listed. Is it listed now? Is it priced reasonably? Is it in good condition? Is it likely to sell?

You may also want to include some protection for yourself in case the house doesn't sell. For example, you may want to keep the house on the market and give the buyers right of first refusal. If you get another offer during that time, the first buyers can remove the contingency and buy the house, or they can withdraw their offer.

Checking the Time Limits

The contract should specify certain time limits. For example, you want the buyers to commit to applying for a loan and having the home inspected within a certain time frame.

In addition, the buyers will want you to respond to the offer by a certain time and to be out of the house by a certain time. The buyers may specify a settlement date (when you close) and an occupancy date (when they move in). Be sure these dates are acceptable. For instance, will you be able to move out by the date specified?

Making a Counteroffer

After evaluating an offer, you have three options. You can say, "Yes! We'll take it." In this case, see the next section, "Accepting an Offer."

You can say, "No! Forget it." In this case, you may want to reconsider. Sometimes buyers like to dangle the worm a little bit to see if you will bite. Even if the offer isn't close to what you want, you may want to consider returning the offer with some changes.

This brings up your third option. When you consider the offer, but want to make some modifications, you make a counteroffer. Making a counteroffer is like saying, "Not this, but how about this?" You may want to up the price or change the terms. Whatever changes you make, your agent will help you complete the counteroffer. You may make changes directly on the original offer or submit a new offer. Refer to the sample counteroffer in Chapter 9 to see what one looks like.

Be sure to spell out all the changes you want to make. Anything not mentioned, the buyer will assume you found acceptable. If you are unsure, write in your conditions again.

Your agent will relay any counteroffers back to the buyers' agent who will relay the offer to the buyers. The buyers can accept the offer or can counter again. Go back to the start!

Accepting an Offer

You have an accepted offer when both parties sign the same agreement. That is, when you accept the buyers' original offer or a counteroffer made by them. Or when the buyers accept your counteroffer.

Congratulations! You've sold your home. You should get a copy of the accepted offer and prepare for the final step—the closing. This topic is discussed in Chapter 26.

What to Do If You Don't Get Any Offers

You are sitting in your house patiently waiting and waiting and waiting. What if you don't get any nibbles? What if your house has been on the market, but not one person has made an offer? When you aren't getting any offers, you should evaluate the situation to find out where the problem lies.

 If you are close on the deal, you may not want to push it. Consider taking the deal and being satisfied. Any time you make a counteroffer, you give the potential buyer the opportunity to walk away. The better the offer is, the more you risk losing that offer when you make a counter-offer.

Have you given yourself enough time? If you don't have an offer in the first week, it's not time to give up. Selling a home takes time—it can take several months or more, depending on the current market. You should ask yourself whether you are being overly anxious or whether you have given enough time and perhaps there is another problem.

Has the house gotten enough exposure? That is, are people coming to see it? Have you had a lot of showings? How many? How many calls? How many open houses? Were the open houses well attended? A buyer can't buy the house unless he knows it is for sale. If you haven't had buyers looking, you can't expect to have buyers buying. If this is the problem, you may want to discuss with your agent what else can be done. Has the agent done enough advertising? Held enough open houses?

What is the current market like? Is it hot, warm, lukewarm, cool, cold, frosty? Real estate professionals like to use a lot of hot/cold and hard/soft terms to describe the market. For a seller, hot is good, cold is bad. Many things can determine the current market. For example, what are the interest rates? If the rates are sky high, buyers may be unable to afford a home. If you are selling in a cool or cold market, you may want to wait for better market conditions. If you can't wait, you may want to offer additional incentives for the buyer, such as help with financing.

What is your neighborhood like? Remember, location is the most important factor in determining the desirability of a home. If you live in a war zone, you may have a hard time selling your house. There's not much you can do about a bad neighborhood. You can try to improve the neighborhood, which is most likely not going to happen overnight. Or you can lower the price.

What is the condition of the house? Go back to Chapter 22 and look through your assessment of the condition of the house. Does the home have curb appeal? What problems do you see? Ask the opinions of others. For instance, you should be getting feedback from the showings. Why weren't the buyers interested? You may also want to get a professional opinion from an inspector. If the condition is the problem, you may want to make improvements or lower the price.

Is the price too high? If you have had a few offers, what price was offered? If you are getting offers, but at a much lower price, you may need to lower the price. Also, get feedback from your showings. What did potential buyers comment about the price? What does your agent think about the price? If you are having serious concerns about the price, you may want to have an appraisal done.

What terms are you offering (or not offering)? Is what you are offering reasonable? Do you need to add incentives to help the buyer? Is there a particular problem with this property that needs to be addressed?

Should You Help with Financing?

When your house won't sell, many sellers are tempted to consider seller financing. You as a seller may decide to help the buyer in a number of ways. You may buy down the mortgage or take back a second mortgage (basically, you loan the buyers the money). Alternative financing is covered in Chapter 15.

Before you agree to help with financing, consider the buyers' motivation. Why can't the buyers get a traditional loan? Do they have bad credit? Won't their income qualify for a loan? Don't they have the money for a down payment? There are usually good reasons why a lender won't lend to a buyer. Are you willing to do what a lender won't do?

In some cases, you may decide to help the buyer. For example, if interest rates are really high, it may be more difficult than usual to qualify for a loan. Or perhaps you want to sell to a couple that just graduated from college. They have good income potential, but just don't have any money for a down payment now.

If you decide to help the buyer, you need to take several precautions. Lending money is risky. You should first check out the buyer. Do a thorough credit report. Get an explanation of any problems. If the buyers have a history of missed payments, are you sure you want to count on them to pay you back, even if they do look really nice?

Make sure the buyers are committed to the property. For example, if you take out a second mortgage on the home for the buyers, you may want to insist on a big down payment. It's also a good idea to keep the loan at a short term. Make sure you are not giving your money away. Insist on a fair interest rate.

Be sure to have a formal, legal agreement. In the agreement, spell out the terms. When do you expect to be paid back? What is the penalty for late payments? Have your attorney review the agreement.

Finally, consider the worst-case scenario. What if the buyers skip town to Tupelo, Mississippi, with four months' worth of overdue payments? Can you get your missing payments? How do you foreclose on a property? What is the cost of foreclosure?

The Least You Need to Know

When you receive an offer, you should first review it to decide whether you find it acceptable. If it's not, you will want to plan a strategy for getting an acceptable offer; for example, countering with another offer to the buyers. Once you have a signed offer, you've sold your house!

➤ Your agent represents your interests. The buyer will also most likely be working with an agent. If the buyer uses a buyer's agent, the agent represents only the interest of the buyer. If the buyer uses a subagent, that agent actually works for you and should pass along any and all information about the price and terms the buyer is willing to accept.

➤ Look over any contingencies included in the contract. Make sure that they are reasonable, acceptable, and limited.

➤ You do not have to accept a buyer's first offer. You may want to counter with your own offer. Countering continues until one party walks away or until the deal is signed by both parties. Be careful not to haggle over frivolous terms.

➤ If you aren't getting any offers on your home, evaluate whether you have given enough time and whether the house has had enough exposure. Take a look at the market conditions, the condition of your home, the price, and terms to see whether you can pinpoint the problem.

➤ In a tough market, you may want to offer the buyer help with financing. Be careful! Seller financing is risky. Be sure to get a thorough credit check on the buyers, and have your attorney review or draft an agreement. Get at least the going market rate for interest and try to keep the term of the loan short. Know the consequences of the worst-case scenario.

Never ask of money spent
Where the spender thinks it went
Nobody was ever meant
To remember or invent
What he did with every cent.

—Robert Frost

YEAH. MICE.

Chapter 26

Handling the Closing: Seller's Point of View

In This Chapter

➤ What is closing?

➤ What the buyer has to do before closing

➤ What you have to do before closing

➤ Handling problems

➤ What happens at closing

➤ Understanding the tax implications of selling your home

➤ Moving out

After months and months of waiting to sell your home, you may get an acceptable offer and then want to know, "Where's my money?" Money is handled at the closing. At this time, you hand over the deed and keys to your property, and the buyer hands over the check.

This doesn't usually occur the day after the offer, and requires some preparation time for both you and the buyer. This chapter explains how to get ready for closing, what happens at closing, and what happens after closing.

What Is Closing?

The term *closing* is used to refer to the final step in the process of selling or buying a home. At this point, documents are signed, and money is exchanged. You may hear *closing* referred to as *settlement*. It doesn't matter what it's called; the function is the same.

Usually the closing is attended by the buyers and their entourage (agent, attorney, lender) and you and your entourage (agent, attorney, psychic advisor, whoever). A closing agent orchestrates the event.

The closing may be held at the title company, attorney's office, escrow company, lending institute, or county courthouse, depending on local custom.

And finally, the closing is scheduled after the buyers obtain financing and have a loan commitment and all other obligations have been met. Your agent should let you know the precise time and place for the closing. The next section explains what has to happen before you can close on your house.

What the Buyer Has to Do

Most of the preclosing work falls to the buyer. The buyer usually has to obtain financing, get insurance, and meet any other requirements of the lender. The buyer will also schedule a home inspection sometime before closing.

As the seller, you should make sure the buyer is moving along with his to-do list. For example, you don't want to find out 60 days after the offer that the buyer hasn't applied for a loan. If there are problems, you will want to know about them as soon as possible, especially problems that can make the deal fall through. You and your agent should keep yourselves informed about the buyer's progress.

What You Have to Do

In addition to checking up on the buyer, you will have some responsibilities to meet. This section explains what you can be expected to do.

Termites and Other Critters

You may need to have a termite inspection done on the house. A termite inspection is usually the responsibility of the seller for FHA and VA loans. Lenders won't approve a loan until the inspection is done, so you will need to schedule the inspection. At the closing, you should bring the inspection report. If you have termites, you will have to have them treated. (I don't know why they use the term *treated*. It sounds as if the termites are checking into the Betty Ford Clinic. A more descriptive term would be—*terminated, zapped, poisoned, fried,* whatever.)

Checking the Chain of Ownership

You will need to have a title search done on the house. A title search traces the ownership of the property from you to the previous owner to the previous owner to the previous owner and so on until God created the property or until the government sold it, whichever came last. You will be required to pay for this search.

The purpose of the title search is to uncover any claims to your property. For example, if your Great-great-granpappy and Great-great-uncle Elmer once owned the property jointly, but your Granpappy took over the property when Uncle Elmer was at war, Uncle Elmer and clan may have a claim to the property. Or if you did not pay your bills, someone may be able to put a lien against your property.

Handling title problems are covered in the section "Handling Problems" later in this chapter.

Collecting Documents

At the closing, you should expect to bring a copy of the sales contract, with documentation showing that any contingencies have been removed and any conditions have been met. For example, if a termite inspection is required, you have to show the original termite inspection report. The title company usually asks for this when the title work is ordered, so you may not have to bring it again.

Bring receipts of paid utilities and taxes. The buyer won't want to pay your water bill for the past month. You may be required to show documentation of paid utilities.

Also, bring any information on your current loan. You should know the mortgage balance and the date to which you have paid. The money you receive from the buyers isn't going directly to your pocket. You will most likely be paying off the loan on the house. The escrow officer will ensure the payment of your current loan. The title company will order the payoff as of the date of closing.

Hiring an Orchestrater

What if you closed on the house, but forgot to pay off your existing loan? What if you sold the house, but the deed wasn't transferred to the buyer's name? What if the buyers assumed the mortgage, but no one made a record of the transaction? You'd be in hot soup, that's what. To make sure everything is done, and done in the proper order, you set up an escrow account and let the escrow agent do the orchestrating.

Comparison shop for escrow companies and compare the fees charged. Different companies charge different fees. Also, the agent's franchise may own an escrow company. You don't have to use the agent's company, and if the agent is affiliated with a company, she must disclose that.

An escrow agent (also called a closing agent) is a third party who handles the title to the property, collects the buyers' money, and concludes the sale. Your agent will probably recommend an escrow company, or you may use the buyers' escrow. Or you can select an escrow company yourself.

The escrow agent or company starts by collecting the sales agreement. This agreement is the blueprint for the proceedings. The escrow agent will use the agreement to prepare a list of instructions for you and the buyer, basically assigning you your homework. The buyers should know what they have to do, and you should know what you have to do.

At the closing, the escrow agent collects all the necessary documents and prepares the documents for signatures. If you have to sign a million pieces of paper, glare at the escrow agent. He's the paper-pusher in the deal.

The escrow agent is also the money handler. He will calculate all figures and tell you who pays what—the total deposit amount, the down payment, the closing costs.

The escrow agent will collect the money due from the sale and then hold the money in trust account, until the sale is final (usually when the deed is recorded, which is also done by the escrow agent).

Proration

A **proration** is a division of bill or payment. For example, suppose that you pay your taxes in arrears (you pay backwards). In the six-month tax period, you will live in the house three of those months, so you should have to pay for those months. To come up with how much you have to pay, the escrow agent takes the total payment, divides it by 6 (the number of months) and then multiplies it by the number of months you are responsible for (3). Proration varies by area.

Finally, the escrow agent will disburse (a fancy word for *hand out*) the money. The escrow agent should take care of paying off your current loan and then pay you your remaining equity.

Handling Problems

Most problems will crop up *before* closing and will have to be dealt with before you can close. Think about hurdles popping up throughout the race course. The number of hurdles you have to jump will depend on your situation. Here are some common hurdles:

Holdups in the loan process. If the lender doesn't approve the loan, the buyer cannot buy the house. For this reason, you will want progress reports on the loan application. If a problem occurs, you will want to know how serious it is. Is the process just delayed? Is the process held up by something you must do? Or have the buyers been denied?

Problems with the appraisal. Before approving the loan, the lender will require an independent appraisal. Usually, a lender will approve a loan for a certain percentage of the appraised value—for instance, 80 percent. If your appraisal comes in a lot lower than the selling price, you may have problems. Either the buyer is going to have to come up with more money or you are going to have to lower the price. If the buyer made the sale contingent on an appraisal, he holds the upperhand.

Problems with the inspection. If the inspection report turns up problems and if the buyers had a contingency in the contract for a successful inspection, you have to mediate the problems. The buyers may ask you to make certain repairs or may ask to renegotiate the price. Your agent can help you deal with any problems on inspection. You can refuse to make the repairs and kill the deal, but you should realize that you are most likely going to be asked to make the same repair on the next offer.

Repairs required for loan approval. Even if the buyers say it's okay to skip some repairs, the lender may require certain repairs. FHA loans, for example, require the approval of an FHA appraisal. You have to make the repairs, or FHA won't underwrite the loan.

Problems with the title. If the title search turns up problems, you have to clear them up before the closing. You can pay off a lien if you have a bad debt, or you can get the person with the claim to sign a release. If the claim is in error, you must have it corrected.

The details of the agreement are spelled out in the contract, so you shouldn't hear any surprises at closing. If you do, you can refer to the agreements. If disputes do pop up, they usually pertain to the deposit, condition of property, or definition of personal property. Check the contract. If you can't come to an agreement, you may want to agree to mediation. A third party hears both sides and then makes a ruling. Some contracts will spell out how disputes are to be handled.

What Happens at Closing

At the closing, the buyers sign their loan agreements, and you sign over the deed. You also go over the final reckoning of closing costs. The closing costs you are expected to pay will vary depending on the local custom, the lender, and what you have agreed to in the sales agreement. For instance, in most areas, the seller traditionally pays for the title search and possibly part of the title insurance. The lender will charge different fees for processing the loan. Usually the buyer pays loan fees, but if you agreed to pay for part of the fees in the sales agreement, you may pay some of the buyers' closing costs.

Fees You Can Expect

Here are some of the fees you as seller may be expected to pay:

Commission You are responsible for the commission fee charged by your agent. This fee should be agreed upon as part of the listing agreement. Seven percent of the selling price is common.

You should get the figures and check them before closing. Your agent is experienced with the closing details, but you should check over the figures to ensure they are correct.

Points A point is a fee associated with the loan and is one percent of the loan amount. For example, if the loan amount is $100,000, one point would total $1,000. You may have, as part of the sales agreement, agreed to pay points for the buyer. A similar fee is the loan origination fee, charged by the lender to process the loan. Again, if you agreed to it, you'll have to pay this fee.

Processing fees The lender will charge various fees for processing the loan. These fees may include a mail or delivery fee, a document preparation fee, an underwriting fee, and other fees. Which fees end up in your column depends on your agreement.

Settlement fee A fee may be charged for the services of the settlement company. This fee can run from $150 to $400.

Title search and insurance You may be charged a fee to perform a title search. Depending on how the title is secured, you may also be charged other examination and binder fees. You may also pay all or part of the title insurance.

Attorney If you have hired an attorney, you will be responsible for the attorney's fees.

Taxes You may owe money for tax prorations.

The HUD-1 Statement: My Column or Yours

At the closing, you will receive the HUD-1 statement, which on the front side lists the names and addresses of those involved (buyer, seller, lender, settlement agent).

If you note any discrepancies, don't sign the document. Signing means that you agree with the document. It is difficult to get agreements changed after you sign. You may want to bring your attorney to review the documents.

The left side shows the amount due from the borrower or buyer. This amount is calculated by taking the sales price, adding the closing costs, and subtracting the earnest money and any other credits such as taxes.

The right side of the form tallies up what money is due to you. This total is calculated by taking the sales price and subtracting the closing costs you owe.

The back side of the form details the closing costs. In the first column, you see a description of the closing costs with two columns. If you are responsible for the fee, the fee is typed into your column. On the other hand, if the buyer is responsible, the fee goes into his column. The bottom of the form totals the closing costs for the buyer and you. See the figures at the end of this chapter that show the front and back of a sample HUD-1 Statement. You may see the abbreviation **POC** on the settlement statement. Remember, POC stands for *paid outside of closing*. That means that the fee was charged, but it was paid before the closing.

Sign on the Dotted Line

You will be required to sign several documents at the closing. Before you sign, make sure the information is correct. Is the commission correct? Is the proration correct? Title insurance and escrow charges correct?

You will also sign the deed transmitting property to the buyer and a vendor affidavit. Then you turn over all your house keys, mailbox keys, and garage door openers to the buyer. After the deed is delivered, you will receive the check for your proceeds.

Tax Implications

The IRS likes to know when you make money, because when you do, they want part of it. For example, if you sell and make a gain on your home, you owe taxes. Fortunately, the tax laws are a little more lenient for homeowners. The laws enable you to defer payment on the gain.

You basically tell the IRS, "I'll pay later." You can continue to postpone the taxes as long as you continue to trade up. Tax laws change every year. When you sell your home, be sure to check with your accountant or attorney to make sure you understand the current requirements.

But I Didn't Gain Anything!

Gain is not the same as profit. Profit is what you earn when you sell the house, and is the sales price minus what you owe on the house. Gain does not take into consideration the amount you have to pay off on the loan.

You are eligible for a deferral if you roll over the gain to a new home within two years. You can defer only on a personal residence (not a rental property or vacation home), and you can defer only once every 18 months for an existing home and every two years for a new home. To get the full deferral, the house you buy must cost more than the one you sold.

If you continue to trade up on your house, you don't owe any taxes. When it comes time to trade down, you may still get a break. The laws provide for a one-time $125,000 exclusion. That means $125,000 is free and clear from taxes. You can claim this exclusion only once, and only if you are 55 or older.

Reporting the Sale of Your Home

In the year that you sell, you are required to report the sale, using one of those easy-to-understand IRS forms. You must fill in the *basis* (your home's value for tax purposes) of your home, sales price of the house you sold, and sales price of the house you purchased. The next section explains how to calculate your basis.

You should keep track of the costs you paid at closing on both the home you are selling and the home you are buying. You should also keep records of any improvements you made to your existing home.

This total affects your basis. It's a good idea to use an accountant for any year you buy or sell a house.

Figuring the Tax Basis

Figuring the tax basis is a four-step process:

1. Find the adjusted basis on the home you are selling, using the following equation:

> *Purchase price*
> *+ Costs of purchase*
> *+ Cost of improvements*
> _____
> *= Adjusted basis*

Not all closing costs can be included. For example, you may not be able to include tax prorations, insurance, and some points.

2. Calculate the adjusted sales price of the house you are buying, using the following equation:

> *Sales price*
> *– Costs of sale*
> _____
> *= Adjusted sales price*

3. Figure the gain on the sale using this formula:

> *Adjusted sales price* (from step 2)
> *– Adjusted basis* (from step 1)
> _____
> *= Gain*

4. Calculate the adjusted basis on your next home—that is, how much you are rolling over.

> *Purchase price*
> *– Costs of purchase*
> *– Deferred gain* (from step 3)
> _____
> *= Adjusted basis for new home*

Notice that the rollover decreases the tax basis. That has nothing to do with what your home is *worth*. You want a lower tax basis because that means you owe less in taxes. Table 26.1 illustrates how to use the above steps to figure your tax basis.

Table 26.1 Calculating Your Tax Basis

Step	Amount	Description
Step 1	$80,000	Price you paid for current house
	+ 5,000	Costs you paid to purchase
	+ 7,000	Improvements
	= 92,000	Adjusted basis
Step 2	120,000	Sales price for current house
	– 10,000	Costs you paid to sell
	= 110,000	Adjusted sales price
Step 3	110,000	Adjusted sales price
	– 92,000	Adjusted basis
	= 18,000	Gain
Step 4	180,000	Purchase price of new home
	– 6,000	Costs of purchase
	– 18,000	Deferred gain
	= 156,000	Adjusted basis of new home

Moving Out!

When it's time to move out, you may have mixed emotions. You've sold your house, possibly made a profit, and may be moving on to another home. This makes you happy. On the other hand, you may really have enjoyed your old home and may have many good memories wrapped up in it. Just keep in mind that you will make new memories in your new home.

Use the opportunity when packing to get rid of items you no longer need. Don't take everything with you. You may want to have a garage sale or donate items to charity. Packing or unpacking is also a good time to make an inventory of your possessions.

Contact the utility companies. Ask for a final reading so that you know what you owe for the bills. Also, have the buyer call at the same time to have the utilities transferred to his or her name. Buyers sometimes must make a cash deposit. Fill out change-of-address cards.

Welcome the new buyers. The sellers of our first home left a bottle of wine with a nice note in the refrigerator. This was a pleasant surprise and made my husband and me really feel welcome in the house.

Start a house file. In this file, keep all the documents pertaining to the sale of your home. You will need this information when you file your tax returns.

The Least You Need to Know

Closing is the final process in selling your home. At the closing, you sign documents and exchange money. A lot has to go on before you can close. After the closing, you receive your money and move on.

➤ The closing is attended by the buyers and their agents. The buyers' attorney and lender may also attend. On your side, you and your agent will attend, as well as your attorney, if you want. The closing agent is the neutral third party who handles the proceedings.

➤ The closing may be held at a title company, lending institute, escrow office, attorney's office, or someplace else, depending on local custom. Your agent will let you know the time and place of the closing.

➤ Buyers have certain responsibilities to meet before closing, including securing a loan, getting insurance, and having the home inspected. You also have certain things to arrange: a termite inspection, title search, and the preparation of certain documents (deed, utility bills, loan payoff).

➤ If there are problems with the loan, the appraisal, the title, or the inspection, they must be handled before the closing.

➤ The HUD-1 statement will list all closing costs as well as who pays them. What you have to pay depends on local custom, charges incurred, and your sales agreement. Some charges, for example, are traditionally paid by the seller. Different lenders and closing agents charge different fees, so what you pay and how much you pay varies. Finally, your sales agreement will spell out any other costs you have agreed to pay for.

➤ When you sell your home, you must report the sale to the IRS and you technically owe taxes on the gain. You can defer payment of the taxes, though, if you buy a more expensive house within two years. You can continue to defer payment until you trade down. At this time, you may owe taxes or you may be able to take the one-time $125,000 exclusion to avoid the tax or to lower the tax amount due. You can take this exclusion when you are 55 or older.

A. SETTLEMENT STATEMENT	U.S. DEPARTMENT OF HOUSING AND URBAN DEVELOPMENT		

ENTERPRISE TITLE
8440 Woodfield Crossing, #100
Indianapolis, IN 46240

OMB No. 2502-0265

B. TYPE OF LOAN

1. ☐ FHA 2. ☐ FmHA 3. ☒ CONV.UNINS.	6. File Number:	7. Loan Number:	8. Mortgage Insurance Case Number:
4. ☐ VA 5. ☐ CONV.INS.			

C. NOTE: This form is furnished to give you a statement of actual settlement costs. Amounts paid to and by the settlement agent are shown. Items marked "(p.o.c)" were paid outside the closing; they are shown here for informational purposes and are not included in the totals.

D. NAME AND ADDRESS OF BORROWER:	E. NAME AND ADDRESS OF SELLER/TAX I.D.No.:	F. NAME AND ADDRESS OF LENDER:

G. PROPERTY LOCATION:	H. SETTLEMENT AGENT:
	Enterprise Title Services of Indiana Inc.

	PLACE OF SETTLEMENT:	I. SETTLEMENT DATE:
	8440 Woodfield Crossing, #100 Indianapolis, IN 46240	07/18/94

J. SUMMARY OF BORROWER'S TRANSACTION		K. SUMMARY OF SELLER'S TRANSACTION	
100. GROSS AMOUNT DUE FROM BORROWER:		400. GROSS AMOUNT DUE TO SELLER:	
101. Contract Sales Price	124,900.00	401. Contract Sales Price	124,900.00
102. Personal property		402. Personal property	
103. Settlement charges to borrower (line 1400)	1,462.78	403.	
104.		404.	
105.		405.	
Adjustments for items paid by seller in advance		Adjustments for items paid by seller in advance	
106. City/town taxes to		406. City/town taxes to	
107. County taxes to		407. County taxes to	
108. Assessments to		408. Assessments to	
109.		409.	
110.		410.	
111.		411.	
112.		412.	
120. GROSS AMOUNT DUE FROM BORROWER	126,362.78	420. GROSS AMOUNT DUE TO SELLER	124,900.00
200. AMOUNTS PAID BY OR IN BEHALF OF BORROWER:		500. REDUCTIONS IN AMOUNT DUE TO SELLER:	
201. Deposit or earnest money	1,000.00	501. Excess deposit (see instructions)	
202. Principal amount of new loan(s)	91,900.00	502. Settlement charges to seller (line 1400)	9,339.00
203. Existing loan(s) taken subject to		503. Existing loan(s) taken subject to	
204. CUSTOMER DEPOSIT	1,319.00	504. Payoff of first mortgage loan 1st IND	80,209.43
205.		505. Payoff of second mortgage loan	
206.		506.	
207.		507.	
208.		508.	
209.		509.	
Adjustments for items unpaid by seller		Adjustments for items unpaid by seller	
210. City/town taxes to		510. City/town taxes to	
211. County taxes to		511. County taxes to	
212. Assessments to		512. Assessments to	
213.		513.	
214. NOVEMBER 1994 TAXES	630.65	514. NOVEMBER 1994 TAXES	630.65
215.		515.	
216.		516.	
217.		517.	
218.		518.	
219.		519.	
220. TOTAL PAID BY/FOR BORROWER	94,849.65	520. TOTAL REDUCTION AMOUNT DUE SELLER	90,179.08
300. CASH AT SETTLEMENT FROM/TO BORROWER		600. CASH AT SETTLEMENT TO/FROM SELLER	
301. Gross amount due from borrower (line 120)	126,362.78	601. Gross amount due to seller (line 420)	124,900.00
302. Less amounts paid by/for borrower (line 220)	94,849.65	602. Less reductions in amount due seller (line 520)	90,179.08
303. CASH (☒ FROM) (☐ TO) BORROWER	31,513.13	603. CASH (☒ TO) (☐ FROM) SELLER	34,720.92

Previous edition is obsolete.

HUD-1 (8-87)
RESPA, HB 4305.2

The front side of the HUD-1 statement.

-2-

L. SETTLEMENT CHARGES		PAID FROM BORROWER'S FUNDS AT SETTLEMENT	PAID FROM SELLER'S FUNDS AT SETTLEMENT
700. TOTAL SALES/BROKER'S COMMISSION			
based on price $ 124,900.00 @ 7.00 %= 8,743.00			
Division of Commission (line 700) as follows:			
701. $ 4,371.50 to			
702. $ 4,371.50 to			
703. Commission paid at Settlement			8,743.00
704.			
800. ITEMS PAYABLE IN CONNECTION WITH LOAN			
801. Loan Origination Fee %			
802. Loan Discount %			
803. Appraisal Fee to		275.00	
804. Credit Report to		108.00	
805. Lenders Inspection Fee			
806. Mortgage Insurance Application Fee to			
807. Assumption Fee			
808. PROCESSING FEE		125.00	
809. TAX/INS. VERIFICATIO		90.00	
810.			
811. MORTGAGE BROKERAGE FEE 1838.00			
900. ITEMS REQUIRED BY LENDER TO BE PAID IN ADVANCE			
901. Interest from 07/18/94 to 08/01/94 @$ 20.771918 /day		290.78	
902. Mortgage Insurance Premium for months to			
903. Hazard Insurance Premium for 1 years to STANDARD MUTUAL $321.00			
904. Flood Insurance Premium for years to			
905.			
1000. RESERVES DEPOSITED WITH LENDER			
1001. Hazard Insurance months @$ per month			
1002. Mortgage Insurance months @$ per month			
1003. City property taxes months @$ per month			
1004. County property taxes months @$ per month			
1005. Annual assessments months @$ per month			
1006. Flood insurance months @$ per month			
1007. months @$ per month			
1008. months @$ per month			
1100. TITLE CHARGES			
1101. Settlement or closing fee to ENTERPRISE TITLE		240.00	
1102. Abstract or title search to			
1103. Title examination to			
1104. Title insurance binder to			
1105. Document preparation to			
1106. Notary fees to			
1107. Attorney's fees to MICHAEL J. CURRY			35.00
(includes above items numbers:)			
1108. Title insurance to ENTERPRISE TITLE		95.00	550.00
(includes above items numbers:)			
1109. Lender's coverage $ 124,900.00 95.00			
1110. Owner's coverage $ 91,900.00 550.00			
1111. EXPRESS/PO ENTERPRISE TITLE			11.00
1112.			
1113.			
1200. GOVERNMENT RECORDING AND TRANSFER CHARGES			
1201. Recording fees: Deed $ 7.00 Mortgage $ 16.00 :Releases $		23.00	
1202. City/county tax stamps: Deed $:Mortgage $			
1203. State tax/stamps: Deed $:Mortgage $			
1204. DISCLOSURE FEE MARION COUNTY AUDITOR		5.00	
1205. MORTGAGE EXEMPTION MARION COUNTY AUDITOR		1.00	
1300. ADDITIONAL SETTLEMENT CHARGES			
1301. Survey to HAHN & ASSOCIATES		110.00	
1302. Pest inspection to			
1303.			
1304. SETTLEMENT TO NBDMC		100.00	
1305.			
1400. TOTAL SETTLEMENT CHARGES(enter on lines 103,Sect J and 502,Sect K)		1,462.78	9,339.00

I have carefully reviewed the HUD-1 Settlement Statement and to the best of my knowledge and belief it is a true and accurate statement of all receipts and disbursements made on my account or by me in this transaction. I further certify that I have received a copy of the HUD-1 Settlement Statement.

Marion E. Ayers   Marion L. Bugh

Borrowers Elizabeth Ayers Lathrop   Sellers Martha O. Bugh

The HUD-1 Settlement Statement which I have prepared is a true and accurate account of this transaction. I have caused or will cause the funds to be disbursed in accordance with this statement.

07/18/94
Settlement Agent Sarah Gregory   Date

Warning: It is a crime to knowingly make false statements to the United States on this or any similar form. Penalties upon conviction can include a fine and imprisonment. For details see: Title 18 U.S. Code Section 1001 and Section 1010.

The reverse side of the HUD-1 statement.

**Never spend your money
before you have it.**

—Thomas Jefferson

Selling Your Home Yourself

In This Chapter

➤ Mapping out your strategy

➤ Pricing your home

➤ Marketing your home

➤ Showing your home

➤ Understanding financing

➤ Negotiating with the buyers

➤ Closing on the home

➤ Knowing when to call it quits

Approximately one in six home sales close without the work of an agent. Are you one of the six that can sell practically anything? Do you know a lot about your house and neighborhood? Do you understand the real estate market—financing, negotiating, and closing? If so, you may want to forego signing an agent and sell your home yourself. Why go it alone? To save money. Agents typically charge a 7% commission. On a $100,000 house, that comes to $7,000!

Selling a home by yourself isn't easy. Chapter 23 discusses what you should be prepared for if you want to go it alone and explains what services an agent can provide. If you have made your way to this chapter, you are ready to get to work selling your home.

Mapping Out Your Strategy

To begin with, you should understand the entire sales process of selling a home; then you will be able to identify your strengths and weaknesses and see where you need help.

Step 1: Get the House Ready

This process is described in Chapter 22. You first inspect your house and then decide what repairs and improvements you need to make. If you are having trouble deciding what to do, you may want to hire a professional inspector to do a thorough inspection. You may also want to hire contractors to do some of the repair work, if any is needed.

Step 2: Set the List Price

Pricing your home yourself is covered later in this chapter in the section "Setting the Price." You may also want to consult agents or home appraisers in setting your price.

Step 3: Market the Home

Before a buyer can be interested in your home, that buyer is going to have to know it is for sale. The section "Marketing Your Home," later in this chapter, covers how to advertise and show your home. If you have trouble getting the attention of buyers, you may want to consider an open listing with agents. This topic is discussed later in this section.

Step 4: Help the Buyer Get Financing

Getting an offer from a buyer is one thing; getting an offer from a buyer who can actually buy the house is something entirely different. As part of the sales process, you will want to qualify the buyers so that you are sure they can obtain financing for the home. Consider visiting several lenders and collecting information from them on the lending process. Financing is covered later in this chapter.

Step 5:   Negotiate the Sale

Negotiating involves coming to an agreement with the buyers on price and terms. It also involves drawing up a binding contract that protects your interests. You will most likely want to hire a real estate attorney or real estate agent to help you with the contracts. Hiring an attorney or agent is covered later.

Step 6:   Close on the House

The closing is the final process of signing papers, transferring owner-ship, and collecting money. To help you with the closing, you will probably want to use an attorney. You will also most likely want to hire the services of an escrow company to conduct the closing.

Using an Agent

Once you put that For Sale sign in your yard, be prepared for a caval-cade of real estate agents asking you to list your house with them. You may see more agents than buyers at first!

The agents may promise you quick sales, tell you horror stories of "The Fizz-bo That Never Sold," and give you their best sales pitch. You should be firm with the agents—tell them that you have made up your mind to sell the home yourself.

In some cases, you may want to consider using some services from an agent. For instance, you may hire an agent to research comparable home sales and give advice on your list price. In this case, you may want to have a set fee or an hourly fee for the service. You may also let the agents do market reports for you. Some will do so for free in the hopes that you will eventually list your home with them.

Also, you may want to consider an open listing. This type of listing usually pays a lower commission (three percent) to the agent who brings you a buyer. You can sign open listings with more than one agent. Many fizz-bos advertise this type of arrangement with "Brokers welcome at 3%." Keep in mind that many agents won't be interested in this type of agreement.

Finally, you should be willing to work with any buyers who are represented by an agent. A buyer with an agent is usually serious about buying a home and is usually prequalified. You don't want to turn away this type of buyer! The arrangements for the buyer's agent compensation should be discussed with the agent.

Hiring an Attorney

Even if you don't hire anyone else, you will definitely want to hire the services of an attorney. An attorney can advise you on the disclosure laws in your state, can draw up or look over any contracts, and can ensure that your interests are protected. The attorney can ensure that you do everything properly and legally—for instance, that you don't unwittingly discriminate against any buyers.

When looking for an attorney, ask for recommendations from friends, relatives, agents, and co-workers. Keep in mind that you will want to hire an attorney who specializes in real estate. You don't want to use your sister the divorce attorney to handle the transaction.

You will want to understand up front the charges that you will incur. The attorney will most likely charge by the hour. You should draw up a contract that lists the hourly fee as well as spells out what services you want the attorney to help with.

Using an Escrow Company

In addition to an attorney, another consultant you will most likely want to use is an escrow holder. An escrow holder works for an escrow company which, in real estate transactions, serves as a neutral third party. The escrow holder is the maestro of the transaction. You can expect the escrow holder to prepare, obtain, and record documents; handle the mechanics of property transfer; calculate any prorations; and receive and disburse money.

You may want to ask your attorney or any real estate agents you know for recommendations on escrow companies. Again, make sure you know the charges you will incur for using a particular escrow company. Also, be sure you know exactly what duties the escrow agent will perform. For example, an escrow agent cannot offer advice and cannot negotiate with you and the buyer.

Setting the Price

The single most important aspect of the sale of a home is the price. Setting the price is critical to a successful home sale. If you set the price too high, buyers may avoid your property. When a property sits and sits, it becomes a target for lowball bids. On the other hand, you don't want to price the home too low. You want to get the best deal possible! The best way to set the price of your home is to investigate sales of similar homes in your area. This topic is covered in Chapter 24.

Comparable homes are of the same style (brick, frame, bungalow, 2-story), have the same number of bedrooms, bathrooms, have the same room types (dining room, rec room, living room), and are located in the same area. You can find the list price for homes by reading the local paper or by calling agents. You may want to attend open houses of similar homes to see how yours compares.

Be sure you have reasonable expectations when you price your home and plan for your net proceeds. Many fizzbos expect to pocket the entire commission savings. Savvy buyers may want to share in the savings.

To find the sales price of homes, you will have to do some research. These transactions are recorded at the county courthouse, so you can look through public records to find the information you need.

If you do not want to do the research yourself, you may want to hire the services of an agent to do the research for you. You may also consider having the home appraised.

Figuring Your Net Proceeds

To prepare you for negotiation, you will want to figure your net proceeds from the sale of your home. Chapter 24 explains how to calculate this total, and the handy tear-out card at the front of the book contains a worksheet you can use for this purpose. You will want to include the costs you incur for the sale of your home (advertising fees, attorney costs, and so on). You will also want to investigate which closing costs may pertain to your sale—which costs you expect to pay and how much they are.

Defining What Financial Terms Are Acceptable

In addition to the list price, you should decide on the amount of down payment you (and the lender) will require. You will also want to determine the amount of earnest money you expect to accompany an offer.

Marketing Your Home

Marketing the home means getting the attention of buyers. No matter how wonderful your home is, it isn't going to sell unless buyers know it is available. This section discusses some strategies for getting noticed.

Putting a Sign in Your Yard

One of the first steps in marketing your home is to put up a sign. A sign alerts neighbors that you are selling your home (and agents, so watch out!). It also tells others driving through the neighborhood that your home is for sale.

 Before you put up your sign, check any city laws or neighborhood ordinances pertaining to signs in your area. You may be limited in the size or type of sign you can put up.

You can purchase a sign at a local hardware store. It should clearly say FOR SALE BY OWNER and should include space for you to write in your phone number. (Be sure to use a big, black marker so that your number is clearly visible.) When you put the sign in your yard, make sure that it can be easily seen from both directions.

In addition to a yard sign, you may want to put up other signs around the neighborhood, including the main road into your neighborhood.

Be prepared for two things once the sign goes up. First, agents will flock to you. Second, people will stop by, ring the doorbell, and want to see your house. You can handle stop-bys by giving the buyers a tour, if it is convenient for you. Or you can give them an information sheet about your home (described later in this chapter) and schedule an appointment for a showing.

Taking Out an Ad

In addition to signs, you will most likely want to advertise your home in the local paper and perhaps other publications. Usually, most city papers have a large section devoted to real estate in the Sunday paper. You may choose to take out an ad for this edition.

You don't have to take out a full-page ad to advertise your home. A small ad works perfectly well. Most buyers in the home market read all the small ads, so you don't have to worry about size. You *should* worry about making your small ad stand out, and you can do this by making the ad to-the-point, descriptive, and inviting. A good ad should include the following:

In addition to the ads, consider posting notices on bulletin boards in your local library or supermarket. You may also want to advertise in weekly neighborhood papers. The best way to decide where to advertise is to target your audience. Who is likely to want to purchase your house? How can you reach these buyers?

➤ The price

➤ Your phone number

➤ Number of bedrooms and baths

➤ Style of home and condition of property

In the ad, emphasize the benefits of your home. What is its best feature? What do you like best about the house? What will buyers like best? After reading the ad, the buyer should want to visit your home.

Notice that you don't have to put the address in. You can schedule appointments and give the address when interested buyers call. You should, however, put your address in if you hold an open house. Otherwise, how will lookers find your house?

Preparing Fact Sheets

When buyers visit your house, you will want them to remember it after they leave. You will also want to anticipate questions the buyers may have and provide that information in printed form. To do so, create a fact sheet that you can hand out during open houses and showings.

You can study the MLS listings used by agents for ideas of what to include (see Chapter 6). Also, visit other open houses and collect other fact sheets from homes. Here is some information you may want to include on your fact sheet:

➤ The address of your home.

➤ The list price.

➤ The best features of your home.

➤ The number of bedrooms and baths (this is probably the first thing a buyer wants to know).

➤ A description of other rooms in the house (living room, family room, dining room, great room, office, and so on).

➤ Information about the age, construction (adobe, siding, block, brick, frame, stone, stucco, wood), style (bungalow, Cape Cod, Colonial, Contemporary, Dutch Colonial, ranch, Spanish, split level, traditional, Tudor), and condition (move-in, needs work, as-is).

➤ Information about the size of the house—number of stories, total square footage, lot size, and room dimensions of living room, dining room, bedrooms, den, and other rooms.

➤ Any special features—fireplace, patio, pool, and so on.

➤ A description of the garage (if you have one).

➤ The types of major systems (heating, cooling, electricity, plumbing, water heater) and a record of utility costs.

➤ A list of appliances included with the house.

➤ Information about the neighborhood, for example, school district and annual taxes.

➤ Information about the current mortgage.

Give a few of your fact sheets to your neighbors and coworkers and ask them to spread them around. They may know of someone in the market for a home.

To make the fact sheet more appealing, you may want to include a photo of your home. You can also include a drawing of the layout or survey, if you want. You may also want to attach your seller disclosure form. In some states, seller disclosures are required (see Chapter 22).

Showing Your Home

If you have done a good job marketing your home, you will have plenty of visitors. Expect, especially at first, to have a lot of snoopers (curious neighbors, agents, other potential fizz-bos comparing properties) and hopefully some potential buyers.

Handling Sales Calls

Because you do not have an agent to schedule appointments, you will have to do so yourself. You should be prepared to handle phone calls and stop-bys.

For phone calls, you may want to write up a script to follow so that you are sure to tell the potential buyer everything you think is important. For instance, you will want to give the buyer directions to your home, a description of the home, and the list price.

You may want to ask the buyers a few questions also. For instance, you can ask how the caller heard about the house to gauge the effectiveness of your marketing strategy. You will probably also want to ask for the caller's name and phone number. You can write these down in your visitor log so that you know who has called and visited.

You may then want to set up an appointment to show the home if you think the buyer may indeed be interested. You can set up a time that is convenient for both you and the buyer.

In some cases, you may have buyers that just stop by and knock on the door. How you handle this interruption is up to you. If it is convenient, you may want to arrange for a showing right then and there. If it isn't convenient (if your four-year-old has just finger-painted himself, your spouse has decided to dismantle the dishwasher at that moment, and you are in the middle of giving your mother a home perm), you may want to give the buyers a fact sheet and then schedule an appointment for a more convenient time.

Be flexible. One of the benefits of having an agent is that you don't have to be available for showings during the day. If you are selling alone and work, you may be able to schedule all your showings during the evenings, but be flexible. You may have to arrange for weekday showings as well.

341

Showing Your House

When potential buyers visit your house, have them sign some sort of visitor register and list their names and addresses. Doing so will provide you with a record of who visited your home. You can keep your phone calls in the same or in a separate ledger.

To prepare for the showing, make sure the house is clean and clutter-free (see Chapter 22). Also, make sure the home is safe. Are the walkways clear? Is the dog put away? Any poisonous liquids sitting out on the table?

You may want to point out a few things of interest and then let the buyers wander through the house. Or you may want to accompany the buyers on the tour. When you tag along, though, the buyers may feel stifled. Be sure to put away any valuables, especially if you let the visitors tour the home alone.

During the tour, be prepared for questions about the area, your home, and financing. As part of the preparation process, you should get to know the area and your home. You should also look into financing options. If you don't know the answer, say so. Don't lie and don't exaggerate.

Holding Open Houses

In addition to scheduled showings, you may want to hold an open house or two. Open houses are traditionally held Sunday afternoons.

If you plan an open house, be sure to advertise it in the paper. Also, make sure you have enough fact sheets on hand for the visitors. Finally, you may want to put up some additional signs in the neighborhood directing visitors to your home. As with regular showings, have the visitors sign in.

Helping the Buyer with Financing

One of the benefits of using an agent is that the agent can prequalify a buyer and can help a buyer obtain financing. Without an agent, you are going to have to do this yourself.

First, you will want to prequalify any buyers serious about making an offer. Just because Pam and Steve seem like a nice couple doesn't mean they have the money to buy your house. You won't want to spend hours and hours of time working with one buyer only to find out that the buyer can't afford the home.

To prequalify a buyer, you may want to purchase a buyer qualification form from an office supply company. Or you may want to draw up your own form with your attorney's help. You will want to know the buyer's income, job situation, current debt, and other information. Chapter 3 includes information on prequalifying and explains the ratios most lenders use. You can use this information to qualify a buyer yourself. If a buyer gets angry when you ask for financial information, be sure to explain why you need it. After you do so, the buyer should understand.

You will want to help the buyer obtain financing once you have accepted an offer. An offer without financial backing isn't going to do you any good. To do this, you should be familiar with the different types of financing available. You can find this information in Part III of this book. You can also talk to local lenders. You may want to consider putting together an information sheet that lists the names of various lenders, maximum loan amounts, points charged, and other fees. You can include this information along with your fact sheet.

Negotiating an Offer

When you have an agent, all offers are delivered to the agent. The agent serves as a go-between, discussing the offer with the buyers and their agent and then relaying that information to you.

Without an agent, you will have to negotiate face-to-face with the buyers and possibly with the buyers' agent. Put on your poker face and leave your thin skin at home.

Be Prepared

Face-to-face negotiating is tough. You have to be prepared for any negative comments made about your house. If you take the comments personally, the offer process is going to be extremely stressful. If you understand that the comments are probably just part of the buyer's strategy to get more favorable terms, you can be prepared to handle any objections.

You may want to role-play with your spouse or a friend. Have that person say all the bad things about your house—even if they aren't true. "Well, the roof needs to be repaired. The kitchen tile is the worst.

343

And who picked the wallpaper in the living room? It's hideous!" You can then counter with "The roof was replaced last year. The list price takes into consideration the kitchen tile, and if you don't like the wallpaper, you can select something that you do like."

You will also want to prepare by figuring out the bottom line. Knowing what price and terms you will accept can help you when you have to evaluate offers.

Drawing Up Offers

If your buyers are working with an agent, the agent may help them draw up an offer. If not, they may have an attorney do the work. Or the buyers may come to you with their own purchase agreement.

If, on the other hand, the buyers don't have anyone to help them with an offer, and need help, you can offer to do so. You may want to buy some contract forms from an office supply store and have them available. If the standard contract isn't to your liking, you can ask your attorney to draw up a contract.

Reviewing Offers

When a buyer has an offer, you should schedule an appointment—it can be at your house if you like. When you receive an offer, thank the buyers and ask for time to review it. Usually a sales contract stipulates a time for a response (24–48 hours is typical).

During that response time, you can look over the offer. What price are the buyers offering? What terms? How does this compare to what you expected? Reviewing offers and making counteroffers are covered in Chapter 25.

The offer–counteroffer process can continue until someone withdraws an offer or until both parties agree to the same offer. When you have both signed the same agreement you have successfully sold your house!

Closing on the House

The final stage in buying and selling a home is the closing. At the closing, you exchange money and keys, and you sign more documents than you ever imagined.

To handle the closing, you will most likely want to hire the services of an escrow company. The escrow agent will prepare a settlement sheet and will need from you the original purchase contract to start.

Settlement Sheet

When the escrow agent prepares for the closing, he completes a **settlement sheet**. This is the collection of information necessary to prepare escrow instructions, and includes the property description, parties involved, escrow information, sales price, your loan information, and the buyers' loan information.

Using the contract as a blueprint, the escrow agent draws up the instructions for you and the buyers. (Chapter 26 describes the function of the escrow agent.) You should be prepared to carry out all the instructions the agent gives you and to provide any information the escrow agent needs (deed, title report, mortgage, mortgage note, property tax statements, survey, and so on).

Note that the escrow agent will not reveal information about escrow to other parties and will not revise the instructions without authorization by you and the buyer.

Before the closing, the escrow agent will let you and the buyers know the closing costs that must be paid and by whom they must be paid. He will also calculate any prorations. At the closing, the escrow agent will ensure that all the proper documents have been prepared and are signed. The agent will arrange for your original loan(s) to be paid off and for the new deed to be recorded. After the deed has been recorded, the escrow company will release to you your hard-earned check for any proceeds on the sale of your home.

Knowing When to Call It Quits

If you have had your home on the market for a while and have not sold it, take a second look. Why hasn't the house sold? Chapter 25 lists some reasons why a house may not sell, including the price, the market, the terms, and the condition. Review these items and try to pinpoint the problem.

Consider using an agent, especially if it turns out that exposure is the main problem (getting buyers to the house). At the beginning of selling your house, set a time limit. Say "If I haven't sold my house in *x* months, I'll get an agent." After your time limit is up, hire an agent.

Finally, if the market is so slow, or interest rates are so high, that you are not getting any acceptable offers, consider taking your house off the market for a while.

The Least You Need to Know

If you have a knack for sales and an understanding of the real estate market, you may want to forego paying an agent 7% commission, and sell your home yourself.

➤ Be sure you understand what is involved in selling your home. You may want to hire consultants—for example, a real estate attorney, agent, or escrow company—to help with some of the steps.

➤ The most important aspect of selling a home is setting the price. To come up with a price, compare similar homes in the area. You may want to hire an agent to help you with pricing.

➤ To get your house noticed put a FOR SALE BY OWNER sign in your yard, and advertise in the local daily paper and neighborhood weeklies.

➤ Create a fact sheet about your house to hand out to potential buyers when they visit your home.

➤ Negotiating face-to-face with a buyer can be tough. Be prepared to deal with criticism and objections, and know your bottom line.

➤ The final step in selling a home is the closing. You should hire the services of an escrow company to prepare the instructions for the closing, ensure all documents are prepared and properly signed, and to hold all the money and distribute it when the deal is complete.

Loan Payment Tables

You can use the following tables to find out the principal and interest payment on a given loan amount. First find the amount financed (along the left column), then find the appropriate interest rate (along the top of the page).

Keep in mind that your mortgage payment will include principal and interest along with taxes and insurance. Your actual monthly payment will be higher. This table just figures the principal and interest amount.

Amount Financed	Interest Rate						
	4.0%	4.25%	4.5%	4.75%	5.0%	5.25%	5.5%
$ 40,000	191	197	203	209	215	221	227
$ 45,000	215	221	228	235	242	248	256
$ 50,000	239	246	253	261	268	276	284
$ 55,000	263	271	279	287	295	304	312
$ 60,000	286	295	304	313	322	331	341
$ 65,000	310	320	329	339	349	359	369
$ 70,000	334	344	355	365	376	387	397
$ 75,000	358	369	380	391	403	414	426
$ 80,000	382	394	405	417	429	442	454
$ 85,000	406	418	431	443	456	469	483
$ 90,000	430	443	456	469	483	497	511
$ 95,000	454	467	481	496	510	525	539
$ 100,000	477	492	507	522	537	552	568
$ 105,000	501	517	532	548	564	580	596
$ 110,000	525	541	557	574	591	607	625
$ 115,000	549	566	583	600	617	635	653
$ 120,000	573	590	608	626	644	663	681
$ 125,000	597	615	633	652	671	690	710
$ 130,000	621	640	659	678	698	718	738
$ 135,000	645	664	684	704	725	745	767
$ 140,000	668	689	709	730	752	773	795
$ 145,000	692	713	735	756	778	801	823
$ 150,000	716	738	760	782	805	828	852
$ 155,000	740	763	785	809	832	856	880
$ 160,000	764	787	811	835	859	884	908
$ 165,000	788	812	836	861	886	911	937
$ 170,000	812	836	861	887	913	939	965
$ 175,000	835	861	887	913	939	966	994
$ 180,000	859	885	912	939	966	994	1,022
$ 185,000	883	910	937	965	993	1,022	1,050
$ 190,000	907	935	963	991	1,020	1,049	1,079
$ 195,000	931	959	988	1,017	1,047	1,077	1,107
$ 200,000	955	984	1,013	1,043	1,074	1,104	1,136
$ 205,000	979	1,008	1,039	1,069	1,100	1,132	1,164
$ 210,000	1,003	1,033	1,064	1,095	1,127	1,160	1,192
$ 215,000	1,026	1,058	1,089	1,122	1,154	1,187	1,221
$ 220,000	1,050	1,082	1,115	1,148	1,181	1,215	1,249
$ 225,000	1,074	1,107	1,140	1,174	1,208	1,242	1,278
$ 230,000	1,098	1,131	1,165	1,200	1,235	1,270	1,306
$ 235,000	1,122	1,156	1,191	1,226	1,262	1,298	1,334
$ 240,000	1,146	1,181	1,216	1,252	1,288	1,325	1,363
$ 245,000	1,170	1,205	1,241	1,278	1,315	1,353	1,391
$ 250,000	1,194	1,230	1,267	1,304	1,342	1,381	1,419
$ 255,000	1,217	1,254	1,292	1,330	1,369	1,408	1,448
$ 260,000	1,241	1,279	1,317	1,356	1,396	1,436	1,476
$ 265,000	1,265	1,304	1,343	1,382	1,423	1,463	1,505
$ 270,000	1,289	1,328	1,368	1,408	1,449	1,491	1,533

Amount Financed	Interest Rate							
	5.75%	6.0%	6.25%	6.5%	6.75%	7.0%	7.25%	7.5%
$ 40,000	233	240	246	253	259	266	273	280
$ 45,000	263	270	277	284	292	299	307	315
$ 50,000	292	300	308	316	324	333	341	350
$ 55,000	321	330	339	348	357	366	375	385
$ 60,000	350	360	369	379	389	399	409	420
$ 65,000	379	390	400	411	422	432	443	454
$ 70,000	409	420	431	442	454	466	478	489
$ 75,000	438	450	462	474	486	499	512	524
$ 80,000	467	480	493	506	519	532	546	559
$ 85,000	496	510	523	537	551	566	580	594
$ 90,000	525	540	554	569	584	599	614	629
$ 95,000	554	570	585	600	616	632	648	664
$ 100,000	584	600	616	632	649	665	682	699
$ 105,000	613	630	647	664	681	699	716	734
$ 110,000	642	660	677	695	713	732	750	769
$ 115,000	671	689	708	727	746	765	785	804
$ 120,000	700	719	739	758	778	798	819	839
$ 125,000	729	749	770	790	811	832	853	874
$ 130,000	759	779	800	822	843	865	887	909
$ 135,000	788	809	831	853	876	898	921	944
$ 140,000	817	839	862	885	908	931	955	979
$ 145,000	846	869	893	916	940	965	989	1,014
$ 150,000	875	899	924	948	973	998	1,023	1,049
$ 155,000	905	929	954	980	1,005	1,031	1,057	1,084
$ 160,000	934	959	985	1,011	1,038	1,064	1,091	1,119
$ 165,000	963	989	1,016	1,043	1,070	1,098	1,126	1,154
$ 170,000	992	1,019	1,047	1,075	1,103	1,131	1,160	1,189
$ 175,000	1,021	1,049	1,078	1,106	1,135	1,164	1,194	1,224
$ 180,000	1,050	1,079	1,108	1,138	1,167	1,198	1,228	1,259
$ 185,000	1,080	1,109	1,139	1,169	1,200	1,231	1,262	1,294
$ 190,000	1,109	1,139	1,170	1,201	1,232	1,264	1,296	1,329
$ 195,000	1,138	1,169	1,201	1,233	1,265	1,297	1,330	1,363
$ 200,000	1,167	1,199	1,231	1,264	1,297	1,331	1,364	1,398
$ 205,000	1,196	1,229	1,262	1,296	1,330	1,364	1,398	1,433
$ 210,000	1,226	1,259	1,293	1,327	1,362	1,397	1,433	1,468
$ 215,000	1,255	1,289	1,324	1,359	1,394	1,430	1,467	1,503
$ 220,000	1,284	1,319	1,355	1,391	1,427	1,464	1,501	1,538
$ 225,000	1,313	1,349	1,385	1,422	1,459	1,497	1,535	1,573
$ 230,000	1,342	1,379	1,416	1,454	1,492	1,530	1,569	1,608
$ 235,000	1,371	1,409	1,447	1,485	1,524	1,563	1,603	1,643
$ 240,000	1,401	1,439	1,478	1,517	1,557	1,597	1,637	1,678
$ 245,000	1,430	1,469	1,509	1,549	1,589	1,630	1,671	1,713
$ 250,000	1,459	1,499	1,539	1,580	1,621	1,663	1,705	1,748
$ 255,000	1,488	1,529	1,570	1,612	1,654	1,697	1,740	1,783
$ 260,000	1,517	1,559	1,601	1,643	1,686	1,730	1,774	1,818
$ 265,000	1,546	1,589	1,632	1,675	1,719	1,763	1,808	1,853
$ 270,000	1,576	1,619	1,662	1,707	1,751	1,796	1,842	1,888

Amount Financed	Interest Rate							
	7.75%	8.0%	8.25%	8.5%	8.75%	9.0%	9.25%	9.5%
$ 40,000	287	294	301	308	315	322	329	336
$ 45,000	322	330	338	346	354	362	370	378
$ 50,000	358	367	376	384	393	402	411	420
$ 55,000	394	404	413	423	433	443	452	462
$ 60,000	430	440	451	461	472	483	494	505
$ 65,000	466	477	488	500	511	523	535	547
$ 70,000	501	514	526	538	551	563	576	589
$ 75,000	537	550	563	577	590	603	617	631
$ 80,000	573	587	601	615	629	644	658	673
$ 85,000	609	624	639	654	669	684	699	715
$ 90,000	645	660	676	692	708	724	740	757
$ 95,000	681	697	714	730	747	764	782	799
$ 100,000	716	734	751	769	787	805	823	841
$ 105,000	752	770	789	807	826	845	864	883
$ 110,000	788	807	826	846	865	885	905	925
$ 115,000	824	844	864	884	905	925	946	967
$ 120,000	860	881	902	923	944	966	987	1,009
$ 125,000	896	917	939	961	983	1,006	1,028	1,051
$ 130,000	931	954	977	1,000	1,023	1,046	1,069	1,093
$ 135,000	967	991	1,014	1,038	1,062	1,086	1,111	1,135
$ 140,000	1,003	1,027	1,052	1,076	1,101	1,126	1,152	1,177
$ 145,000	1,039	1,064	1,089	1,115	1,141	1,167	1,193	1,219
$ 150,000	1,075	1,101	1,127	1,153	1,180	1,207	1,234	1,261
$ 155,000	1,110	1,137	1,164	1,192	1,219	1,247	1,275	1,303
$ 160,000	1,146	1,174	1,202	1,230	1,259	1,287	1,316	1,345
$ 165,000	1,182	1,211	1,240	1,269	1,298	1,328	1,357	1,387
$ 170,000	1,218	1,247	1,277	1,307	1,337	1,368	1,399	1,429
$ 175,000	1,254	1,284	1,315	1,346	1,377	1,408	1,440	1,471
$ 180,000	1,290	1,321	1,352	1,384	1,416	1,448	1,481	1,514
$ 185,000	1,325	1,357	1,390	1,422	1,455	1,489	1,522	1,556
$ 190,000	1,361	1,394	1,427	1,461	1,495	1,529	1,563	1,598
$ 195,000	1,397	1,431	1,465	1,499	1,534	1,569	1,604	1,640
$ 200,000	1,433	1,468	1,503	1,538	1,573	1,609	1,645	1,682
$ 205,000	1,469	1,504	1,540	1,576	1,613	1,649	1,686	1,724
$ 210,000	1,504	1,541	1,578	1,615	1,652	1,690	1,728	1,766
$ 215,000	1,540	1,578	1,615	1,653	1,691	1,730	1,769	1,808
$ 220,000	1,576	1,614	1,653	1,692	1,731	1,770	1,810	1,850
$ 225,000	1,612	1,651	1,690	1,730	1,770	1,810	1,851	1,892
$ 230,000	1,648	1,688	1,728	1,769	1,809	1,851	1,892	1,934
$ 235,000	1,684	1,724	1,765	1,807	1,849	1,891	1,933	1,976
$ 240,000	1,719	1,761	1,803	1,845	1,888	1,931	1,974	2,018
$ 245,000	1,755	1,798	1,841	1,884	1,927	1,971	2,016	2,060
$ 250,000	1,791	1,834	1,878	1,922	1,967	2,012	2,057	2,102
$ 255,000	1,827	1,871	1,916	1,961	2,006	2,052	2,098	2,144
$ 260,000	1,863	1,908	1,953	1,999	2,045	2,092	2,139	2,186
$ 265,000	1,898	1,944	1,991	2,038	2,085	2,132	2,180	2,228
$ 270,000	1,934	1,981	2,028	2,076	2,124	2,172	2,221	2,270

Amount Financed	Interest Rate							
	9.75%	10.0%	10.25%	10.5%	10.75%	11.0%	11.25%	11.5%
$ 40,000	344	351	358	366	373	381	389	396
$ 45,000	387	395	403	412	420	429	437	446
$ 50,000	430	439	448	457	467	476	486	495
$ 55,000	473	483	493	503	513	524	534	545
$ 60,000	515	527	538	549	560	571	583	594
$ 65,000	558	570	582	595	607	619	631	644
$ 70,000	601	614	627	640	653	667	680	693
$ 75,000	644	658	672	686	700	714	728	743
$ 80,000	687	702	717	732	747	762	777	792
$ 85,000	730	746	762	778	793	809	826	842
$ 90,000	773	790	806	823	840	857	874	891
$ 95,000	816	834	851	869	887	905	923	941
$ 100,000	859	878	896	915	933	952	971	990
$ 105,000	902	921	941	960	980	1,000	1,020	1,040
$ 110,000	945	965	986	1,006	1,027	1,048	1,068	1,089
$ 115,000	988	1,009	1,031	1,052	1,074	1,095	1,117	1,139
$ 120,000	1,031	1,053	1,075	1,098	1,120	1,143	1,166	1,188
$ 125,000	1,074	1,097	1,120	1,143	1,167	1,190	1,214	1,238
$ 130,000	1,117	1,141	1,165	1,189	1,214	1,238	1,263	1,287
$ 135,000	1,160	1,185	1,210	1,235	1,260	1,286	1,311	1,337
$ 140,000	1,203	1,229	1,255	1,281	1,307	1,333	1,360	1,386
$ 145,000	1,246	1,272	1,299	1,326	1,354	1,381	1,408	1,436
$ 150,000	1,289	1,316	1,344	1,372	1,400	1,428	1,457	1,485
$ 155,000	1,332	1,360	1,389	1,418	1,447	1,476	1,505	1,535
$ 160,000	1,375	1,404	1,434	1,464	1,494	1,524	1,554	1,584
$ 165,000	1,418	1,448	1,479	1,509	1,540	1,571	1,603	1,634
$ 170,000	1,461	1,492	1,523	1,555	1,587	1,619	1,651	1,683
$ 175,000	1,504	1,536	1,568	1,601	1,634	1,667	1,700	1,733
$ 180,000	1,546	1,580	1,613	1,647	1,680	1,714	1,748	1,783
$ 185,000	1,589	1,624	1,658	1,692	1,727	1,762	1,797	1,832
$ 190,000	1,632	1,667	1,703	1,738	1,774	1,809	1,845	1,882
$ 195,000	1,675	1,711	1,747	1,784	1,820	1,857	1,894	1,931
$ 200,000	1,718	1,755	1,792	1,829	1,867	1,905	1,943	1,981
$ 205,000	1,761	1,799	1,837	1,875	1,914	1,952	1,991	2,030
$ 210,000	1,804	1,843	1,882	1,921	1,960	2,000	2,040	2,080
$ 215,000	1,847	1,887	1,927	1,967	2,007	2,047	2,088	2,129
$ 220,000	1,890	1,931	1,971	2,012	2,054	2,095	2,137	2,179
$ 225,000	1,933	1,975	2,016	2,058	2,100	2,143	2,185	2,228
$ 230,000	1,976	2,018	2,061	2,104	2,147	2,190	2,234	2,278
$ 235,000	2,019	2,062	2,106	2,150	2,194	2,238	2,282	2,327
$ 240,000	2,062	2,106	2,151	2,195	2,240	2,286	2,331	2,377
$ 245,000	2,105	2,150	2,195	2,241	2,287	2,333	2,380	2,426
$ 250,000	2,148	2,194	2,240	2,287	2,334	2,381	2,428	2,476
$ 255,000	2,191	2,238	2,285	2,333	2,380	2,428	2,477	2,525
$ 260,000	2,234	2,282	2,330	2,378	2,427	2,476	2,525	2,575
$ 265,000	2,277	2,326	2,375	2,424	2,474	2,524	2,574	2,624
$ 270,000	2,320	2,369	2,419	2,470	2,520	2,571	2,622	2,674

Amount Financed	Interest Rate							
	11.75%	12.0%	12.25%	12.5%	12.75%	13.0%	13.25%	13.5%
$ 40,000	404	411	419	427	435	442	450	458
$ 45,000	454	463	472	480	489	498	507	515
$ 50,000	505	514	524	534	543	553	563	573
$ 55,000	555	566	576	587	598	608	619	630
$ 60,000	606	617	629	640	652	664	675	687
$ 65,000	656	669	681	694	706	719	732	745
$ 70,000	707	720	734	747	761	774	788	802
$ 75,000	757	771	786	800	815	830	844	859
$ 80,000	808	823	838	854	869	885	901	916
$ 85,000	858	874	891	907	924	940	957	974
$ 90,000	908	926	943	961	978	996	1,013	1,031
$ 95,000	959	977	996	1,014	1,032	1,051	1,069	1,088
$ 100,000	1,009	1,029	1,048	1,067	1,087	1,106	1,126	1,145
$ 105,000	1,060	1,080	1,100	1,121	1,141	1,162	1,182	1,203
$ 110,000	1,110	1,131	1,153	1,174	1,195	1,217	1,238	1,260
$ 115,000	1,161	1,183	1,205	1,227	1,250	1,272	1,295	1,317
$ 120,000	1,211	1,234	1,257	1,281	1,304	1,327	1,351	1,374
$ 125,000	1,262	1,286	1,310	1,334	1,358	1,383	1,407	1,432
$ 130,000	1,312	1,337	1,362	1,387	1,413	1,438	1,464	1,489
$ 135,000	1,363	1,389	1,415	1,441	1,467	1,493	1,520	1,546
$ 140,000	1,413	1,440	1,467	1,494	1,521	1,549	1,576	1,604
$ 145,000	1,464	1,491	1,519	1,548	1,576	1,604	1,632	1,661
$ 150,000	1,514	1,543	1,572	1,601	1,630	1,659	1,689	1,718
$ 155,000	1,565	1,594	1,624	1,654	1,684	1,715	1,745	1,775
$ 160,000	1,615	1,646	1,677	1,708	1,739	1,770	1,801	1,833
$ 165,000	1,666	1,697	1,729	1,761	1,793	1,825	1,858	1,890
$ 170,000	1,716	1,749	1,781	1,814	1,847	1,881	1,914	1,947
$ 175,000	1,766	1,800	1,834	1,868	1,902	1,936	1,970	2,004
$ 180,000	1,817	1,852	1,886	1,921	1,956	1,991	2,026	2,062
$ 185,000	1,867	1,903	1,939	1,974	2,010	2,046	2,083	2,119
$ 190,000	1,918	1,954	1,991	2,028	2,065	2,102	2,139	2,176
$ 195,000	1,968	2,006	2,043	2,081	2,119	2,157	2,195	2,234
$ 200,000	2,019	2,057	2,096	2,135	2,173	2,212	2,252	2,291
$ 205,000	2,069	2,109	2,148	2,188	2,228	2,268	2,308	2,348
$ 210,000	2,120	2,160	2,201	2,241	2,282	2,323	2,364	2,405
$ 215,000	2,170	2,212	2,253	2,295	2,336	2,378	2,420	2,463
$ 220,000	2,221	2,263	2,305	2,348	2,391	2,434	2,477	2,520
$ 225,000	2,271	2,314	2,358	2,401	2,445	2,489	2,533	2,577
$ 230,000	2,322	2,366	2,410	2,455	2,499	2,544	2,589	2,634
$ 235,000	2,372	2,417	2,463	2,508	2,554	2,600	2,646	2,692
$ 240,000	2,423	2,469	2,515	2,561	2,608	2,655	2,702	2,749
$ 245,000	2,473	2,520	2,567	2,615	2,662	2,710	2,758	2,806
$ 250,000	2,524	2,572	2,620	2,668	2,717	2,765	2,814	2,864
$ 255,000	2,574	2,623	2,672	2,722	2,771	2,821	2,871	2,921
$ 260,000	2,624	2,674	2,725	2,775	2,825	2,876	2,927	2,978
$ 265,000	2,675	2,726	2,777	2,828	2,880	2,931	2,983	3,035
$ 270,000	2,725	2,777	2,829	2,882	2,934	2,987	3,040	3,093

Amount Financed	Interest Rate							
	13.75%	14.0%	14.25%	14.5%	14.75%	15.0%	15.25%	15.50%
$ 40,000	466	474	482	490	498	506	514	522
$ 45,000	524	533	542	551	560	569	578	587
$ 50,000	583	592	602	612	622	632	642	652
$ 55,000	641	652	663	674	684	695	706	717
$ 60,000	699	711	723	735	747	759	771	783
$ 65,000	757	770	783	796	809	822	835	848
$ 70,000	816	829	843	857	871	885	899	913
$ 75,000	874	889	904	918	933	948	963	978
$ 80,000	932	948	964	980	996	1,012	1,028	1,044
$ 85,000	990	1,007	1,024	1,041	1,058	1,075	1,092	1,109
$ 90,000	1,049	1,066	1,084	1,102	1,120	1,138	1,156	1,174
$ 95,000	1,107	1,126	1,144	1,163	1,182	1,201	1,220	1,239
$ 100,000	1,165	1,185	1,205	1,225	1,244	1,264	1,284	1,305
$ 105,000	1,223	1,244	1,265	1,286	1,307	1,328	1,349	1,370
$ 110,000	1,282	1,303	1,325	1,347	1,369	1,391	1,413	1,435
$ 115,000	1,340	1,363	1,385	1,408	1,431	1,454	1,477	1,500
$ 120,000	1,398	1,422	1,446	1,469	1,493	1,517	1,541	1,565
$ 125,000	1,456	1,481	1,506	1,531	1,556	1,581	1,606	1,631
$ 130,000	1,515	1,540	1,566	1,592	1,618	1,644	1,670	1,696
$ 135,000	1,573	1,600	1,626	1,653	1,680	1,707	1,734	1,761
$ 140,000	1,631	1,659	1,687	1,714	1,742	1,770	1,798	1,826
$ 145,000	1,689	1,718	1,747	1,776	1,804	1,833	1,862	1,892
$ 150,000	1,748	1,777	1,807	1,837	1,867	1,897	1,927	1,957
$ 155,000	1,806	1,837	1,867	1,898	1,929	1,960	1,991	2,022
$ 160,000	1,864	1,896	1,927	1,959	1,991	2,023	2,055	2,087
$ 165,000	1,922	1,955	1,988	2,021	2,053	2,086	2,119	2,152
$ 170,000	1,981	2,014	2,048	2,082	2,116	2,150	2,184	2,218
$ 175,000	2,039	2,074	2,108	2,143	2,178	2,213	2,248	2,283
$ 180,000	2,097	2,133	2,168	2,204	2,240	2,276	2,312	2,348
$ 185,000	2,155	2,192	2,229	2,265	2,302	2,339	2,376	2,413
$ 190,000	2,214	2,251	2,289	2,327	2,365	2,402	2,440	2,479
$ 195,000	2,272	2,310	2,349	2,388	2,427	2,466	2,505	2,544
$ 200,000	2,330	2,370	2,409	2,449	2,489	2,529	2,569	2,609
$ 205,000	2,388	2,429	2,470	2,510	2,551	2,592	2,633	2,674
$ 210,000	2,447	2,488	2,530	2,572	2,613	2,655	2,697	2,739
$ 215,000	2,505	2,547	2,590	2,633	2,676	2,719	2,762	2,805
$ 220,000	2,563	2,607	2,650	2,694	2,738	2,782	2,826	2,870
$ 225,000	2,622	2,666	2,711	2,755	2,800	2,845	2,890	2,935
$ 230,000	2,680	2,725	2,771	2,816	2,862	2,908	2,954	3,000
$ 235,000	2,738	2,784	2,831	2,878	2,925	2,971	3,018	3,066
$ 240,000	2,796	2,844	2,891	2,939	2,987	3,035	3,083	3,131
$ 245,000	2,855	2,903	2,951	3,000	3,049	3,098	3,147	3,196
$ 250,000	2,913	2,962	3,012	3,061	3,111	3,161	3,211	3,261
$ 255,000	2,971	3,021	3,072	3,123	3,173	3,224	3,275	3,327
$ 260,000	3,029	3,081	3,132	3,184	3,236	3,288	3,340	3,392
$ 265,000	3,088	3,140	3,192	3,245	3,298	3,351	3,404	3,457
$ 270,000	3,146	3,199	3,253	3,306	3,360	3,414	3,468	3,522

Creditors have better memories than debtors.
—**Proverb**

Resources

American Society of Appraisers
800-272-8258

> Gives you a referral for an appraisal. The association requires five years' experience, and member appraisers must pass exams in their specialty.

American Society of Home Inspectors
1735 N. Lynn Street, Suite 950
Arlington VA 22209

> Provides a list of ASHI-certified firms when you send a self-addressed, stamped envelope.

Appraisers Association of America
212-867-9775

> Gives you a referral for an appraisal. The association requires five years' experience, and member appraisers must pass exams in their specialty.

Buyer's Broker Registry
PO Box 23275
Ventura CA 93002
800-729-5147

> Prints a directory of buyer's brokers that gives advice on using a buyer's broker and employing a broker.

Equifax
PO Box 740241
Atlanta GA 30374
800-685-1111

Provides a copy of your credit report, for a fee.

Fair Housing Information Clearinghouse
PO Box 6091
Rockville MD 20850
1-800-343-3442

Publishes a free book on fair housing (your rights).

Fannie Mae
Customer Education
3900 Wisconsin Avenue NW
Washington DC 20016

Provides free consumer information on buying a home.

Farmers Home Administration
U.S. Department of Agriculture
Washington DC 20250

Provides you with information about FmHA loans.

Federal Housing Administration
Washington DC 20410

Provides you with information about FHA programs.

Home Buyers Companion
Parsons Technology
One Parsons Drive
Hiawatha IA 52233
(800) 223-6925

Sells a software program designed for the home-buying process. Includes an interview that leads you step-by-step through questions about income, debts, and interest rates so that you can figure out how much you can afford. Includes a closing estimator, a loan viewer which creates amortization tables, a tax saver, living indexes, and other features. The list price is $49.

Home Buyers Warranty
Customer Service
HBW
1400 Montreal Rd
Suite 240
Tucker GA 30084

Provides you with a list of members.

Home Owners Warranty
PO Box 152087
Irving TX 75015

Provides you with a list of member builders.

HSH Associates
1200 Route 23
Butler NJ 07405
800-873-2837

Real estate industry publisher. Also will survey mortgage programs and rates in your area and give you a list of 25 to 50 lenders.

National Cooperative Bank (NCB)
Share Loan Services
1630 Connecticut Avenue NW
Washington DC 20009

This is the largest co-operative lender. Write for information.

National Institute of Building Inspectors
424 Vosseller Avenue
Bound Brook NJ 08805
Trans Union
PO Box 7000
North Olmstead OH 44070
312-408-1050

Provides a copy of your credit report for a fee.

TRW
PO Box 2350
Chatsworth CA 91313
800-392-1122

> Provides a copy of your credit report for a fee.

Veteran's Administration
810 Vermont Avenue NW
Washington DC 20420

> Provides you with information on VA loans.

U.S. Department of Housing and Urban Development
Fair Housing Division
451 7th St. SW
Washington DC 20410
800-669-9777

> Handles discrimination complaints. You should always report discrimination.

adjustable-rate mortgage A type of mortgage in which the interest rate is keyed to a certain economic index and is adjusted as the index rises and falls. If you have this type of mortgage, your monthly payment could go up or down, depending on the prevailing rates.

agent A person authorized to work on another's behalf—for instance, a person authorized to sell or buy a house on your behalf.

amortization The process of paying off the loan balance. As you make payments, a certain amount is applied to the principal and a certain amount to the interest. The schedule or table of amortization shows the declining balance as you make payments.

annual percentage rate The true rate of interest for a loan. This rate will include the costs of any points paid, mortgage insurance, and other costs.

appraisal An estimate of the value of a certain property by a qualified, independent individual.

assumption A type of purchase in which the buyer assumes the responsibility of making payments on the seller's home.

balloon mortgage A type of mortgage in which the loan amount is amortized over the full length of the loan (usually 30 years), but the loan actually comes due after a few years (usually 5 or 7). The first payments go mostly toward interest. The balance of the loan is due in one final installment, called the balloon payment.

basis Your home's value for tax purposes.

basic policy A homeowners insurance policy that covers certain perils. Also called *HO-1*.

broker An agent that is authorized to open and run his or her own agency. All real estate offices have one principal broker.

buy-down A type of financing in which a developer or seller arranges for the buyer to get a loan at a rate below the current market rate. The developer or seller pays interest costs in order to lower the interest rate, but usually raises the price of the house to recoup this loss.

buyer's agent An agent hired by the buyer to help the buyer find a home and negotiate the purchase of a home. This agent works for the best interests of the buyer, not the seller.

cap A limit on an adjustable-rate mortgage. Depending on the ARM, the loan may have a cap on how much the interest rate can increase, for instance.

closing The process of finalizing all the dealings associated with the sale and purchase of a home. Also called the *settlement*.

commitment letter A formal offer of a loan by a lender. The letter will state the terms under which it has agreed to the loan.

commission The fee an agent earns for the sale of a home, usually a percentage of the selling price.

comprehensive The most expensive type of homeowner's insurance, also covers the most potential damages.

co-operative (co-op) A form of home ownership in which the owner owns shares in a corporation. In return for the purchase of shares, the owner is allowed to live in a unit in the co-op building.

condominium A form of home ownership in which the owner owns the airspace within the walls, but doesn't own the actual walls, ceilings or floors of his home; the owner may also own a percentage of the common areas, such as the swimming pool.

contingency A provision included in a sales contract that states certain events that must occur or conditions that must be met before the contract is valid.

conventional mortgage A type of mortgage made by banks and other lending institutions.

counteroffer A subsequent offer that makes changes to the original offer. Can be made by either the seller or the buyer.

credit report A report of all your debt information compiled by an independent agency. The credit report will show all outstanding debt as well as a record of payment on outstanding debts.

deed The legal document that conveys the title to a property.

default To fail to make payments on a loan.

down payment The money you pay up front for the purchase of the home.

earnest money A deposit you make when you make an offer on a house.

easement A right given by the landowner to use the property. For example, you may have easements on your property for phone lines, utility poles, and so on.

equity The financial interest or cash value of your home, minus the current loan balance, minus any costs incurred in selling the home.

escrow A trust account created by a neutral third party to hold money for the seller or buyer. For example, when you put down a deposit on a house, it should be put into an escrow account. When the sale is complete, the money can be released from this account to the seller.

Also, an account set up for your taxes and insurance. Your monthly mortgage payment includes payment for 1/12 of your taxes and insurance. This money is kept in an escrow account. When the bill comes due, your mortgage company uses the escrow money to pay it.

FHA mortgage *FHA* stands for Federal Housing Authority. FHA loans are guaranteed by the government. You can put down a smaller down payment on an FHA loan, but you will also be required to pay mortgage insurance.

fizz-bo See *FSBO.*

fixed-rate mortgage A type of mortgage in which the interest rate is fixed for the life of the loan.

foreclosure The legal process in which a mortgage property is seized because of default and then sold.

FSBO For-Sale-By-Owner; pronounced "fizz-bo." A home that is offered for sale without the use of an agent.

gift letter A letter that is required if you receive a down payment from any individual as a gift.

home warranty A guarantee for certain features of a new home—for instance, the materials and workmanship, the main components of the house, and so on.

housing ratio The percentage of your housing payment (principal, interest, taxes, and insurance) to your monthly gross income. Lenders will use this ratio to qualify you for a loan. Sometimes this ratio is called the *front ratio.* A common ratio is 28%.

index An economic indicator that is used in setting the rate for adjustable-rate mortgages.

inspection A close and thorough examination of a house and property. The inspection is usually done by a licensed individual.

interest rate The percentage the lender charges you for borrowing money.

joint tenancy An equal, undivided ownership in a property by two or more individuals.

loan origination fee A fee charged by the lenders, usually one percent of the loan amount.

lien A claim against a property.

lock in To guarantee a certain interest rate for a certain period of time.

LTV   Loan-to-value ratio. Used by lenders to state how much you have financed. If you put down 20% on a purchase, you finance 80% and have an 80% LTV.

maintenance fee   A fee charged by condominium associations, co-ops, or other homeowner's associations for the upkeep of the property.

mortgage insurance premium (MIP)   The up-front insurance premium you must pay if you get an FHA loan. The insurance helps cover the costs of reselling your home if you default on the loan.

mortgage   A legal document that pledges your property as security for a loan.

mortgage banker   A company that originates mortgages and then sells them to a secondary market.

mortgage broker   An intermediary between the borrowers and lenders used to ensure a loan. The broker takes the loan and then packages it for the lender.

mortgagee   The lender.

mortgagor   The borrower.

MLS   A computerized listing of all the homes for sale in an area. Agents are granted access to this multiple listing service and can use it to find a house in a particular price range or area.

negative amortization   A type of loan situation that occurs when the monthly payments do not cover the principal or interest. Rather than declining, the balance on the loan will actually increase.

overall debt ratio   The percentage of your overall debt (housing payments plus any other long-term debt) to your monthly gross income. Lenders will use this ratio to see whether you qualify for a loan. This ratio is sometimes called the *back ratio*. Common ratios used are 33 or 36 percent.

PITI   Principal, interest, taxes, and insurance—the total monthly payment you make on a house.

point   One percent of a loan amount. Lenders charge points in exchange for lowering the interest rate.

prequalify   Meeting or talking with a lender, providing the lender with your financial information, then having the lender qualify you for a loan for a certain amount. You can prequalify formally or informally.

principal   The amount of money borrowed and still owed on a loan.

private mortgage insurance (PMI)   Insurance that protects lenders in case of a loan default. Some loans require this type of insurance.

proprietary lease   A lease used for co-ops that gives the share owners the right to live in a particular unit.

proration   The division of certain fees. For example, if the sellers have paid for taxes six months in advance, they may want a portion of that payment back for the months you are living in the house.

qualifying ratio   The percentages that a lender will compare to see whether you qualify for a loan. See *overall debt ratio* and *housing ratio*.

Realtor®   An agent or agency that belongs to the local or state board of Realtors® and has an affiliation with the National Association of Realtors® (NAR).

RESPA   Real Estate Settlement Procedures Act. This act requires the lender to disclose certain information about a loan, including the estimated closing costs and APR.

sales contract   The contract you draw up when you want to make an offer on a home. Sometimes called the *purchase agreement.*

seller takeback   A type of financing in which the seller arranges for the financing on a property.

subagent   The agent who works with you to purchase a house, but is paid by the seller. Compare with *buyer's agent.*

subdivision   A piece of land divided into several plots on which homes are built.

survey   An examination of the property boundaries to find out the quantity of land, location of improvements, and other information. Usually, the surveyor creates a map or drawing of the legal boundaries of the property.

term   The length of a loan.

title   The right of property ownership.

title search   The process of reviewing court and other records to ensure that there are no liens or claims against the property you are buying.

title insurance   Insurance that protects the lender and buyer against any losses incurred from disputes over the title of a property.

underwriting   The process of evaluating a loan to determine whether the loan is a good risk.

VA loan   A type of loan available to veterans and guaranteed by the Department of Veteran's Affairs.

zoning   Laws that establish how a property can be used and what codes must be followed when building new buildings.

'Tis against some men's principle to pay interest, and seems against others' interest to pay the principal.

—Benjamin Franklin

Index

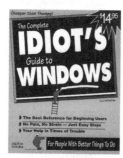

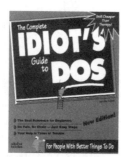

Also Available!

Everyone's talking about
The Complete Idiot's Guides!

"Thanks for helping me get started."
Jim Ellars, Greenfield, IN

"It is written in plain, old English and tells me what I need to know to do what I want to do."
Craig Connolly, Lincoln, NE

"I've made friends with my computer."
Marjorie Bock, Slidell, LA

"...quite helpful in gaining familiarity and confidence in various computer topics."
Martin Bondy, New York, NY

"...most of all, the books helped build a much-needed confidence."
Bill Shepson, Sacramento, CA

"I could hardly put it down—anxious to find out a little more and more."
June Littlejohn, Irving, TX

"...covered the basics of the entire program without getting too bogged down in details."
Robert Matson, New York, NY

"...one of the best introductory computer books that I have come across in the past few years. It's refreshing to have instructional material written at the level of the beginner and not making many assumptions regarding prior computer ability."
Daniel Green, Saratoga Springs, NY

"It teaches in such a simplified, straightforward manner."
Richard Boehringer, Miramar, FL

"This book taught me that I'm in control."
Greg Wright, Ashmore, Australia

"...simple, easy to read, and enjoyable. I felt like someone was talking to me."
Jon Marshall, Dover, OH

"The best thing about the book is the readability."
Gerard van Os, The Netherlands

"I appreciate material that assumes me to be lacking in information rather than lacking in intelligence."
Holly Waldrop, Nashville, TN

"I have to say that this is THE book for teaching in this area."
Richard Caladine, University of Wollongong, Australia

"After really close review, I have found it to be superb. The concepts are as clear as I have seen."
Barry Owen, San Juan, CO

"Lest I forget, your bright orange cover and cheat sheet proved to be invaluable amongst a cluttered desk."
Darryl Pang, Honolulu, HI

The Complete Idiot's Guides—For People With Better Things To Do